"RECOMMENDED. . .

As Hellerstein recounts his family history—the story of five generations of physicians—it evolves into something larger: a chronicle of the changes in medicine from the nineteenth century to the present as seen through the experiences of his family."

—*Library Journal*

"A briskly flowing narrative. . .In lively portraits and anecdotes culled from family attic archives, Hellerstein describes early, more primitive, medical procedures together with his ancestors' romances, scandals and travels."

—*Publishers Weekly*

"Engrossing. . .After reading this expertly written chronicle of a century of medical history enriched by five generations of related physicians, no reader can doubt that there will be a sixth generation in a family of doctors."

—*Cleveland Jewish News*

"This remarkable family memoir is at once the remembrance of American medicine past and a hopeful sign of its future. Hellerstein's wise and very human book reassures us that not only medical practice but also its literature are in the hands of a new breed of idealists."

—GERALD WEISSMANN, M.D.
Author of *Woods Hole Cantata*

A FAMILY OF DOCTORS

David Hellerstein

IVY BOOKS • NEW YORK

Ivy Books
Published by Ballantine Books
Copyright © 1994 by David Hellerstein

Library of Congress Catalog Card Number: 93-3194

ISBN 0-8041-1332-7

This edition published by arrangement with Hill and Wang, a division of Farrar, Straus and Giroux, Inc.

Manufactured in the United States of America

First Ballantine Books Edition: August 1995

10 9 8 7 6 5 4 3 2 1

*For Sarah, Benjamin, and Jason,
and for Jessica, Julie, Rebecca, Jonah, Leah,
Nellie, and Andrew—a new generation*

CONTENTS

FAMILY

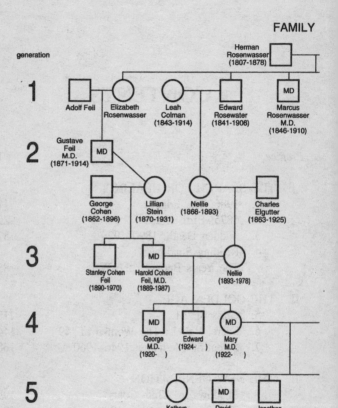

generation

1

Herman Rosenwasser (1807-1878)

Adolf Feil — Elizabeth Rosenwasser

Leah Colman (1843-1914)

Edward Rosewater (1841-1906)

Marcus Rosenwasser M.D. (1846-1910) — MD

2

Gustave Feil M.D. (1871-1914) — MD

George Cohen (1862-1896)

Lillian Stein (1870-1931)

Nellie (1868-1893)

Charles Elgutter (1863-1925)

3

Stanley Cohen Feil (1890-1970)

Harold Cohen Feil, M.D. (1889-1987) — MD

Nellie (1893-1978)

4

George M.D. (1920-) — MD

Edward (1924-)

Mary M.D. (1922-) — MD

5

Kathryn (1952-)

David M.D. (1953-) — MD

Jonathan (1955-)

TREE

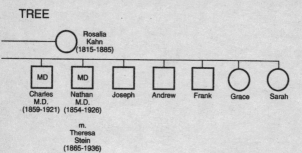

Rosalia
Kahn
(1815-1885)

Charles
M.D.
(1859-1921)

Nathan
M.D.
(1854-1926)

m.
Theresa
Stein
(1865-1936)

Joseph

Andrew

Frank

Grace

Sarah

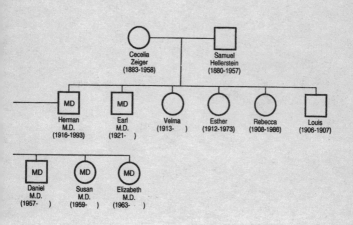

Cecelia
Zeiger
(1883-1958)

Samuel
Hellerstein
(1880-1957)

Herman
M.D.
(1916-1993)

Earl
M.D.
(1921-)

Velma
(1913-)

Esther
(1912-1973)

Rebecca
(1908-1986)

Louis
(1906-1907)

Daniel
M.D.
(1957-)

Susan
M.D.
(1959-)

Elizabeth
M.D.
(1963-)

PREFACE

IT is Dad's patients we remember most. Mr. Alonzo Wright, for one, the black millionaire who lived on a vast estate on County Line Road. Our father kept him alive for years, through three heart attacks, an aortic aneurysm, and assorted other diseases, delicately adjusting medications so that his failing heart continued beating. And Sid Meadow, the businessman who refused to give up on life after developing heart disease in his sixties. Defying doctors, he began running, and put a wooden track on the roof of the local YMCA. He became lean and sinewy, a wrinkled marathoner who celebrated each birthday by running seven miles in fewer minutes than his age: seven miles in sixty-five minutes at the age of seventy!

Most of all from our 1960s Cleveland childhood, we recall Mr. Laugesen. An old-time newspaperman, Victor Laugesen had chainsmoked from one deadline to the next, until he was felled by a heart attack. Doctors advised him to retire not only from journalism but from life, and so, utterly demoralized, he did. Until Dad encountered him. Then he cut out cigarettes, eggs, red meat. He owned an old farm on S.O.M. Center Road, a house dating from the early 1800s. With Dad's encouragement, he started a new life as a dairy farmer, buying one cow, then two, then four.

Dad and Mom used to pile all six kids into the big-finned blue Plymouth on Sunday mornings for a trip to Mr. Laugesen's farm. We'd park on a rutted country lane and run back to the barn. There we'd find him, a ruddy old fellow in overalls. He'd grab Dad's hand and lead us into the barn's fragrant darkness to show us a just-born calf or demonstrate the workings of the stainless-steel milking machine. Once he walked us through high-grass fields to a pond at the back of his property, still as midnight, where he handed us fishing rods and had us cast for bluegills.

These patients would have been dead or, if alive, condemned to a limbo of despair and ill health, if not for the progress of medicine—this was apparent to all six Hellerstein kids from a very early age. New drugs, new technologies, new operations saved many patients' lives; the doctor's artful management helped make those lives meaningful again.

As children, we realized that we were part of a great adventure, the conquest of disease by scientific medicine. These were the Kennedy years—a time of boundless optimism. Sure, we feared the atom bomb, and brainwashing by North Koreans. During air-raid drills we cowered in the basement gymnasium, scared of mushroom clouds. We debated whether we should have a bomb shelter, and whether we would let our next-door neighbors share it. But we were miraculously hopeful. Projects Mercury and Apollo were sending astronauts into space. In the South, Martin Luther King, Jr., was helping blacks gain equality and justice. And the Peace Corps was spreading democracy around the world.

Doctors, too, it seemed, could do almost anything. They had discovered penicillin, which cured strep throat and prevented rheumatic fever. They conquered polio with medicine hidden in little sugar cubes you dissolved under your tongue. There were artificial kidneys, and open-heart surgery. Close to home, doctors were heroes, too. Besides Dad, Dr. Herman K. Hellerstein, who told heart-attack victims not to give up, there was Dr. Harold Feil, our grandfather, a pioneer with the EKG machine. There was Dr. Claude S. Beck, who pioneered in heart surgery before World War II, and Dr. F. Mason Sones, Jr., who had accidentally begun arteriography of the coronary arteries in 1959, and Dr. René G. Favaloro, who first performed a coronary-artery bypass operation in 1967. To us, they were like baseball all-stars; we were astonished to discover our friends did not know their names. Just as democracy would save the world from Communism, medicine would bring health and longevity to all. It was only a matter of time.

Yet death was omnipresent, a fragile heartbeat away. There were new diseases, new side effects, new complications. And so our telephone rang late at night and we'd hear Mom, the pediatrician, asking questions: How high is the child's fever? Is he having difficulty breathing? What did the culture show? Or when it was for Dad: What do you see on the rhythm strip? Did you try epinephrine? The "pO$_2$" [the level of oxygen in the arteries] was *what*? His digoxin level? Have you talked to the wife? The door to the kitchen would swing shut, Dad's voice dropped, and we strained to hear what he was saying over baby Beth's crying or Jon and Susie's squabbling. Sometimes Dad put his coat on and hopped in the car and backed down the driveway into the dark Ohio night, not to reappear until long after we had gone to bed; later, as we grew older, he would ask me or Jonny or Susie, "Do you want to come along?" "Herm, it's so *late*," Mom would say. "We'll be home soon," Dad always promised. And we'd zip up our winter coats and follow him out back to the car, and head down the hill to the hospital. He'd park in the doctors' lot, and we kids, his little shadows, would follow him inside, past the security desk and up four or five flights of stairs, to the polished hospital ward.

Other times we found him catching up on his correspondence, sitting in the breakfast room with his Dictaphone, a sleek gray machine which recorded on red phonograph disks. Before him, long EKG tapes unfolded across the checked vinyl tablecloth and onto the blue linoleum-covered floor; he showed us the bumps and jiggles of the heart's electrical dance, and then returned to his dictation, ending, "Cordially yours, HKH." We would help him fold the long, long tapes, and bind them carefully with rubber bands. When hungry, we sizzled some bologna in a frying pan and doused it with ketchup, or cooked up onions with paprika. Gathered around the table, we drank ice water from tall, sweaty glasses, listening to the crickets outside.

Dad's life, Mom's life, the whole family's life was healing. Almost all the grownups were doctors: Mom, Dr. Mary Feil Hellerstein, was a pediatrician; Dad, and Papa, Mom's father, were cardiologists; Uncle George, her brother, was an internist in Shaker Heights; and Dad's brother, Uncle Earl, was a pathologist in Boston; and his sister's husband, Uncle Morrie, was a GP in Collinsville, Illinois. Aunt Maren was a nurse; Aunt Esther was a social worker; and except that Aunt Velma lost a kidney when she was in college, she would have become a doctor, too.

When we were very young, we were swept up in Dad's adventure. Yet when he showed us the pile of EKGs our attention tended to wander, and after a while the stories of Alonzo White and Sid Meadow and even Mr. Laugesen began to sound overly familiar. As we got older, other stories became more compelling. For instance, Billy McCallum from across the street, whose family summered at Cape Cod with the Kennedys, and whose dad drove us around on summer afternoons on an antique red fire engine. Billy's older brother, Robert, had muscular dystrophy. A sickly, pale thirteen-year-old with long white hairless arms, Robert spent afternoons in the darkened sunroom painstakingly gluing together model airplanes. He kept getting weaker and weaker, until one day he was gone.

Why did he die? Why couldn't doctors save him? The mystery of that haunted us. Then there was Mrs. Collins, another neighbor, who never slept. Late at night, if we got up to go to the bathroom or to get a snack and looked out the window, the light in her room would be on; and if we went over in the afternoon to visit her son Jeff, she would be wandering around in her bathrobe, her face puffy and creased by pillows. Why couldn't all the pills she took help her sleep? There was Jamie Newton's father, who died of cancer when we were Cub Scouts. And the Donohues, who lived behind us. Their daughter Patricia was a prodigy of fat, a mountainous miserable girl who once donned her father's size 11 shoes and stepped onto the wet cement behind our garage to draw swastikas and write: KILL THE KIKES! How come she was so fat? And why was she possessed with hatred for us, who had done nothing to her?

The intriguing stories became those with mystery, stories of suffering not yet alleviated, diseases of body and mind not yet understood and cured.

Each generation of doctors needs to find haunting stories. What diseases cry out for treatment, what terrible suffering demands to be soothed? Gripping case histories or dry statistical tables or brilliant nuclear magnetic images may define the bounds of these stories, whose form varies greatly from one century to the next. But, in the end, doctors in every generation find stories to help chart their mission. Just as their tasks invariably differ from those of prior generations, so do the tales that compel them to heal.

Thus, our eventual irritation with Dad's stories was no doubt predestined. Once exciting, evidence of his dedication, of his courage and originality, they became oppressive, even stifling. His medical advice became so widely accepted it became a new orthodoxy. It was one thing when Dr. Paul Dudley White called from the White House to consult with Dad—who was an expert in the rehabilitation of heart patients—after President Eisenhower's 1955 heart attack. In the 1960s we were the only family on the block, if not in the entire city of Cleveland, doing aerobic exercise and eating low-cholesterol meals; and Dad's research project in an old downtown mansion, his Work Classification Clinic, which prepared heart patients to go back to work, was one of few such centers in the country. Yet, by the mid-seventies, everyone, it seemed, was buying bicycles and running shoes and cutting out eggs, and virtually all heart patients were being advised that life was not over and they should plan to return to work.

Each of us kids struggled with Dad (and in a less obvious way with Mom) over family myths of sickness and healing. Our struggles, sometimes comic, other times bitter and angry, were part of a necessary process. Eventually, four of us became doctors: more compelling than any other stories, we found, were those of disease and cure.

It was also perhaps inevitable that after becoming M.D.s we should reject cardiology—that we should turn toward new continents, what appeared to be open territory, the frontiers of medicine. Dan chose urology, Susie obstetrics, Beth pediatrics. I picked the mind. I chose psychiatry with my gut, my heart. I chose defiantly—taking the risk of disappointing my father, of breaking with family tradition.

And yet we still became doctors, four of the six kids. What propelled us into healing? What was it that drove our family for so many generations into medicine? What history created a family's need to cure, central as chromosomes, and what sustained it over the decades?

There were also questions of the future, some intimidatingly difficult. What did we have to contribute? Which of our stories would rival those we'd grown up with?

One thing was certain: first as witnesses, then as healers, we lived for tales of sickness and cure.

I

THE SEARCH FOR HEALING

1

1986: THE EDGE

I was late; the conference had already begun. Dozens of doctors in white coats sat in the darkened amphitheater at Case Western Reserve University Hospital in Cleveland, Ohio, images of dye-infused human hearts flashing above them. I slid quietly into an aisle seat. The speaker's professorial tone immediately transported me back to my medical-school days.

He was asking a breathtaking question: Could coronary-artery disease be reversed? Did new drugs actually strip cholesterol from the walls of coronary arteries, reversing the supposedly irreversible deadly blockage? Would bypass surgery soon become irrelevant? Not exactly my field, but angiograms and 12-lead EKGs and radionuclide scatter-images flashed before us, sweeping the audience into his high-tech medical passion.

I settled in, trying to banish thoughts of my clinic, my patients, all the things waiting for me back in New York. I tried to forget the harried drive in my rented Avis subcompact to find this place, a rush through a labyrinth of roads. Every time I came home to Cleveland, the streets around the Case Western Reserve University Hospital seemed to have been rerouted once again so another vast new gleaming hospital building could fit on campus, replacing an obsolete laboratory or nurses' residence. Like medicine itself, the hospital was constantly being remade.

That was why I got lost. Or was it that I was more than a trifle preoccupied today, distracted and bemused?

As a white puff of angiogram dye flowed through constricted vessels on the large screen before us, I scanned the crowd, looking for Dad.

I finally found him, sitting next to Mom in the second row. By the flicker of video, he looked young again, lean, energetic, his black hair slicked down, his white coat fresh-pressed, his body tense with purpose. There beside him, Mom looked pretty, even girlish. For a moment it was 1962 again and I was nine years old, plump, curly-headed, in a checked shirt and ebony-rimmed glasses. I looked around the auditorium, searching for brothers and sisters, little kids perched on folding seats, poking and squirming.

But then, as the lights came up and the next speaker was introduced, the illusion dissolved and I saw that we were indeed all grown, and that it was 1986.

My sisters sat together. There was Susan, beautiful as Kate Hepburn. In June, she finished medical school at the University of California in San Francisco. She still looked gaunt from malaria contracted the previous year when she was delivering babies in China. Beside her sat Beth, the "baby" of the family, age twenty-three, and Kathryn, our oldest sister, the Yiddish scholar, with her fiancé.

My two brothers were even later than I. Jon, the environmental scientist, arrived twenty minutes after I did and took an aisle seat. Then, just before lunch, wearing hospital whites (which matched his pallid complexion), Dan, the third-year surgery resident, slipped in with practiced silence. Almost immediately, he dozed off.

We were reunited: the whole family was in one room. A rare event—the first time in years.

During a short break, we began catching up. Called back

from diaspora as we were by Dad's forced retirement (a retirement celebrated this weekend by receptions, dinners,
and by this *Festschrift*, a presentation of scientific papers in
his honor), we were all, I could tell, bursting with stories,
tales of the latest news from hospitals in California and
New York and Cleveland. No sooner did we start talking,
though, than Dad broke in to introduce us to a Stanford
physiologist, a Harvard cardiologist, an Oregon monkey researcher, whose visits to our house or to Dad's lab we
vaguely recalled from two decades before. Interrupted, we
assumed our best public smiles.

At lunch there wasn't enough to go around: just as at
home, a crowd of hungry visitors had dropped in. Jon and
Dan headed for the cafeteria and returned with cheeseburgers, Cokes, and chocolate layer cake, which the rest of us
eyed greedily over our lunch of tuna, iceberg lettuce, and
carrot sticks.

Healthy food—the bane of our existence! From our early
childhood, at Dad's insistence, our diet was low in cholesterol and saturated fats. Two decades before the rest of
America, we had ice milk, not ice cream; margarine, not
butter. We shunned eggs, we exercised aerobically. In Dad's
lab, electrodes strapped onto our chests and limbs, we
climbed on treadmills and bicycle ergometers and ran up
imaginary mountains. Dad measured our "vital capacity,"
the breathing volume of our lungs, and pinched fat folds in
calipers, for the laudable goal of determining our fitness,
our cardiac reserve, our exercise capacity in kilogram-
meters of work, our percentage of lean body weight. At
once we were Victorian and post-modern, provincial and
European. We had no television; we read. As a young soldier, Dad had stood at the entrance of Bergen-Belsen by
piles of starved Jewish corpses, and was haunted by what
he had witnessed; and so, through our childhood, it was as
though any night all six, no, all eight of us, might have sud-

denly to run into the darkness, fleeing Nazis, leaving our peaceful Midwestern street behind.

Dad made us want to be doctors—that is, when he wasn't driving us crazy. His example alone would have sufficed: we saw his day-in-and-day-out dedication, his willingness to hop in the old Corvair in the middle of the night to run down to the hospital to stabilize a sick patient in the ICU, and we observed a thousand satisfactions of the doctor's life which had nothing to do with money. Unfortunately, Dad didn't always trust the effect of his example, and tried to bolster it with words. Didactic, professorial words. And thus, our relationships—father and sons, father and daughters—had their rocky moments, even when there was no real disagreement.

There had been a moment of that yesterday, for me, when Dad and I had lunch at the doctors' dining room. We sat with a group of other doctors—talking about how medicine had changed since World War II, with the advent of cardiac resuscitation, and coronary-care units and heart transplants, and malpractice suits, and managed care—and when they left, Dad asked the usual wrong question: "Are you doing any research?"

He knew I always answered "No," with the unspoken "And I'm not interested in doing it." Maybe he posed the question with the best of intentions, but it always felt like a challenge, a complaint. My brother Dan had no trouble laughing it off. But I never had an answer. What he asked, no, *demanded*, was for us to define ourselves as doctors in the context of the past, to state bluntly how our professional attainments, our production of new medical knowledge, would stack up against those of previous generations.

That day, though, I surprised him: I *had* started doing research. Of a sort. Not laboratory work, not the massive clinical, ecological studies he had always done, but instead an analysis of previously collected data on 789 hospitalized patients, in a computerized database. My paper on "command hallucinations" had just been accepted for publication in a psychiatric journal. Schizophrenic patients often hear voices, and sometimes the voices command them to do things—to cut themselves, to jump off a bridge. Conventional wisdom held these to be dangerous voices. But my study showed that it was rare for schizophrenics to act on the commands: usually they were able to ignore them.

"A *research* paper," Dad said dubiously.

I nodded.

Rather than being pleased, Dad seemed distracted, even annoyed. "Let's go. I'll show you around the new buildings."

All the way out of the dining room, he introduced me to one colleague after another. Then he took me on a whirlwind tour of the new outpatient building. The entryway, as broad as a hotel lobby, led to a skylit atrium with a fountain around which dozens of doctors and medical students and visitors sat having lunch, and then to brightly carpeted corridors where patients and their children waited to be seen. A far cry from the yellowed marble and cracked plaster of the old clinic, the new outpatient building resembled a shopping mall more than a hospital. We proceeded through laboratories, inpatient units. The familiar old hospital through which we used to wander on Saturday afternoons on our way to meet Dad was gone—or, if still there, was so changed as to seem new.

Dad ducked into a stairwell and began bounding up two steps at a time. I ran after him.

Four flights up, we stepped out onto a carpeted corridor; he darted to the right and we were in his office.

I looked around: the usual clutter of books and papers, plaques and awards, plastic multicolored hearts, massive blue volumes containing hundreds of his medical papers (Kathryn spent a high-school summer cataloguing them). To the right, his laboratory, once a gloomy place filled with round oscilloscope screens and slate-gray electronic consoles, now was alive with color. The speckled linoleum floor was hidden beneath bright carpeting, and rowing machines, stationary bicycles, a fancy treadmill filled the room. Except for instruments measuring oxygen consumption, and a bank of computers, it looked like a health club. Or, to be more precise, health clubs had come to look like Dad's lab—they, too, had become places for retraining the heart.

Our conversation continued. My talks with Dad, once immeasurably difficult, had become more civil in recent years, even friendly, but also increasingly distant. Each of us told about articles written, books in progress, patients seen, lectures given.

That day, the eve of his retirement, there was a surprise. For the first time ever—or at least the first time since his heart surgery ten years before—there was uncertainty in Dad's voice.

"So, what are you going to do next?" I asked, trying to imagine what life would be like without *this*—the laboratory, patients, the hospital.

There was a long pause.

"I don't know," he answered. "I'm still not sure. There . . . there are a lot of possibilities." Ever since he had turned sixty-five, the Medical Center's retirement age, this question had been raised, but each year he had wangled an extension. Now he was seventy, and there was no room for delay. Hence Dad's riffs of conversation, of inspired ideas. A Ph.D. in medical ethics. A multimillion-dollar grant on how exercise slows osteoporosis in women. "Or," he concluded glumly, "maybe we'll pack up and move to Florida, where your mother and I can rot on a beach."

"Oh, you couldn't possibly do that!"

Another long pause. "Well, I'll probably just hang on here at Western Reserve." Conversation veered to the practicalities of emeritus life, how your salary stopped but you could keep seeing patients. "Plus"—an awkward laugh—"a free parking space for life."

I could imagine him all too easily as one of those frail old professors you see hobbling out of Grand Rounds, those retired doctors who won't or can't let go of medicine. As he talked about how he would have to pack up everything in the laboratory in a few months and move, I felt his sadness, his vulnerability—and my own unease.

I hadn't realized how much stake I placed in Dad's utter certainty.

Here I was, thirty-two years old, married, and living in Manhattan. I had finished medical school in June of 1980, and residency training in psychiatry four years later, followed by a year of fellowship at Columbia. In the summer of 1985, I had begun my current job in the outpatient psychiatric clinic at Beth Israel Medical Center in lower Manhattan. I had spent the past year seeing patients, teaching residents and medical students, and working with the sickest of psychiatric patients, schizophrenics who also were severe drug abusers.

After a decade of striving, of sleepless nights and endless studying, I had come to the end of my medical training. Finally, I was in a position to begin contributing my own stories of healing to the familiar ones of childhood, to add to the family's oral tradition of doctoring. Furthermore, my literary career had finally been launched: with articles and essays in magazines, two books accepted for publication.

In brief, everything was settled. Yet, in some difficult-to-define way, I felt at loose ends, unsettled. And so, I sensed, did my siblings.

Perhaps it had to do with family. Dad's retirement—the

intimation of a generation's passing—shook the certainties that had guided our lives since infancy. We were losing our emotional compass, and now we had no choice but to find our own direction.

For our family, medicine always provided these certainties, a mix of privilege and responsibilities. Yet medicine had changed radically, becoming almost unrecognizable. Mom's father, Dr. Harold Feil, had practiced in Cleveland since before World War I; Dad graduated from medical school in 1941, six months before Pearl Harbor; and Mom finished in 1949. All three spent their careers affiliated with one hospital, one medical school. They followed patients for decades, keeping them alive in defiance of all odds. They devoted everything to healing; in return, patients idolized them. Loyal nurses and secretaries and lab technicians spent whole careers at their side.

In 1986, such dedication was virtually unheard of. Doctors moved from one hospital to another, one city to the next, like baseball players traded between rival teams. They complained of mountains of paperwork, of constant second-guessing of their decisions, of the ever-present threat of litigation. Patients complained that care had become impersonal, high-priced, deadeningly bureaucratic. They told tales of corruption and greed—of unnecessary procedures, of doctors fraudulently billing insurance companies for work not done.

Beyond that, as I could see every day at the hospital—and even more by walking the Manhattan streets—was medicine's failure to live up to its 1960s promises of health and longevity for all. Despite the "miracles" of liver and heart transplants, of magnetic resonance imaging scans and angioplasty, of fetal surgery, and gallstone lithotripsy, by the mid-1980s American health care was in a dismal state. Costs were rising ten to fifteen percent a year; medical care consumed over ten percent of the gross national product. At the same time, tens of millions of Americans, lacking medical insurance, lived in terror of hospitalization. Millions of others, even with health insurance, couldn't find good care.

In the Reagan years, as fortunes were being made on Wall Street, as stretch limos double-parked outside trendy restaurants, and as two-bedroom apartments sold for half a million dollars, legions of sick and homeless people filled the city. A subway ride became a live medical textbook, a satyricon of disease, physical and mental: emaciated AIDS sufferers, gaunt tuberculars, wheezing emphysemics, jittery crackheads, prancing unmedicated schizophrenics. Moreover, the mood at my hospital was hardly boundless optimism, hardly the expectation that medicine was about to cure such ills. Instead, there was battle fatigue, anger, dread of the next health crisis around the corner. Ignorance, bureaucracy, greed, miscommunication, expensive technology—and incurable disease—tarnished the glitter of science. No wonder that, over lunch, my fellow doctors debated whether it was a mistake to have gone into medicine.

On one side was our family tradition of selfless service—and on the other, the harsh, cynical world I saw every day in New York City. Did our devotion to medicine still make sense, or did it result from some misguided loyalty to a world that no longer existed?

Now that I was married and considering beginning a family, these questions acquired new urgency. How did I want my family to be, especially compared to the family in which I had grown up? And because I come from a very particular kind of family, would I want my children to be doctors?

Questions I couldn't begin to answer—yet impossible not to ask.

* * *

The afternoon sessions continued our whirlwind tour of late-twentieth-century medicine. A Stanford professor showed how public education on diet and exercise dramatically decreased heart-disease deaths in five California towns. A cardiologist-marathoner hobbled forward on inflamed knees to discuss how exercise affects longevity, his complex statistics showing (as far as I could tell) that running a hundred miles a week will increase your life expectancy by several months—hardly worth the effort, it seemed. A Harvard psychiatrist told of the newest evidence that, after a heart attack, dying muscle sends chemical messages to the brain, often causing depression. A rainbow of PET scans and regional cerebral blood-flow maps showed the heart conversing with the brain.

Next Beth, our youngest sister, age twenty-three, talked about her research project. Under the supervision of an Israeli scientist, she had used plasmids, tiny circles of DNA, to snag bits of human genetic material. Then she transplanted these genes to e. coli bacteria, and grew them on agar plates, one colony for each gene. From an enormous hodgepodge of genes you could, remarkably enough, select the one which had coded for insulin. Eventually, genetically transformed insulin-producing cells might be injected back into diabetic patients, to cure their disease. Beth described their work effortlessly. It was brilliant.

Then former Fellows from Dad's lab presented research, and told stories. They told how Dad refused to give up when a patient was in a coma for weeks, and how she miraculously recovered. How Dad developed a machine to take EKGs on fish in aquariums, as a "bioassay" of digitalis levels. How Dad rode shotgun in airplanes, testing the cardiovascular responses of parachutists. And how, one time, late for a plane, Dad and his Fellow roared down I-90 toward the airport at eighty miles an hour.

Jon nudged me: "Remember?"

"A thousand times," I whispered.

"We arrived at the instant the plane was scheduled to take off," the doctor continued. "We're in the lobby, carrying suitcases, briefcases, big heavy boxes of lantern slides. Suddenly Herm stops. He hands me his suitcase, his slides. He says, 'Here, take these. Now run ahead, tell them to hold the plane.' " Everyone laughed.

"That's Dad, all right," said Jon.

After the last presentation we headed home, and I lay down for a brief nap in Daniel's room, where I was staying. There was a reception at seven at the Automobile Museum, followed by a formal dinner at eight. I could hear brothers and sisters thumping up and down stairs. Dad's voice, calling: "Mary, where'd you put my clean shirt?" The shower running, stopping, running again.

Three floors, seven bedrooms, a full attic and basement, a two-story garage—ours is a big house. The kind Midwesterners fill with six or seven kids and a century of ancestors' belongings. That day, however, creaking and shuddering under our adult weight, it felt tiny, claustrophobic.

It was hard to believe we grew up here. It seemed like a lifetime ago, someone else's lifetime.

Dangerously restless, I wandered out of Dan's room and up the stairs to my old attic room. Ever since Jon had bought my grandparents' house two years earlier, my old room had been used as a storeroom for family possessions; recently Jon had cleared out his basement. Besides human hearts in lucite blocks, and a lampshade with EKG patterns, and the metal hospital bedside stand with which I had grown up, my room was now occupied by boxes of the past. A seemingly infinite archive covered my bed and proceeded shoulder-high across the floor.

Century-old dust covered everything—cardboard hat-boxes of nineteenth-century postcards, tin bread boxes crammed with family photographs, suitcases of clippings from Midwestern newspapers. And cartons of medical records of my grandfather Dr. Harold Feil's long-dead patients, some going back to the 1920s. Within a few minutes I discovered issues of Volume I of *The Omaha Bee*, a newspaper founded in 1871 by my great-great-grandfather Edward Rosewater. And letters in Yiddish and German dating to the 1860s, and a telegram announcing my grandmother's birth.

I hunkered down on the floor, looking at old medical books from my grandfather's library. A stack, no, a collection, of various editions of Osler's *The Principles and Practice of Medicine*. Starting with the first edition, a leather-bound book dated 1892, it ended in the 1950s with the fourteenth. In one volume, dated 1910 and inscribed "Ex Libris Harold S. Feil," my grandfather had scrawled notes to himself: "Death and Sudden Death—Brouerdel," and "Read up works of Paget, Hunter, Gross."

Must have been Papa's medical-school textbook. A large part of it, I noticed, was taken up with "Specific Infectious Diseases." I scanned chapter headings: Typhoid Fever, Typhus Fever, Relapsing Fever, Small-Pox, Measles, Rubella, Whooping-Cough, Influenza, Dengue, Rheumatic Fever, Cholera Asiatica, Yellow Fever, Syphilis. All horrible scourges seventy-five years ago; now largely eradicated in America. The thick section on Tuberculosis contained separate chapters on infection of the lungs, the digestive tract, the liver, the brain—not unlike what you would see today in a medical textbook under AIDS.

I turned to Treatment. Natural or spontaneous cure. Open-air treatment. Treatment in sanatoria. Climatic treatment: "The first question to be decided is whether the patient is fit to be sent from home." Under "General medical treatment," Osler notes: "No medicinal agents have any special or peculiar action upon tuberculous processes."

I closed the book. TB in 1910 *was* like AIDS in 1986. Except that, in the world Papa faced as a young doctor, almost *all* diseases were incurable. Even in the 1940s, when Mom and Dad graduated from medical school, the situation had hardly changed.

The flyleaf of another old medical textbook was inscribed: "Dr. Gustave R. Feil." Who could that have been? I wondered. I made a mental note to ask Mom.

I heard voices downstairs, attenuated as on winter mornings long ago when Mom tried, usually unsuccessfully, to get me out of bed in time for school. Eventually, the entire family would gather before the intercom (scavenged from the hospital) and sing reveille:

> *You've got to get up, you've got to get up,*
> *You've got to get up in the morning!*

Now again came a chorus: "Come down! Come down! We're leaving!"

I straightened, wiping dust off my trousers. My forehead brushed the ceiling as I ran downstairs.

It was surreal. At the Automobile Museum, on East Drive in Cleveland near the Art Museum, Western Reserve Historical Society, and Cleveland Institute of Music, we stood surrounded by enormous gleaming Duesenbergs, by Packards and Pierce-Arrows larger than some New York apartments. Carrying non-alcoholic drinks and plates of low-cholesterol hors d'oeuvres, we wandered through the reception, among dozens of doctors, hordes of grateful patients ("Your father is wonderful, he saved my life," sounding more than ever like a rebuke). Patrons of research, longtime secretaries and lab assistants, family friends. These old cars were the hoarded jewels of faded industry in this rusty Midwestern city which once produced more cars than Detroit. Now the city's biggest glories are its gleaming, ever-expanding hospitals, its booming business is disease.

In this gallery we six kids finally caught up with each other.

Tonight Dan carried two beepers. For once he was out of hospital whites, but he was still on call. He asked me about clinic work, and about my books, and told me about urology.

Motor-vehicle accidents, shootings, stabbings, and blunt trauma—he was in his first full year of urology, his third year of surgery residency, and tonight, he told me, he was covering urological emergencies for the entire West Side of Cleveland. Last night a truck-accident victim came in with a pelvic fracture and a perforated bladder. Dan had been in the OR until 4 a.m., doing an "exploratory laparotomy," and then sewing up the bladder. Later a kid came in with a "torsed testicle"—painful twisting of the blood vessels to the testicle, requiring immediate surgery to avoid gangrene. A few weeks before, a schizophrenic with his penis in a paper bag checked into the emergency room. Amputated in protest of world violence.

Susan approached. She, too, had stories to tell. In two months she would begin residency in obstetrics and gynecology in Boston: four years, the first two made up largely of every second night on call. Graceful and confident, Susan has always had an adventurous streak, first expressed at the age of ten when she traveled alone to visit a friend in California. She is fluent in Spanish (she worked in a cardiology clinic in Mexico City), and French (junior year abroad in Paris), and can get by in Mandarin. The previous year, she spent nine months in China studying obstetrics—in Shijiazhung, an industrial city, and in Shanghai, at the Second Medical College. It was amazing, she told us, how different Chinese ideas of privacy were from ours. In China, when doctors examined a patient, the other patients on a floor gathered around to watch. Even pelvic exams! She and her boyfriend traveled into newly opened parts of Kunming and Szechuan Province, near the Mekong River, and then up to Tibet. Dancing had just been legalized—they spent hours teaching the twist to Chinese peasants.

Beth joined us, her long blond hair tied with a blue ribbon. We congratulated her for the lecture: at least someone in the family was doing real science! Susan mentioned that Beth just moved out of the house, into an apartment.

"It's weird," Beth said, "leaving Mom and Dad. They're totally at loose ends without kids at home."

Susan laughed. "Just look in the refrigerator! Mom still buys for eight."

Beth described her latest dilemma: whether to go to medical school or to get a Ph.D. in geology. She'd taken the medical-research job to help make up her mind.

"Well," I said, the helpful older brother, "don't let anybody pressure you. All this nonsense about family tradition—you know, you don't *have* to be a doctor."

Beth's anger surprised me: "What do you mean?"

"What I'm saying. You don't have to . . ."

"Why does everybody *else* get to be a doctor?" she responded passionately, as if I was withholding her inheritance. "Why can't I?"

"Beth!" I said. "Of course you *can*. If you—"

Fortunately, we were interrupted by Kathryn and her fiancé, David Stern, who were getting married in Cleveland in July and were struggling to make Orthodox wedding arrangements from Philadelphia. Dan wandered back, telling about wind-surfing on Lake Erie, and Jon, a huge Nikon in hand, came up to immortalize us on 400 ASA film. Then came dinner, healthful as ever. And then, of course, speeches.

The chairman of medicine, the president of the heart association, famous heart doctors. All talking about how Dad's work had revolutionized the care of heart patients, improving millions of lives. Of course, Dad had a few words to add.

When the guests had scattered, we gathered in the Auto Museum lobby and wandered out to our cars. It was raining softly, a mild spring Midwestern drizzle. Since Shabbat had begun, Dad and Mom followed in their yellow Oldsmobile behind Kathryn and her fiancé, who were walking home (Dan informed me that it was Sid Meadow's old car, bought from his widow after Sid died the year before at age ninety-one). The rest of us piled into Jon's TransAm and my rented car.

For once, the bantering and teasing had stopped.

Silence.

As I drove, I remembered the trips we used to take up to Canada—seven hundred miles in one day, Dad at the wheel of the Plymouth or the Rambler station wagon, Mom and a couple of babies up front, three or four kids in the back seat. We'd bicker, play games, occasionally vomit out the window. We would reach Niagara Falls after dark, then roar into the vast flatlands of Ontario, driving long after midnight. Above us on the roof, the heavy luggage rack made the whole car sway and lurch, as though we were shaken by giants.

Tomorrow we would each head back to our own lives. Beth to finish moving out, and to decide whether to apply to medical schools (I had a clue to which way she was leaning). Susan to pack for her cross-country move, for an obstetrics and gynecology internship starting June 15.

Kathryn to get married. Dan and Jon and I to operating room and field site and clinic.

Dad would begin sorting through papers, packing up his laboratory.

I could see at that moment how it would be for the six of us, having children, living our lives, telling our stories until they began to turn into myths; myths for each of us, that we would need to propel us on our own trajectories, in six directions, from a common source. I could see, for those who chose to become doctors, how we would struggle with twenty-first-century medicine to make our own tales of healing, to find a disease or disorder that demanded to be cured, to find new ways to alleviate suffering. There was quite a story there, it seemed to me: the story of doctoring in our family, how each generation related to the last one and to the next, the types of medicine they practiced, how that changed over the decades. Perhaps even a book. I had been debating what to write next; and had even begun a second novel. Might this be a more compelling story?

For me, who needed to cure but also to tell, to doctor and to write, there was a new mystery. According to Mom, Gustave Feil was Papa's stepfather (I had never heard his name mentioned before), and he *had* been a doctor—until he got tuberculosis. Dad mentioned in passing that Nana's great-uncle Nate was a doctor, too, who had encouraged Papa to enter medicine back before World War I.

So the family's doctoring was older than I had known. Not just three generations, it was four, or perhaps even five. Must be over a hundred years. Where it started, and why— that I didn't know. I could barely imagine what medicine must have been like back then. Obviously, there was a lot more digging to be done in the attic.

I followed Jon's car up the rain-slicked streets, along the familiar curves of Cedar Hill, past darkened stores and apartments, rising toward home.

2

1875: BIRTH NOTES

CONSIDER the case of Catherine Steiner, a thirty-year-old Bohemian woman whom Dr. Marcus Rosenwasser examined at her home in Cleveland at 8 a.m. on June 16, 1875. For three days Mrs. Steiner had been in labor, but the baby would not come. She was exhausted. Instead of being engaged head-first in her pelvis, the baby, Rosenwasser discovered, lay sideways, head left, feet right, in a position that prevented birth. Only its right arm protruded. Furthermore, the umbilical cord had stopped pulsating, indicating that the mother's blood supply to the baby was threatened. Both mother and child were endangered.

Rosenwasser reached into the birth canal, but Mrs. Steiner screamed with pain, so he instructed his student, Mr. Orwig, to administer chloroform. He reached again. After several fruitless efforts, he seized the baby's right knee and pulled a seven-pound baby girl into the world.

Amazingly, both mother and baby survived.

Four weeks later, after several routine deliveries, he came to the bedside of Anna Schneider, whose labor also had stopped progressing. His notes read:

Called at 6 a.m. Os 2″ in diam. No part presenting—externally diagnose transverse position—at 9½ a.m. ad-

minister chloroform (Orwig) & after seizing left foot
(child lying feet to left, head to right, back to front) rup-
ture membranes & extract; in freeing second arm (left) it
is fractured—head is brought by Prague method & fingers hooked into lower jaw, bringing chin to chest—child
soon cries & mother does well. Placenta by Credé's
method.

It was like having a ghost come suddenly into view, a
ghost whose existence I had not even suspected, but only
dumbly sensed. The package, sent by Federal Express, had
arrived at my Beth Israel Medical Center office one late-
summer day in 1990, sent by a Dr. Stan Marguiles of Hol-
lywood, Florida, who is married to Karen Mintz Marguiles,
a great-granddaughter of Marcus Rosenwasser. A distant
cousin had learned of my interest in the family's history,
and after a few phone calls, this had materialized. In the
package was a leather-bound volume with the words *Obstetric Notes* gold-embossed on its spine. It sat on my desk
all afternoon, through several patients, a dozen phone calls,
a minor crisis in the Walk-In Clinic. When things finally
quieted down, I closed my office door and gingerly opened
the cracked leather binding.

I read eagerly. *Obstetric Notes* was exactly what I was
hoping to find. It consisted of a log of over a thousand deliveries performed between the years 1875 and 1893 by Dr.
Marcus Rosenwasser, my great-great-grandfather's brother,
who practiced in Cleveland, Ohio. In an elegant, precise
surgeon's hand, using medical shorthand easily decipher-
able more than a century later, he detailed his practice case
by case, patient by patient, describing complications and triumphs.

I say a ghost, because, like Gustave Feil, Marcus
Rosenwasser had been unknown to me; yet, once I discovered his existence (in a mimeographed family history done

by a distant relative during World War II, and supplemented by yellowed clippings and old photographs in boxes in my parents' attic), the entire history of my family had to be rewritten. As ghosts, Gustave and Marcus had been defined by their absence, not their presence, by their very lack of substance. It is fitting in a way that the first doctor in the family was an obstetrician, because Marcus Rosenwasser brought into life not only thousands of babies but also a tradition—a tradition of healing that has lasted, so far, five generations.

What I had begun casually during my visit home for Dad's retirement celebration was now approaching the dimensions of a quest and an obsession. I was looking not just for family secrets but for origins. The need to know, to tell a family history, had gradually become something larger; a desire to reconstruct and re-create changes in medicine—as seen through the experience of my family. And not only for my own benefit, not only to come to terms with the family's history for myself, but—the idea had returned again and again over the following year—to write a book that would tell the story from its beginning to the present. I hardly knew what I was getting into.

On semi-annual visits home to Cleveland, I spent afternoons looking through the cartons and boxes of records in my old attic room and going through medical-school libraries and historical-society archives. Soon, foot-high piles of documents covered my desk at the hospital, and cartons full of old medical textbooks and stacks of photocopied letters and journals and ancient newspaper clippings filled my study at home. I put my novel aside, uncompleted, to focus on the family's history. I carried manila folders full of documents back and forth on the bus as I commuted, scribbling in the margins when we were trapped in gridlock on the way up First Avenue, between Beth Israel and the Fifty-ninth Street Bridge. In this fashion, I slowly discovered a complicated genealogy of healing, one that went back to the Civil War.

I had never suspected that. Not only was my grandfather's stepfather, Gustave Feil, a doctor, but so were three brothers from the previous generation—Marcus Rosenwasser and Charles and Nathan Rosewater (who had anglicized their name). The three brothers were great-uncles to *both* my mother's parents. (My grandmother and grandfather had become cousins by circumstances of adoption and remarriage, members of a large Midwestern Jewish family that had been in the United States since the 1840s; and even though I had diagrammed a dozen pages of genealogies going back to 1799, at first I found it impossible to keep all the relationships straight!)

But one thing was clear: Marcus was the first doctor in the family. And—so far as I could reconstruct from the records available—a doctor daring and accomplished in his practice.

In 1875, Marcus was twenty-eight years old; he had been in practice in Cleveland for seven years. As a nineteenth-century doctor, he had severely limited tools. He knew nothing about optimal prenatal care. He had no drugs to speed—or to slow—labor. Though he could feel the umbilical cord's pulsations to determine whether blood was still getting to the fetus, he had no real means of fetal monitoring. Many of his patients were infected with tuberculosis or syphilis or gonorrhea, but he had no antibiotics to treat them. Most medications of his day, complex mixtures of various plants and minerals crushed and dissolved in alcohol, and labeled with long Latin names, were utterly useless to treat disease. Typhoid fever, for instance, which spread through contaminated drinking water, was treated with leeches, tar water, and bark tonic, which had little influence on whether the patient survived the severe bouts of fever, rashes, mental depression, and intestinal hemorrhages. He could not monitor or correct dehydration or electrolyte imbalances. Should a woman start bleeding uncontrollably during childbirth, there were no intravenous lines or fluids for transfusions. He lacked X rays and ultrasounds and electrocardiograms. Like other obstetricians, he delivered babies in his street clothes, and probably only sporadically washed his hands. He wore neither mask nor gloves, and his deliveries were done in the unsterile environment of patients' homes or, even worse, in the contagion-inducing setting of the hospital's maternity ward (in which the maternal death rate was sometimes as high as fifteen to twenty percent!). Furthermore, when labor did not progress, Marcus could not resort to the cesarean section: this ancient operation—which had been performed since the early Christian era—was nearly always fatal, and was not done successfully in the United States until 1894.

What Marcus had were forceps, which could reach high in the birth canal to grasp the baby's head; and chloroform (or occasionally "aether") for anesthesia in cases where the pain of childbirth became unbearable. And he had various dressings of sponge or gauze, and probes and catheters of rubber and metal. Only two decades earlier, obstetricians had broken the taboo that prevented them from looking at women's genitalia as they worked, so he had the speculum (an instrument which opens the vagina to allow examination), and his eyes. But, most of all, he had his hands—with which he palpated abdomens, felt for fetuses or tumors, and vigorously rotated, repositioned, and extracted babies, babies by the hundred, babies living and dead.

Reading through his logbook, I tried to imagine how it must have been to practice under such conditions, what it was like, for instance, when a baby was irreversibly impacted in its mother's pelvis, to be forced to choose between crushing its skull with forceps or watching the woman bleed to death. The skill that I could sense as I read the log became most apparent when Marcus tabulated the results of his work. He compiled numbers every hundred deliveries. In his third hundred deliveries, he noted:

Of 100 females there were born 101 children
" 101 children " " 59 boys, 42 girls
" 101 " " " 93 living, 8 dead
" 8 dead, 2 were blighted, 6 dead or died during or before delivery . . . *Mothers all recovered.*

In his fourth hundred, there were 104 children, of which ten died; one mother died (from peritonitis); in his fifth hundred, three babies out of a hundred died and no mothers died, though three had serious complications. On the back of a hospital memo, I added up his results, then I pulled a few medical reference books off my bookshelves for comparison. Despite a lack of available treatments, only one out of Marcus's three hundred women patients died, or 0.3 percent; yet almost 7 percent of babies died. My medical-history book cited numbers from 1915, the first year that national U.S. statistics were kept: a maternal death rate of sixty-one women per ten thousand births, or 0.6 percent, and an infant mortality rate of 4.3 percent.

Marcus's statistics compared well with those of forty years later. They were even more remarkable if one considers that most of his patients were poor immigrants, highly vulnerable to infection and malnutrition.

In the back of *Obstetric Notes*, I found Marcus's comments on his most difficult and puzzling cases. "Vaginismus—Contracted Pelvis—Abortion," one of the most perplexing, showed him at the peak of his obstetrical career, making the most of limited tools. He wrote:

Aug 4, 1875
Mrs. Mary Rowe; age 24; English; married 15 months;

pregnant for first time. Husband came first to inform me that since marriage has not enjoyed sexual intercourse on account of extreme sensitivity of wife—any attempt on his part was at once followed by expressions of intense suffering on the part of his wife, culminating in complete fainting—Is not aware of ever having had complete connection. Mrs. R—— is a well-developed, muscular brunette, black hair & eyes, quite agitated, nervous . . .

She begged him to perform an abortion. While doing an exam ("In attempting vaginal touch, patient at once clenches thighs & evinces great pain"), he measured her pelvis and concluded that (for anatomical and perhaps psychological reasons) she was unable to have a baby successfully. Reluctantly, after consultation with one of his colleagues, he decided to yield to her entreaties. Thus, he introduced a speculum into her vagina and dilated her cervix with a "tent." Eventually, the uterus emptied "and expelled a pair of twins."

During the abortion, Marcus was able to determine that while Mrs. Rowe's pelvis was too small to deliver a baby at full nine-month term, it might be large enough for a premature baby: "Think she might give birth to medium child at 7 mos."

Two years later, Mrs. Rowe returned to him. "The vaginismus has continued since the abortion, though not in so high a degree. The husband occasionally effected an entrance into the vagina, though the pat.[ient] sometimes fainted from pain," he wrote—revealing his ignorance of what would now be seen as a treatable psychological problem. She had, however, managed to become pregnant again, and this time wanted to have the child.

The dilemma was this: how to deliver a baby small enough to pass through her pelvis, yet physiologically mature enough to survive. The time—seven months—was right, he judged. Therefore, he worked to induce premature labor. What could be easily accomplished today with injections of oxytocin, a drug that precipitates labor, at that time required a massive, almost heroic, intervention. First he advanced a "flexible bougie" into her cervix, then the "smallest size Barnes dilator," then a "large size sponge tent," and next began injecting warm water every few hours; then he tried a second tent, and finally a "flexible catheter no. 22 size," which did the trick.

After four days in which the cervix was progressively dilated, Mrs. Rowe's water broke, and at 2:30 a.m. of February 25, 1877, he delivered a "medium sized living boy." Three days later he noted triumphantly: "*Feb 28*. Mother & child doing well."

Any historian or biographer trying to reconstruct past lives must be frustrated by the vagaries of survival. Letters may refer to events that remain everlastingly ambiguous, or to people whose importance can be only guessed; a diary may end suddenly just before or after the crucial events one is investigating, and descendants or intimates may have distressingly vague memories. Most difficult to reconstruct is the mundane, the routine of daily life: How many patients did Marcus usually see? What did his office look like? *Obstetric Notes* provided only a partial description, a tantalizing skeleton. I am sure such problems exist for any historian, but they are even more vexing for a writer from another discipline who lacks the experience of the professional historian.

Instead, as I read through archives and letters and medical reports and newspapers, doing my best to identify the characters in the hundreds of century-old photographs (the Rosenwassers/Rosewaters loved to have their pictures taken!), I was continually baffled, certain that I was missing something important, and constantly doing my best to create a pattern from the fragments available, but without any conviction that it represented more than a reasonably plausible fiction.

The questions that most immediately preoccupied me, once I had a picture of Rosenwasser at work, were these: Why—and how—did he become a doctor?

The nearest to "why" was in an 1863 letter to Edward Rosewater. Edward, his oldest brother (who had also anglicized his surname), was a telegrapher who had recently left the War Department in Washington, D.C., to go to the frontier town of Omaha, Nebraska Territory, on the edge of what maps referred to as the Great American Desert. On December 25, Marcus, age sixteen, wrote to Edward:

> The small pox has been raging among neighbors, and other diseases have swept from the earth some of our good old friends and acquaintances . . . death is now so frequent that it is uppermost in my mind; that Mrs. Weidenthal, the mother of the Bros. Weidenthal, passed to another world is not surprising, she was old and weak, and after a sickness of three weeks she departed to the place where we all expect to meet. But what was our surprise when soon after her death came a letter from New York, that young and healthy Mrs. Ganz died of the Typhoid fever, leaving a mourning widower and two orphans! You can imagine how that struck the heart of her parents, especially the mother, who to this time, half with and half without her senses, was completely deranged by the information, which could not be kept secret from her—Mr. Woditzka was really to be pittied [sic] at this time: the son [a soldier?] not yet heard of, the daughter dead, the wife insane . . . And what is all this, to the sudden death of that robust, rosy cheeked young maiden, Ms. Menges? On the 8th of Dec there were two funerals, *the one* attended by all the citizens, martial music and

honors, for they followed to their last resting place the brave, lamented heroes of the 7th, Colonels Creighton and Crane, *the other* by only few who had the courage to follow and perform the last services for that girl. She died of the small pox and leaves behind a childless father and a mother not to be consoled . . .

The pitiful deaths of friends and neighbors, and the heroic deaths of soldiers in the Great War—these scenes haunted Marcus. The lakefront town of Cleveland was plagued by contagious disease in the mid-nineteenth century, by epidemics of typhoid, smallpox, malaria, and other infections spread by crowding, contaminated drinking water, swamp-bred insects, and inadequate sewage disposal. Fully a third of babies born in mid-nineteenth-century Cleveland died before they reached the age of five years. And then there was the carnage of the Civil War, in which it is estimated that two-thirds of the 300,000 Union soldiers' deaths came from disease, not gunfire. Combine the omnipresence of death and disease with an immigrant's drive toward self-betterment through education, a religious tradition of good deeds, of *tzedakah*, and an imagination stirred by the beauties of science (the microscope, Marcus wrote in his high-school oration, allowed one to "behold with enthusiasm and leap in ecstasy at the sight of the mere paring of a hoof, that has perhaps been trodden in the dust for months past, so gorgeous are its colors, so regular its outline and so beautiful the whole!"), and with luck you get a doctor.

Some pieces were missing, though. Marcus was the first family member to receive any advanced education—in an era when only one percent of the population had any education beyond high school. As one of five brothers, why was he chosen? Then there is the notation in a mimeographed family history, dating from 1942, that Marcus did not want to go to medical school at all but really wanted to enter West Point, to earn his commission as a Union officer. If so, why did he acquiesce? Moreover, why did his family send him all the way back to Europe for medical school? Was it to escape the horrors of war, or was it because they knew he could get better training in the old country?

After all, the family had moved to America only a decade before. Marcus's father, Herman Rosenwasser, orphaned at the age of seven, had been apprenticed to a butcher in Libna, Czechoslovakia, before becoming a tutor through a process of self-education. After migrating to Cleveland in 1854 with his wife, Rosalia, and nine children, he made his living (like many other Jewish immigrants) in the dry-goods business. Marcus's brothers, Edward and Joseph, went to work immediately to help support the family. After the trauma of immigration, it is surprising that only ten years later plans were made to send Marcus back to Prague.

Even more surprising, I found Marcus's record of these events in a diary he kept from the years 1864 to 1868, a small dark leather-bound volume now in the collection of the Western Reserve Historical Society in Cleveland. It tells how Marcus and his father, leaving Cleveland on June 29, 1864, began an arduous trip by train to New York, then by steamer to Bremen, Germany, then overland to Dresden, Leipzig, bribing corrupt customs officials along the way to prevent their baggage from being confiscated, finally arriving in Prague.

"The scenery is very romantic," seventeen-year-old Marcus wrote in his journal as they traveled through the countryside. "The mountains stretching their lofty tops toward the sky, many of them covered with vineyards or patches of grain and potatoes, some entirely barren, the craggy rocks projecting from their steep sides. I could perceive in every thing that I was in Bohemia, the land of my birth."

On July 22, Marcus and his father entered Bukovan, the small town fifty miles south of Prague (not far from the ancient silver mines of Pribram) where the family had lived in a rough-hewn shack with a large chimney and thatched roof, humans in one room and animals in the other. After weeks of waiting, after innumerable trips to neighboring towns, synagogues, markets, and fairs—and evenings spent watching Pa's card games with various uncles—the euphoria of the returned immigrant began to wane. Then, at noon on August 24, "came a letter from uncle Bernhard announcing my admission as extraordinary hearer to the University" at Prague, his medical studies to begin in October 1864.

After arranging for lodgings, getting a part-time job teaching English, and saying good-bye to his father, who had to return to America, Marcus paid his tuition at the University of Prague and began attending classes. During 1865 and the early part of 1866, Marcus completed courses in botany, anatomy, and zoology (in which he got high honors), and heard lectures on vaccination and trichinosis. One day he noted with excitement: "Began for the first time to dissect—a new era in my life's career." Innumerable dissections followed. He dissected the head, the arm, the leg, the corpse of a child.

For the next three years, until his return to the United States in January 1868, Marcus devoted himself to the study of medicine. Whether chosen fortuitously or deliberately, Marcus's European medical education was much better than any he could have gotten in the United States at that time. Perhaps ten thousand Americans went to Europe between 1870 and 1914 to study medicine. The universities of the Continent—first Edinburgh, London, and Leyden, and then Paris, and finally Vienna and Berlin—were the setting for the world's most sophisticated medical training and research. While native-born Americans often went to medical school in the States, and only afterward went to Europe to pursue specialty "postgraduate" education, the American sons of European immigrants (like Marcus) often returned to the Continent for their entire medical education. Berlin and Vienna were the primary sites Americans visited, but many also attended medical school in Heidelberg, Dresden, Göttingen, and Leipzig, as well as Prague.

Since the 1840s, empirically minded European scientists had forged an enormous revolution in medicine. There was Rudolf Virchow, who discovered the cell as the essential unit of the living organism, and described disease as a result of the disturbed structure of function of cells. And Johannes Müller, who established laboratory studies of body functions, and Jacob Henle, who investigated the microscopic structure of organs, and Robert Koch, who isolated the tuberculosis bacillus. In Paris, the great Louis Pasteur established the validity of the germ theory of disease. And later there was Paul Ehrlich, who produced Salvarsan, the first treatment for syphilis, in 1906. Such great scientists inspired generations of students. The most ambitious young Americans, especially those interested in research careers in physiology or histology or bacteriology, were drawn to the Continent by these remarkable advances. They formed a seemingly endless parade that did not stop until the beginning of World War I—by which time American medicine, led by the German-influenced Johns Hopkins Medical School, was well on its way to becoming the world's most advanced.

Marcus Rosenwasser's focus in his years of European study was not the research laboratory, though, but the lecture hall, the dissecting table, and the clinic. In late 1865 he began to visit the hospital for the first time. This seemingly prosaic activity was in fact remarkable. In most of the world, medical training was still a matter of rote book learning and isolated apprenticeship. The early-nineteenth-century European fusion of the clinic and the lecture had been a major advance. Marcus received clinical training by striking a deal: in exchange for giving English lessons to a certain Dr. Deutschmann, he was permitted to "see and practice upon cases in the hospital . . . on Sunday forenoon."

War was never far off, however. In March 1866, Marcus notes: "Martial law declared over districts of Prague, Plzeň, Písek, Tábor on account of mobs in various parts of the country against the Jews." And in June he writes that war had been declared between Austria and Prussia, and the medical school closed.

The wounded were arriving at the hospital all day; more than three hundred in a few days. "Panic seizes on the people," Marcus wrote, "for the post offices are closed, the military leaving, and likewise the police—it is thought the Prussians will enter in the night or tomorrow." He and a cousin Carl fled Prague. "The immense number of fugitives; the heaps of trunks, the crowding, pushing, crying, can deprive you of your senses—such a sight I never saw in my life—half the city of Prague has fled to this, the only exit from the city." A week later, safely back in Bukovan, he heard the news that eight thousand Prussian soldiers had taken possession of Prague. There he waited. "July 31. All dull and quiet—not a drum heard nor a fife—all the time leading a secluded life, almost entirely ignorant of the outside world, of which all I know is: the *Austrians* are being beaten to *mash*, and that *cholera* is spreading in Bohemia."

The war ended in August 1866 with victory for Bismarck's Prussian troops, but medical school did not begin regularly until November—by which time Marcus was passionately in love with a second cousin from the town of Nadějkov, whose name he records only as Jane. On September 25 she accompanied him to a ball in Tanselikow, where they danced until dawn. A few days later, he confided: "Declare love to Jane—Do I need explain? I'm happy."

With the ebbing of hostilities, Marcus was able to spend ten weeks in a student barracks while completing his clinical work in obstetrics. In the spring he received his diploma from the University of Prague. Following this, he traveled to Bavaria's ancient university city of Würzburg for a week of examinations: it was from there, not Prague, that he was to receive his medical degree, on the condition that he pledge not to practice in Germany. First Marcus passed his written and oral examinations, then he prepared to defend his thesis.

On August 1, 1867, he awoke early and put on his swallowtail jacket and girded his rapier, a ceremonial sword. Anxiously, he paced back and forth in his room until his carriage arrived at 10 a.m. to take him to the examination hall. His turn came at 11:15, and he read a prepared lecture and then was engaged in disputation by three professors. His thesis defense was successful, and later that day the dean pronounced him "doctor of medicine, surgery and midwifery."

In celebration, Marcus purchased a beautiful anatomical and surgical atlas, and photographs of several great professors. The following day he presented the Würzburg Police Department with a note stating that "there was no objection on part [of] the University to the police returning Dr. Rosenwasser's passport," and thus he was able to return to Prague.

There, a note from Edward awaited him—ordering him to break off his relationship with Jane. Reluctantly, Marcus did so. He was crushed: "How happy might I have felt myself? How tedious, how lonely is the world now to me? I never thought I could feel as indifferent to everything around me. Another disappointment [added] to the many of my experience."

Like other heartbroken lovers before and since, Marcus plunged into work and travel—heading to Vienna, "the celebrated grand capital of central Europe," to continue his desultory postgraduate medical education. Besides riding lessons, theater, and coffeehouses, he managed to find the energy to go to lectures by eminent Viennese professors, including Theodor Billroth, a distinguished German surgeon who was the first to do successful radical operations on the throat and stomach—operations which remove every trace of possibly diseased tissue, to minimize the risk of recurrence. He heard a lecture on "The Learned and Their Malheurs" by a Professor Goltz. And he began work in what was to be his field of specialty, obstetrics. As Thomas Bonner writes in 1963 in his book *American Doctors and German Universities*: "The 'touch' courses in obstetrics were the most popular of all" with visiting Americans in Vienna. "Limited in size to four or five students, these classes gave ample experience in examination of the pregnant woman, diagnosis of the position of the fetus, and delivery of the infant at term. From six to eight women were examined hourly and twenty-five to thirty births occurred daily." Marcus even began to spend several nights in "watch" in Professor Brancusi's midwife clinic, presumably delivering babies.

Marcus's medical Grand Tour continued through the cities of Heidelberg and Paris (where he attended a lecture on "the American method of healing the vesico-vaginal fistula," an 1852 surgical advance by Dr. J. Marion Sims, an Alabama doctor who discovered how to repair birth injuries, tears between the vagina and bladder or anus that often left women debilitated for life); then he went on to England.

On the last day of 1867, Dr. Marcus Rosenwasser, age

twenty-one, embarked from Southampton on the ship *America*, heading back to the United States. A violent storm several days out caused the ship's timbers to creak like a pair of new boots. The *America* arrived safely in New York Harbor two weeks later, and when he reached Cleveland, his own brother Joe did not recognize him.

The city to which Marcus returned after a three-and-a-half-year absence was perhaps equally unrecognizable to him. In 1850, Cleveland had been an agricultural town of 17,000; by 1860 there were 43,000 inhabitants, and by 1870 it was to become a commercial city of 100,000. Its growth was spurred first by transportation (the opening of canals in the 1830s and 1840s, and the vast expansion of railroads from the 1860s through the 1890s, connecting Cleveland to Chicago, Pittsburgh, and New York, among other cities) and then by an enormous surge in iron and steel production and oil refining, and an increase in commerce. Along with this came a torrent of immigrants from Western and Eastern Europe. By 1910, the year of Marcus's death, the city's population was 560,000, making it the sixth largest in the country; three-quarters of its inhabitants were immigrants or the children of immigrants.

The city's growth was dramatic, but its problems were depressingly familiar. As a newly minted doctor with the most up-to-date European training, Marcus found himself a leader in a medical community struggling to keep up with the city's growth. There were too few doctors, and most of them were poorly trained. Hospital beds were so lacking that over half the city's deaths occurred without the sick receiving any medical care. Epidemics of contagious disease swept the city, everything from malaria (much of the city lay in mosquito-infested marshes and riverbanks) to typhoid (caused by polluted water supplies) to diphtheria, smallpox, and tuberculosis. The average life expectancy in 1860 was only 40.9 years.

Marcus kept no diary after his return to Cleveland, and few of his letters have survived; so I can only guess at the internal compass of his life. Most likely his practice soon became busy, though not necessarily profitable, since the doctor's financial lot in those days was precarious, and Marcus's patients were often poor immigrants. Perhaps he missed the vital social and scientific interchanges he had found in Europe, in returning to a provincial city without museums or cafés, with few theaters, and with little of the scientific excitement of the medical capitals. Although Cleveland at the time had five medical schools, the city did not have a single medical library.

The greatest crisis concerned children—children orphaned as a result of the Civil War and the smallpox and yellow-fever and typhoid epidemics that followed in its wake. The few orphanages in the Midwest were overwhelmed by thousands of orphans and half orphans (children who had lost one parent, and whose remaining parent was unable to care for them) left to their care.

Though he had little training in the care of children (few doctors received formal education in pediatrics until early in the twentieth century), Marcus became associated with the Cleveland Jewish Orphan Asylum from its beginning in 1868. As a volunteer, he was the sole physician for the institution's 250 children, and later cared for over five hundred at a time. His unpaid service was to continue for forty-two years. As epidemics swept through the city, he made vigorous attempts to isolate and treat sick children, to block the spread of contagion. In 1878, an outbreak of yellow fever in the South flooded the institution with new orphans, and under dangerously crowded conditions, diphtheria spread. In 1881, sixty children were infected with measles; the following year, ten contracted diphtheria during a citywide epidemic. After four deaths, Marcus set up a contagious-disease unit at the orphanage, separate from the infirmary, to segregate the afflicted from the other sick.

Marcus ran his private practice from an office in his home on Woodland Avenue. It was the eastern fringe of a crowded, now-demolished neighborhood, populated initially by German and Czech Jews, and later by Italians, Russian Jews, and blacks. Later, in 1905, Marcus moved to a large Victorian house on East 82nd Street, the center of the turn-of-the-century German Jewish community; in addition to an office at home, he had a practice in a fashionable down-town building. In 1877, at the relatively late age of thirty, he married Ida Rohrheimer, the nineteen-year-old daughter of a prosperous German Jewish family (whether this delay resulted from prolonged heartbreak over his aborted love affair with Jane, or whether it reflected a young doctor's desire to establish himself professionally to improve his so-cial prospects before marrying, we'll never know). In *Obstetric Notes*, he reported that on August 16, 1878, at 10:45 p.m., after a five-hour labor, he delivered a five-pound baby boy whose parents, ages thirty-one and twenty, were "Marcus Rosenwasser (Austrian)" and "Ida Rohrheimer (American)." Besides his first son, named Herman in honor of his father, he delivered his three other children as well, in 1880, 1883, and 1889—hardly something a doctor of our century would do.

Except for *Obstetric Notes*, and offhand references in a handful of medical publications and newspaper articles, I could find only fragmentary information about his practice. His wife's sister Flora worked for many years as his office assistant; she never married. He traveled around his neigh-borhood by horse and buggy, and did deliveries at St. Ann's maternity home and at patients' homes. According to one of his granddaughters, he was adored by neighborhood chil-dren, who often came to his house in the evening to listen to him read stories. His personal life appears to have been happy, with the exception of the tragic loss of his second son, Walter, who fell through an upper-floor window screen to his death at the age of two.

In addition to his practice, Marcus became active in medical organizations, including the Cleveland Medical Society (serving as its president in 1897–98) and the American Society of Obstetrics and Gynecology. He railed against the claims of quacks, who far outnumbered the graduates of legitimate medical schools. In 1901 and 1902, Marcus was president of the Cleveland Board of Health, under the reform mayor Tom Johnson, and helped to avert a smallpox epidemic by a vigorous program of vaccination, including compulsory vaccination of schoolchildren. He was initially a general practitioner specializing in obstetrics, but round-the-clock work took a toll on his health, and in the 1880s he began to specialize in gynecological surgery, a new field in which he soon developed a national reputation.

In short, he invented himself as a modern clinician. No matter that his formal training was limited to three brief, interrupted years, and that his postgraduate education consisted of a handful of lectures; and no matter that his countrymen believed that the doctor who "specialized" was likely to be a quack. Clearly, the European model he had studied grew and flourished within him, and even in a distant part of the world he continued to adhere to its principles.

His younger brother, Nathan, a pharmacist and chemist, had been enthusiastic about antisepsis since he'd seen its earliest American demonstration at New York Hospital in 1877, a through-the-knee amputation of a tumor, performed by Dr. Lewis Atterbury Stimson. But Marcus was skeptical by nature and had been unconvinced. Since he believed that a modern doctor must continually improve his knowledge and keep up with the latest medical advances, Marcus traveled to New York, Philadelphia, Chicago, and Baltimore to train in advanced medical and surgical techniques. On one such trip in the 1880s, he observed antiseptic surgery at Women's Hospital in Boston.

In the early 1860s, Glasgow surgeon Joseph Lister had noted that bone fractures healed well if the skin was not broken, and poorly when exposed to the air. Relating this observation with Pasteur's 1856 description of the importance of microscopic bacteria in fermentation, Lister concluded that airborne bacteria caused the infection of wounds. He stressed the importance of killing bacteria and keeping them away from the vulnerable patient with a fine mist of carbolic acid sprayed over the open wound during an operation. Lister's findings were published in 1867, but even two decades later many American surgeons remained unconvinced.

Marcus's visit to Boston made him a convert. He wrote to Nate: "Thus far I have not seen a single death." Marcus incorporated some but not all elements of antisepsis into his surgical technique. In an 1890 paper describing twelve cases of gynecological surgery he had done in the past year, Marcus stated:

> My method of operation has been to use no chemicals on patient, instrument, or sponges, except sublimate [antiseptic] for integument [skin] and operator's hands. Boiled hot water on and in all else. Chloroform or ether as anesthetics. The incision is made short and extended when necessary. Catgut is used as ligature ... Through-and-through sutures are introduced, about three to the inch, and the wound then painted with iodoform collodion.

Such a technique was apparently successful, since none of the twelve patients died of sepsis; eleven survived, and the only death was caused by heart failure.

Changes in surgical technique—whether as simple as washing hands between patients, or changing dressings frequently, or as complex as a constant noxious spray of acid—were symptomatic of a larger revolution in medicine, of which Rosenwasser was acutely aware. For instance, there was gonorrhea, which the German doctor Albert Neisser had shown to be caused by diplococci, small round bacteria found in pairs. Such advances, Marcus wrote in 1896, "have revolutionized our ideas, transposing the disease [gonorrhea] from the list of slight, benign ailments to the list of those of serious, dangerous, tragic import." Fully twelve percent of women patients seeing the gynecologist had gonorrhea; and it caused fifteen percent of "puerperal fever" (fever after childbirth)—and seventy percent of sterility in women. "What are the facts now accepted?" he asks. "The statement that 'a certain case of gonorrhea might have arisen from making water in the night air' is no longer tenable. The gonococcus of Neisser, in whatever diseased tissue present, is positive evidence of its gonorrheal origin." Yet understanding the cause of a disease was only a first step. In these pre-antibiotic years, treatment consisted of crude palliations such as surgical removal of infected glands, and dusting the vagina with boric acid. Abstinence from sex was the only way to prevent the spread of infection.

In one woman he saw, infected by her husband soon after marriage, gonorrhea had caused pelvic abscesses and was transmitted to her newborn infant. "The bride, wife or mother," he wrote, "comes to us in her innocence and ignorance often too late to avert the havoc wrought. We are even obliged to keep from her the real cause of her troubles."

Keeping up with—and participating in—medical advances did not always ensure one's patients the best treatment. Rosenwasser was not immune from his era's

gynecological fads, among them the conviction that mis-
alignments of the uterus were the cause of many feminine
symptoms. In 1901, he wrote about techniques of resus-
pending the uterus. While he cautioned against excessive
surgery, he still believed that such conditions caused much
suffering. "It has been doubted that retroversion, as such,
causes any symptoms; that it does produce symptoms on its
own is proved by the almost immediate relief from local
and reflex disturbances after replacement." In most cases,
instead of surgery he advocated the use of "pessaries,"
molded hard-rubber devices that were placed in the vagina
for purposes of holding the cervix, and thus the uterus, in
its "normal" position. But he still believed surgery had a
place. (In reading such a paper today, one can only wonder
how many present-day medical procedures and treatments
will look in a hundred—or even twenty—years, and recall
the aphorism of Hippocrates quoted by William Osler in his
epigraph to *The Principles and Practice of Medicine*: "Experience is fallacious and judgment difficult.")

Increasingly, Marcus's need to cure became a need to
teach healing. Medical schools in Cleveland then included
the well-regarded Western Reserve University, and several
homeopathic medical academies, and a women's medical
college. In the late 1870s, Marcus began teaching operative
obstetrics at a small institution, Wooster Medical School
(later known as the Cleveland College of Physicians and
Surgeons). It was not much of a school. Like most programs of its day, Wooster required only a high-school education for admission, and gave an M.D. degree after two
terms of classes and an informal preceptorship under a local
doctor. Classes were held in a building that had been condemned as unfit for use as an elementary school twenty
years before. Furthermore, after an abortive 1881 effort to
merge with Western Reserve University, Wooster had lost
its teaching privileges at Charity Hospital, the city's main

hospital. In order to provide patients for the Wooster students (besides those who could be seen at the county poorhouse!), a new hospital was founded in two old houses adjacent to the medical-school building. Given the grand name of University Hospital, it had all of thirty beds.

Marcus became dean of little Wooster Medical School in 1891, a position he held until 1896 (when he was ousted, one newspaper story reported, because of anti-Semitism). Facilities were so lacking that the Histology Department did not even own a microscope! According to George Crile, a famous alumnus who founded the Cleveland Clinic, the school's professor of anatomy, a Dr. Cotton, obtained cadavers for his classes in midnight horse-and-carriage rides to raid local cemeteries.

On one trip to Cleveland, I met my father at the now-vast University Hospital (950 beds), descendant of that little two-house hospital in name only (the original University Hospital was dissolved following the merger of Western Reserve Medical School and University of Wooster Medical School). I followed him behind the Case Western Reserve University engineering school to a back-lot archive. There a librarian fetched for us some ancient 1870s Wooster Medical School course catalogues, and several frayed ledger books containing minutes of Wooster Medical School faculty meetings, their pages too fragile even to photocopy. The professors debated issues such as whether they should graduate students who had not paid all their tuition, and, on a more institutional level, whether Wooster should again try to merge with the larger and more established Western Reserve University—a goal not accomplished until 1910.

In addition to teaching, Marcus influenced others by example. Through much of his career he was in debt, because of expenses incurred in putting his younger brothers, Charles and Nathan, through medical school—debts his wealthy in-laws the Rohrheimer family did not see fit to help pay off. After twenty years as a pharmacist and chemist, Nate went back to get his M.D. from Wooster in 1897. His youngest brother, Charles, first attended Wooster Medical School, then followed Marcus's path to Vienna, Prague, and Würzburg; he, too, became an obstetrician, practicing in Omaha.

There was also Marcus's nephew, Gustave Feil, son of Elizabeth, the oldest Rosenwasser sister. Originally trained as a bookkeeper, Gustave injured his back as a young man, and after Marcus successfully treated him, Gustave decided to become a doctor. He graduated from Wooster Medical School in 1891 and began practice in Cleveland. He seemed to have a bright future.

"Dr. Rosenwasser, the great Mogul in gynecology," irreverently reported *Pes Anserinus*, the 1909 yearbook of the Cleveland College of Physicians and Surgeons, "is seeking green fields and pastures new beyond the broad expanse of the Atlantic." *Pes Anserinus* was my grandfather Harold Feil's medical-school yearbook; he was its assistant editor. A well-crafted volume, it reads more like a high-school or college yearbook than any publication that would come out of a modern medical school. The text's anonymous author or authors (my grandfather? I wonder) both poke fun at and celebrate the institution they attend.

That year, 1909, Marcus, age sixty-three, formerly dean of the college, and now professor of diseases of women, took his family to Europe. He spent several months in advanced study in Vienna with the great gynecologist Ernst Wertheim, who had done one of the first hysterectomies for cancer of the uterus, a radical operation which excised the uterus, most of the vagina, and many lymph nodes. He and his family also spent time in Bohemia, where he revisited his hometown of Bukovan, and then continued on with his son Herman, a dentist, to Palestine. Just as his medical career had begun with a trip to Europe, it ended there with another round of study and travel.

Marcus's photograph is first among the faculty listing in *Pes Anserinus*, befitting his prominence as physician and teacher. It shows an elegantly groomed man in late middle age, balding, with a mustache and a goatee. He wears a monocle and a wing collar, and his expression is intent and forbidding, as if by his gaze alone he holds his students to the highest European standard.

In an 1894 address to the medical school's graduating class, Marcus had reflected on the enormous changes in medicine. "All around us," he said, "we recognize evidence of the educational tidal wave [of change] coming from the east with irresistible force." Indeed, the 1909 yearbook offers ample evidence of this revolution. In the past quarter century, the Medical College had grown into a solid and well-rounded school for physicians. The initial two-year course of medical training at the school's inception in 1863 had been expanded by 1909 to "four years of eight months attendance." Instead of a mere nine faculty members, "the entire teaching force now comprises sixty-one." It brags of the prominence of its professors, and of the medical texts they have written. It adds that "this College was the first in the country to produce diphtheria antitoxin, the most marked triumph in serum therapy," in which the serum of an animal that has been made immune to diphtheria is injected into a patient, neutralizing the bacterial toxin—which had decreased the death rate in diphtheria from fifty percent to only ten percent.

Photographs of the Medical College's three-story brick building illustrate these advances. They show long wooden lab benches, covered with glass flasks and bottles, and a busy library, and a high-ceilinged free-dispensary waiting room, with half a dozen patients sitting on benches before the desk of a registrar, a young woman in a long-sleeved

white blouse and flowing dark skirt. The college-laboratory
building testifies to ongoing scientific research by medical-
school professors, and an interior shot of the bacteriology
laboratory shows fifteen young men and two women in
class, bent over their microscopes, deep in scientific observation. There is a photo, too, of the dissecting room, where
white-coated young medical students work over eviscerated
cadavers.

The hospitals affiliated with the college had grown substantial, suggesting that science had begun to illuminate
clinical care. There is St. Luke's, a high brick building with
two long wings connected by a columned portico; and St.
Alexis Hospital, looming and Victorian; and the sprawling
vastness of the City Hospital, which cared for Cleveland's
indigent. The tile-floored and -walled operating room at St.
Luke's is obviously an aseptic place, with its glass-
windowed cabinets, high four-wheeled metal carts for surgical equipment reflecting the triumph of Pasteur and Lister,
and of the forgotten work of Ignaz Semmelweis (the Hungarian obstetrician who proved that hand washing could
radically decrease deaths after childbirth), over the previous
century's firmly held beliefs in "laudable pus"—that draining pus in a wound promoted healing, and should be encouraged, by use of dressings and salves. Tanks of ether on
wheeled stands bear witness to a half century of the scientific relief of surgical pain.

It is clear from *Pes Anserinus* that medicine was no
longer a guild or craft, but increasingly a scientific pursuit
in which basic biological discoveries are integrated with patient care, in which doctors can often make a definitive
diagnosis—and someday may be able to cure disease.

But the era of cure had not yet arrived.

The limits of medical progress by the first decade of the
twentieth century, and its impotence in the face of death,
must have been brought home full-force to Marcus after his

return from Europe in 1910, when he was disabled by attacks of chest pain. Despite great medical advances, the triumphs in infection control, in successful and painless surgery, heart disease remained mysterious, inevitably progressive, and incurable.

It was a family illness. Only four years earlier, his older brother, Edward, distinguished journalist and owner of *The Omaha Bee*, had failed to come home one night; the next morning he was discovered sitting in a chair in an empty courtroom, dead of a heart attack. And in 1909 Marcus's younger brother, Andrew, an engineer, died of a heart attack in Omaha's Paxton Hotel.

The stabbing pains of angina were a death sentence. After the first warning signs, Marcus ceased his medical work, no longer even visiting the hospital, and, according to his brother Nathan, he "made earnest preparations for final rest." On September 4, 1910, in "an acute attack of angina pectoris," Marcus died. As one of his obituaries stated: "In the last days of his long agony an increasing sweetness and resignation stole over him and when the end came it was the end of a long and well rounded career."

3

SUDDEN DEATH: 1890–1920

THOUGH the sudden deaths of Marcus and his brothers were tragic, more heartbreaking were the diseases, acute and chronic, that afflicted their children's generation. After all, Marcus and Edward and Andrew survived into their sixties in an era when the average life expectancy was less than fifty years. They had faced the trauma of immigration, prejudice, adversity, yet their photographs and letters and journalism and diaries bear witness to decades of prosperity and good health. The next generation, though, was devastated by disease. They were bright, well educated, privileged, and they died young.

There was the illness of Dr. Gustave Feil, the first second-generation Rosewater physician. The son of Elizabeth, Marcus's oldest sister, Gustave was my grandfather Harold Feil's stepfather. After graduating from Wooster Medical School in 1891 at the age of twenty, Gustave became an assistant to a prominent Cleveland surgeon. He began to establish a lucrative practice. In the late 1890s he met Lillian Cohen, a young widow with two sons. It was a happy match, and in 1899 Gustave and Lillian were married. Two years later Gustave formally adopted the two boys, Harold and Stanley, ages twelve and eleven.

Then tragedy struck: Gustave contracted tuberculosis. Perhaps from a patient (it was distressingly common for nineteenth-century doctors to succumb to "phthisis" or "consumption" contracted in the sickroom)—or perhaps from a friend or colleague. Regardless of its source, tuberculosis was a curse. Though German bacteriologist Robert Koch had briefly raised hopes that tuberculin, an extract of cultured tubercle bacilli, might cure tuberculosis, medicine in 1900 offered nothing in the way of specific cures. The best hope lay in flight—leaving the smoky damp city for the calm of a sanatorium, and for the dry thin air of the mountains. Consumptives spent nights on open-air sleeping porches. They ate large quantities of eggs, milk, and meat. Sitting on reclining chairs, wrapped in blankets, they faced the sun day after day, praying for cure.

Gustave opted for Colorado, known for its pine-scented mountain air, its romantic vistas, and the chance it offered the afflicted to earn a living should they even partially recover. After six months in Colorado Springs, he apparently recovered from his tuberculosis, and soon he was able to begin to practice again. In 1907, he joined the staff of the National Jewish Hospital for Consumptives as a member of the Department of Medicine, and served on its Medical Advisory Board. He became one of Denver's most prominent physicians, specializing in diseases of the nose and throat, and his family enjoyed a return to middle-class life.

I say "apparently" for two reasons: first, because his recovery was a remission and not a cure; and second, because (as I found in the course of my researches) the details of Gustave's illness—even the particulars of his life—remain shrouded in secrecy and silence. In contrast to the vast archive of letters and journals and newspaper articles and professional writings produced by the previous generation, and carefully preserved by their descendants, during my trips to Cleveland I had found virtually nothing about Gustave. There were no letters, no stories, no memories. Only a few fugitive photographs of Gustave survived—a young dandy in a high collar, a lean, bearded man on a horse. It was almost as though he had never lived.

Then there was the tragic death of Edward Rosewater's second daughter, Nellie, my great-grandmother. A graceful girl who painted luminescent floral still lifes in oils and watercolors, she grew up in Omaha in a prosperous Jewish household that was a center of Western journalistic and political life. After high school, she daringly came to New York to study painting. She graduated from Cooper Union in 1890 and then returned to Nebraska to marry Charles Elgutter, the eldest son of a wealthy Nebraska pioneer family. Charles, a graduate of Exeter and Harvard College, had gone to work as a journalist at Edward's newspaper, *The Omaha Bee*. Nellie soon became pregnant. On June 16, 1893, her father telegraphed his wife, Leah, who was visiting relatives in Cleveland:

> NELLIES GIRL BABY BORN LAST NIGHT
> ALL WELL CONGRATULATIONS.
> E. ROSEWATER

All was not well, however. Within days, puerperal fever set in. While advances in hygiene and cleanliness had dramatically lowered the incidence of this dreaded illness by the 1890s, once the fever began—the torn tissues of the birth canal allowing bacteria into the mother's bloodstream—there was no effective treatment. The family watched in horror as their twenty-four-year-old daughter succumbed to fevers, chills, hemorrhage, aware that even her doctor uncles were powerless to help her. Barely two weeks later, Nellie was dead.

Her body lay in the front parlor of her family's house, beside her a bouquet of white roses and carnations surmounted by a white dove, its outstretched talons holding a

tiny white rosebud. Relatives and friends gathered to hear
the eulogy by the Reverend Dr. Franklin, who spoke of
how Nellie had met death at the altar of love, at the altar
of noblest motherhood; her twenty-nine-year-old husband
was unable to contain his grief. Their child, a plump,
healthy girl named Nellie in her mother's honor, was given
to her grandparents Edward and Leah Rosewater to raise.

Papa, Harold Feil, my grandfather, never once talked about
his stepfather, Gustave. And my grandmother, Nellie
Elgutter Feil (who had married her step-cousin), had nothing to say about Nellie Rosewater Elgutter, the mother she
had never known. All that their children, including my
mother, knew of their grandparents were their names. It was
as if silence could undo disease, as if deliberate suppression
of painful facts could undo them, annulling the past. A particularly Victorian response, perhaps the reaction of people
all too familiar with the incurable. Driven by their century's
dramatic scientific advances into a willful optimism, they
found themselves helpless against death.

Consequently—except for a few photographs and newspaper clippings—Gustave Feil and Nellie Elgutter disappeared. If Dr. Marcus Rosenwasser was a family ghost to
be emulated, even though outwardly forgotten, then Dr.
Gustave Feil and Nellie Rosewater Elgutter were ones to be
feared, their examples to be avoided at all costs, mere mention of their names bringing their sad lives perilously close.

Barely a year after my father's retirement, I came home to
attend my grandfather's funeral. Papa had been in a nursing
home down Cedar Hill for five years, and each time home,
we would visit him there, shake his warm, leathery hand,
be soothed by his gracious doctorly manner; each time he
seemed to have sunk a little deeper into the wheelchair,
frailer, his head heavier on his shoulders, until finally in

1987, when he was ninety-seven, his heart gave out. The funeral at the old Temple, in what once was the center of Jewish life in the city but now is a ramshackle ghetto neighborhood, had its moments of sadness and poignancy, when Uncle George became tearful during the eulogy, and in Mom's and Uncle Ed's hushed conversations. Yet for us kids it was as much as anything a moment of mystery, and awareness of questions never to be answered.

Up in the attic the next morning before I caught my plane to New York, I again made a foray into the endless family archive. Inside a tin bread box crammed with old photographs I found a Greek tragedy written by Charles Elgutter, my great-grandfather, Nellie's widower, who later remarried and became a lawyer and poet. Entitled *Iphigenia*, it was printed in Omaha in 1902, a decade after his wife's death, "for private circulation."

"More than the gods we mortals must endure," read the book's epigram. Did these creamy pages hold any clue to Charles's loss? Standing in the musty attic, I read of Iphigenia, daughter of Agammemnon, and lover of Achilles, who sacrificed herself for her country. Charles wrote:

> *Will not the mother in her child-birth pangs*
> *Surrender life to give her infant breath?*
> *Is Greece less worthy of a woman's love?*

And then, beneath piles of 1950s postcards from Arizona and Hawaii, I discovered a thick leather notebook, held together with rubber bands, its pages filled with my grandmother Nellie Feil's handwriting. Inside were genealogies dating back to the 1700s, and charming century-old notes from Charles Elgutter to Nellie Rosewater during their courtship:

Dear Miss Nellie

Many thanks for your umbrella. I found it exceedingly "dry" and comfortable not only last night but today. I shall know where to go in the future for one when caught out.

> Yours in a shower
> C.S.E.

Then came the surprise. The neatly trimmed clipping from an unnamed newspaper, held to the loose-leaf page by a gob of library paste. The headline read:

DOCTOR, HAUNTED BY ILL HEALTH, BLOWS OUT BRAINS WITH PISTOL

Holding the fragile paper, I stood there breathless. There were two clippings actually, two accounts of Gustave's death in 1914, both gruesome, revealing yet obscure.

DOCTOR SHOOTS SELF TO DEATH; WIFE FINDS BODY

was how the other newspaper put it. One account clearly stated it was a suicide; the other noted: "Members of his family said last night they believed the shooting had been accidental. The revolver, they declared, lay in a bureau drawer, and Dr. Feil was in the habit of handling it."

G. R. Feil Fires Bullet in Mouth; "I Don't Want To Live as Sick Man" He Tells Family

LEADING DENVER PHYSICIAN

Mental Condition of Surgeon, Due to Illness, Blamed for the Tragedy

Dr. Gustave R. Feil shot himself to death by firing a bullet through his brain at his residence, 678 Humboldt Street, last night. Dr. Feil was among the leading Denver physicians. A door, closed but unlocked, separated him from the room where his wife was. He died instantly . . .

Mrs. Feil rushed into the room a moment later. She was prostrated last night from shock and her condition was regarded seriously. A nurse and physician attended her. Melancholia, brought on by ill health, is believed to be responsible for the tragedy. Yesterday, according to the coroner, Dr. Feil told his wife that he did not care to live in his condition.

There was also a late photograph of Gustave Feil, showing a man of indeterminate age wearing a fedora, with a mustache and neatly trimmed beard. His face is drawn and gaunt; he looks not at the camera or the photographer, not even aside (as though distracted by something in the photographer's studio), but instead stares intently downward, even inward. It is a haunting photograph, the image of a suffering man.

After going into remission for nearly a decade, in 1913 Gustave's tuberculosis had recurred; he would experience fits of breathlessness and cough blood, and have excruciating head pain. On the evening of January 16, 1914, came the tragedy his stepson never spoke of.

On the plane to New York, and on the crowded bus back to Manhattan, I puzzled over this discovery. Did it explain the paradox I had long observed, my family's differing attitudes toward the past? One side of the family wanted to remember; the other side tried to forget. Yet the side that wanted to remember (my father's) threw everything away, and the side that wanted to forget (my mother's) kept everything, every clipping and photograph, every letter and postcard, so that a casual browser was at risk of awakening an endless archive of ghosts. And thus the boxes of Nana's and Papa's "effects" up in my old attic room.

Here was the fundamental paradox: the side that wanted to remember told the same stories over and over again until they were ossified and chant-like, entirely unrevealing—and the side that wanted to forget told you nothing until you asked exactly the right question, and then answered off-handedly (as they did when I asked about Gustave's death): "Oh yes, I know about that, but we never discussed it." And if pushed, if needled endlessly, they would add reluctantly: "We felt it wasn't proper to ask." Or: "I don't know *how* I know, Papa never mentioned it to me." Or: "Maybe Cousin Jo told me—in passing. We never went into it."

Did this explain everything?

Did it explain the reticence, the scatteredness, the stiff silence of my mother and her brothers, did it explain Harold's taciturnness and Nellie's brittle cheer? Did it somehow explain the family's stubborn emphasis on doctoring, on healing?

Every doctor is a patient; every life ends in death, whether its coming is prolonged or sudden. Family cushions the pain of loss; it offers succor and relief; it can reconfigure around the missing until it almost seems there is no emptiness, no scar. Is this what happened to my grandmother and grandfather, marrying cousins?

Disease took almost an entire generation. And thus, I realized, so many of the carefully posed photographs showed Rosewaters in funeral attire: Leah Rosewater and her two daughters in embroidered black dresses, after Nellie's death; the surviving siblings after Edward's sudden passing; Stanley and Harold as little boys leaning against their mother Lillian, all three in black. The bounds of kinship were strained but not broken. What maintained continuity were the interlacings of cousins and uncles and great-aunts, a reduplicative enfolding of kin. And what added hope to togetherness was medicine.

For none of the family members was this more true than for Harold Feil. Still mourning his death in 1987, I saw him anew in the 1909 medical-school yearbook I had taken from home. There he was, eighty years earlier, in the third row of the sophomore-class picture; and in a photo of the yearbook's editorial board—six young men—he stood second from right. In both pictures I saw a handsome young man wearing a suit and high rounded collar, his thick wavy hair slicked to the side, his expression serious, intent, perhaps a touch mournful.

Indeed, Harold had ample reason for somberness. Gustave's lingering illness was not the first tragedy in Harold's life. He had already lost a father. His biological father was George Cohen, a Yale College and Columbia Law School graduate, a lawyer practicing in Pennsylvania. On October 9, 1896, while arguing a case at the Wilkes-Barre County Court House, George, age thirty-four, suffered a heart attack and collapsed. He died before reaching the hospital. Harold was seven.

That was when Harold's mother, Lillian, overcome with grief, moved to Cleveland to be with her sister Theresa, and when, temporarily unable to care for her two young sons, she put them in a Catholic orphanage, where they lived for nearly a year. And that was when Lillian met Dr. Gustave Feil, and married him, so that she and the two boys were enfolded into the large, warm Rosewater family, attaining a tenuous security that lasted only until Gustave got sick.

I had no idea how Harold took his father's sudden death, or his year among the Catholic boys at St. Joseph's on the Lake, or his stepfather's illness; his quiet and studious mien, his infinite reserve, remained impenetrable until his death. What I did know is that the decision was made early for him to enter the profession of medicine, and that soon after graduating from high school at eighteen, he was packed off to Cleveland to begin medical school at the College of Physicians and Surgeons, where his stepfather's uncle, Marcus Rosenwasser, was a professor. In 1909, a college degree was still not necessary to become a doctor. It was a move into familiar territory, a practical move—but, I suspect, a disappointing one. It meant giving up hopes of following his father George Cohen's footsteps to Yale. During summers, while studying medicine, Harold went back home to Colorado, working to get his B.A. from the University of Denver.

In Cleveland, Harold moved in with Uncle Nate and Aunt Tessie in a house on East 55th Street, in the middle of the Jewish community. He was doubly related to them: Nate was Gustave's uncle, and Tessie was his mother Lillian's sister. Nate and Tessie, too, had suffered the ravages of incurable illness, having lost both their children— their daughter, Louise, soon after birth, and their son, Herbert, at age five, from tuberculous meningitis. Nate and Tessie and Harold reconstituted into a family, a family with healing at its center.

Originally trained as a chemist, Nate had become a doctor with a special interest in sudden death. He was a scientist who had observed the American debut of antiseptic surgery, and claimed to have invented the first antiseptic wound dressing used in this country. He patented methods of preserving eggs to prevent spoilage, and of treating coffee to remove a chemical that he regarded as a poison: caffeine. In Nate's view, both eccentric and prescient, numerous compounds in daily use were actually dangerous toxins. Foremost among these was nicotine. Late in his career, in 1925, Nate published a book, *Old Nic in Nicotine: Tobacco Lure and Cure,* showing on its cover the leering faces of demons arising from the smoke of an ashtray full of cigarette butts. With graphic case histories, *Old Nic* warned that tobacco was a great public-health problem and caused shortening of life from a variety of conditions—in particular from heart disease. "No doctor can foretell," Nate wrote, in a paragraph I recall first reading at the age of ten, "how soon, weakened by nicotine, a heart may fail in its work, without warning the victim may be seized with a sudden crampy, agonizing spasm, or series of spasms . . . or even without a pain—be stopped in death." He went on:

> The truth about tobacco—told by school books, encyclopedias, and medical books—is indisputable; tobacco leaf is poisonous, due to its active, baneful principle, nicotine, which is a quick, powerful, deadly poison . . . Pure nicotine is so powerful that one drop, placed on its tongue, will instantly kill a grown cat.

The plan was that Harold, after finishing medical training, would join Uncle Nate's practice.

In the midst of Harold's medical-school education, the tidal wave of educational reform crested. In 1909 Abraham Flexner, an obscure educator from Louisville, Kentucky, who had become a critic of educational systems, began a grand survey of the state of American medical education, sponsored by the Carnegie Foundation. He passed through Cleveland in December of that year and visited three medical schools—Western Reserve University, the Homeopathic Medical College, and the Cleveland College of Physicians and Surgeons. He spent a day at each school. Flexner was impressed with Western Reserve Medical School. He praised its "[e]xcellent laboratories, in which teaching and research are both vigorously prosecuted," its clinical facilities, "thoroughly modern in construction and equipment," and the close relation in medical training between bedside and laboratory work. "The situation is one," he wrote, "that might be reproduced with infinite advantage in New York, Boston, Chicago, etc." He criticized the Homeopathic Medical College, noting caustically that its clinical facilities were limited to the city hospital three miles distant from the medical school, and that its dispensary's "equipment is poor; no complete or lasting records are kept." He ranked the College of Physicians and Surgeons only slightly better: its laboratory facilities had "a meager supply of apparatus"; the affiliated hospitals "are at a considerable distance from the school"; and the dispensary is "small and poorly organized."

In 1910, Flexner's monumental volume *Medical Education in the United States and Canada: A Report to the Carnegie Foundation for the Advancement of Teaching* was published. Its effect was electric. All over the country, marginal schools collapsed, or merged with stronger rivals. Of 162 American medical schools in 1906, only eighty-three remained by 1921. In the surviving schools, a new model of medical education, based on German schools (first transplanted to America in the 1890s), now took firm hold. Curricula were improved and standardized, and admissions criteria were drastically tightened.

The local effects of these dramatic changes are reflected in a footnote from the Cleveland College of Physicians and Surgeons: "As this report goes to press, it is announced that this school has been consolidated with the Medical Department of Western Reserve University." Harold's graduation certificate thus reads Western Reserve University, not Cleveland College—his degree came from the more prestigious school.

A new ideal of the doctor now dominated medicine: the doctor no longer only attended the sick and comforted the dying; he was a "clinician-scientist," a researcher as well as a healer—a physician who practiced like a scientist, a scientist profoundly influenced by his daily contact with the sick. The hospital, once a place where the sick went to die, was to become a center for research and treatment. New instruments, including the sphygmomanometer to measure blood pressure (1891), the X-ray machine (1895), and the electrocardiograph, which could chart the flow of electricity through the living heart (1903), showed graphically how the doctor-scientist might directly investigate disease. A great age of discovery, of scientific investigation of disease, was beginning.

Despite all these changes, Harold seemed destined to become an old-fashioned M.D., a tradesman wedded to his community, to his patients and his practice. After receiving his medical degree in 1911, Harold served two years of internship at Michael Reese Hospital in Chicago. Then he returned to Cleveland, where he joined Nate's practice. As a concession to modernity, rather than a horse and carriage he bought a Model T to go around to hospitals and patients' homes—a car so lacking in power that Harold regularly had to turn it around and back all the way up Cedar Hill. His life seemed settled—headed toward financial security but little excitement.

Here is where the mystery begins. Only six years later, Harold left almost everything behind, making his one great break with the familiar, the expected. He remade his life.

The first influence was Nellie Elgutter, his step-cousin. Harold had known her since he was two or three, from the time he was still Harold Cohen, son of attorney George Cohen of Pittstown, Pennsylvania. Their families had summered together in upstate New York, at the town of Bemus Point at Lake Chautauqua. My parents have a much-loved photograph of them as small, plump-cheeked children standing before the white columns of the Columbian Inn, Harold with his arms around Nellie and Cousin Anna, his brother Stanley standing impishly to the side, a ball in his hands.

The death of Harold's father had led to a difficult and penurious early life; the tragic loss of Nellie's mother led to a life of opulence and adventure. Her grandfather Edward Rosewater (Marcus Rosenwasser's older brother) was perhaps the most prominent newspaperman in the West. He had been a telegrapher at the War Department under President Lincoln during the Civil War. What particularly impressed me as a kid was that Edward was one of three telegraphers who transmitted the Emancipation Proclamation to the nation on January 1, 1863. Afterward, demobilized, Edward made his way to Omaha, where he became manager for the district branch of the Pacific Telegraph Company; and in 1871 he started *The Omaha Bee*, which was destined to become one of the most powerful newspapers in the American West.

Zelig-like, Rosewater was everywhere in the West. He was on speaking terms with all the Presidents for half a century; twice he ran (unsuccessfully) for the U.S. Senate; he was prime organizer for the Trans-Mississippi Exposition of 1898. Buffalo Bill paid visits to his house in Omaha, and held my grandmother on his knee and gave her a beaded Indian tobacco pouch. Other visitors who signed my grandmother's autograph book included Thomas Edison, Andrew Carnegie, John Hay, Israel Zangwill, and Charles W. Fairbanks. In 1896, at a meeting of the Republican Bi-Metallic League, Edward challenged thirty-six-year-old Nebraska congressman William Jennings Bryan to a great debate over the issue of free silver; in May he and Bryan spoke for hours in St. Louis before the Republican National Convention. Afterward, Bryan continued on his way to Chicago to give his famous "Cross of Gold" speech ("You shall not press down upon the brow of labor this cross of thorns, you shall not crucify mankind upon a cross of gold!") and to receive the Democratic Presidential nomination; Rosewater went back to Omaha and the relative anonymity of journalism. As a little girl, Nellie accompanied her grandfather on his travels to Rome, to Paris, to Pompeii, and wrote about her adventures in *The Omaha Bee*.

For Harold, his cousin Nellie opened the door to a larger, brighter world: one *could* act on the stage of history; one could dare to meet the world's great men on one's own terms. Not that Harold had political or journalistic aspirations: what became increasingly irresistible was the idea of becoming part of the great world of science. Nellie and Harold corresponded through her years at Smith College, and around the time of her graduation in 1914 and her return to Omaha, their letters turned romantic. Their temperaments were well matched: Nellie was a spirited, extroverted, and gregarious young woman with a sharp tongue and a sense of style, who had many friends and loved Shakespeare and the Italian language; Harold was serious, gentle, and courtly, with what could have become an excess of scholarly withdrawal if not for Nellie's influence.

They announced their engagement in the spring of 1915 and were married in Omaha on July 29, in an opulent ceremony held at Aunt Stella's house. They honeymooned in upstate New York, driving through the Finger Lakes and stopping at Lake Placid.

As his childhood had been clouded by his father's premature death, and his adolescence by his stepfather's recurrent suffering and transient recoveries from tuberculosis, a then-incurable illness, Harold and Nellie's wedding must have been touched by the tragedy and scandal of Gustave's suicide a year before.

One way to deal with scandal is to pretend it has not happened, to go on stubbornly with normal life. And so Harold and Nellie, to all outward appearances, did. Their wedding reports and correspondence mention nothing of

Gustave's suicide. On their return to Ohio, they took an apartment with Lillian, Harold's mother, and Harold continued practicing medicine and teaching as a volunteer at the medical school.

Nonetheless, the death of his stepfather had a profound impact. What gradually began to awaken within Harold was a need to do more than practice. It was a need to conquer disease, which had held him and his family hostage so many times, which had taken so many lives prematurely, which had caused so much agony. The way to act was clear: as the European scientists taught, as Abraham Flexner emphasized, disease could be vanquished by investigation, by scientific discovery. Only the opportunity to act was missing.

This was provided by the war. After endless vacillation by President Wilson and Congress, with one U-boat attack after another upon American ships and the loss of thousands of innocent lives, finally on April 6, 1917, America entered the Great War. The horrors of trench warfare—350,000 French soldiers died at Verdun; nearly 600,000 French and British soldiers at the Battle of the Somme—dwarfed any personal or family tragedy. In 1918, Harold volunteered to join the medical corps. He was stationed first at Camp Dodge, Iowa, and then at Fort Dix in New Jersey, where he treated patients struck by that year's devastating influenza epidemic, which killed twenty million people worldwide, including 57,000 American soldiers, a greater number than the 49,000 killed in combat. Initially, Nellie stayed in Cleveland with Lillian, but later she moved to Browns Mills, near Fort Dix, to be close to Harold. There she spent her time organizing women to make bandages from bedsheets for the wounded.

For doctors, World War I was a time of great turmoil and great frustration. There was vast destruction of human life—more than ten million soldiers killed in battle. The effects of shrapnel and machine-gun fire and mustard gas and bombs dropped from zeppelins—and of the new lethal war vehicle, the tank—left perhaps twenty million injured and disabled soldiers. For many of them, little could be done. Pensioned off, filling hospitals and rest homes, veterans were condemned to lives of invalidism, infection, and pain.

For one group of disabled soldiers, though, there seemed to be some hope. These were the veterans with "soldier's heart" or "effort syndrome"—in Britain, the third-largest group of disabled veterans, over 36,000 by 1918. Their symptoms included shortness of breath, palpitations, rapid pulse, chest pain, fear of sudden death, and led to inability to perform the physical exertion required of a soldier. In Hampstead, England, a four-hundred-bed hospital was set aside for the study of this mysterious disorder, and Dr. Thomas Lewis, a "cardiologist" who had made his reputation before the war by studying the electrical function of the heart, was put in charge by the Medical Research Committee. In short order, Lewis cut the length of hospitalization for soldier's-heart patients from an average of 5.5 months to 1.5 months, and while the cause of their illness (whether infection, bacterial toxins, hyperthyroidism, mental strain, or heart disease) remained uncertain, the possibility of recovery had become clear. Cardiology, the study of the heart, had been given new prominence.

This "new" disease, and the great focus of public attention, resonated with Harold Feil's own experience. At Camp Dodge, Harold had begun his own work on the heart, writing a paper about the 443 men he had examined for heart disease among the base's 25,000 soldiers. He had seen five cases of "effort syndrome," and he cautiously okayed them for further military training, knowing that Lewis found most such patients could be rehabilitated by a program of graduated exercise.

Besides the focus of public attention, there was the promise of a new medical instrument, the electrocardio-

graph, or EKG machine. The warring armies had introduced one brutal killing machine after another—U-boats,
warplanes, poison gas, and the murderously effective tank,
which had its debut on the Plain of Mars—new technologies for ensuring deaths by the thousand. In contrast, the
EKG, a machine of science and healing, had a quiet debut.
Lewis had installed the first one in Great Britain in a basement room at London's University College Hospital in
1908. It was not yet able to save lives, but it could provide
new knowledge of life's electric force.

A complex instrument, the EKG machine was sensitive
to the small, rapidly fluctuating electrical changes produced
by the heart, and displayed them in a visible and meaningful form. An early version developed in the 1880s, called
the capillary electrometer, amplified the heart's electrical
signal by projecting a light across the top of a column of
mercury, which moved up and down as the heart produced
electric currents. In the early 1900s a Dutch researcher,
Willem Einthoven (who won the 1924 Nobel Prize for his
work), began to apply to the heart an instrument called the
string galvanometer, which had been invented by French-
man Clément Ader to speed the rate of telegraphic transmission between Marseilles and Algiers. Its key advance
was a fine string, only .003 millimeters across, through
which passed electrical impulses conducted from the heart.
The string was stretched in a magnetic field, and depending
on the fluctuations of current, the string moved rapidly in
one direction or another. A bright light shone across the
string and passed through a narrow slit. As the string
moved, it cast a shadow on a moving strip of photographic
paper. This long, narrow photograph, once developed, provided a tracing of the heart's electrical currents. In the first
decade of the twentieth century, Einthoven began to test the
string galvanometer on the human heart, writing classic papers that defined the electrical course of the normal heart-

beat. The heart's electrical impulse began in the atria, the upper chambers, then passed through the heart muscle. The EKG showed the P wave, which coincided with atrial contraction, and the QRS complex, which initiated the ventricle's contraction, followed by a recovery phase (the T wave) as the heart muscle repolarized, awaiting the next beat.

In 1908, Thomas Lewis began to use the EKG to study heart disease, particularly abnormal rhythms, or arrhythmias. In the process, he revolutionized thinking about heart disease. Previously, doctors were only able to listen to the heartbeat (amplified perhaps through the stethoscope), or feel the pulse, or examine the heart's anatomical changes on autopsy. But now the EKG showed physiological processes in the living patient. Doctors had always thought of heart disease in terms of anatomical abnormalities—calcified valves, abnormally thickened or dilated muscle. These old ideas were still valid, but in a large proportion of heart-disease cases there was no obvious anatomical abnormality—instead, illness resulted from subtle disorders of rhythm. Arrhythmias were a result of dysfunction of the heart's electrical conduction system. Heart disease was also understood to be a matter of function, not just structure; and the heart's function was understood to be, to a large extent, the result of its electrical state. Indeed, a person might drop dead after his heart suddenly stopped beating, and on autopsy the heart's anatomy might be found to be entirely normal: death could result from a short circuit.

The early EKG was an enormous, cumbersome, and temperamental machine that initially filled two rooms and required five people to operate, but its importance can hardly be overemphasized. It was perhaps a thousandfold that of nuclear magnetic resonance imaging (MRI) or computerized tomography (CT) scanners seventy years later. Yet the average doctor still looked with suspicion on diagnostic instruments, which seemed to be no substitute for the physician's eye and ear and hand. Moreover, diseases of the heart were notorious for being untreatable. To most doctors, the EKG machine seemed no more than a scientific curiosity.

Some doctors saw great promise in the EKG, however. In the years prior to World War I, ambitious young Americans had begun to flock to England to study with Thomas Lewis and with other researchers, including the great University of London physiologist E. H. Starling, who did pioneering research on the pumping properties of the heart, as well as James Mackenzie, a Scottish general practitioner who systematically studied heart patients using an instrument called the "ink polygraph," demonstrating how various heart diseases affected the pressure waves in different blood vessels. These Americans, including Paul Dudley White and Samuel Levine, both later to become prominent Harvard Medical School professors, were particularly interested in learning to use the EKG machine, for laboratory research as well as evaluation and treatment of patients. The war had stopped the flow of visiting students; but after the Germans signed the Treaty of Versailles in June 1919, it slowly started again.

As Harold's army discharge approached, his plans began to crystallize. He would go to England to study cardiology. His mother opposed this decision; she felt he should stay in Cleveland and expand his general practice. He was opposed as well by tradition. Doctors in those days were generally suspicious of colleagues who called themselves "specialists." Since all bodily systems were interrelated, the thinking went, a doctor who focused on one system alone would be doing so to the patient's detriment—though possibly to his own enrichment.

Since medical-research careers were foreign to American tradition, few grants or fellowships were available for advanced training. Fortunately, Aunt Tessie and Uncle Nate approved of Harold's plan and agreed to help finance a year of study abroad. Several decades earlier, Marcus Rosenwasser had put himself into debt to finance Nate's medical education; perhaps this was Nate's way of repaying his older brother.

In October 1919, Harold and Nellie (then four months pregnant) boarded the S.S. *Mauretania*, headed for England. After a very rough passage, they arrived in London and settled in a hotel near Russell Square. Within the week, Harold had begun his research at Lewis's laboratory in the University College Hospital Medical School. He was one of two assistants, and spent two days a week doing research on dogs, two days in the clinics, and the rest of his time seeing patients in the hospital.

He wrote to his patrons:

10/23/19

Dear Aunt Tessie and Uncle Nate
I really am learning much in a clinical way—Uncle Nate—and often a point comes up which you have impressed before. Lewis is a man of about 40—a great follower of Mackenzie's teachings—but withal very original. He is really a good clinician—. . . he is a very clever experimental worker & his exactness & precision are quite remarkable. The few months spent here will help me greatly. I am learning a great deal in the technique of the Electrocardiograph. London continues to amuse us greatly . . .

As usual, Harold was keeping up appearances. What he omitted from his cheerful letter home (but would confide to my father fifty years later) was that Thomas Lewis was treating him abominably. During his first weeks in the laboratory, Lewis scarcely looked at or spoke to him; and almost to the end of his stay, Lewis was brusque to the point of cruelty. Harold eventually realized that it was not personal. Lewis was a genius, possessed by an intolerable need to know.

Thomas Lewis had grown up in Cardiff, Wales, the sickly son of a mining engineer who was educated at home, then went to college, where his scientific bent was quickly recognized, and he began publishing major scientific articles while still an undergraduate at University College, Cardiff. By the age of twenty-seven, he was editor of his own journal, *Heart*, which became the most important journal dealing with cardiology. Moody and short-tempered, ready to cut to the bone if one interrupted his train of thought, Lewis had no time for social conventions. When faced with a scientific problem, he was inclined to be brooding, idle, fretful, and irritable for weeks at a time, and then, once he had figured out the right experiments to perform, to work feverishly around the clock along with his assistants until the studies were done.

Paul Dudley White had studied with Lewis in 1913. He notes in his autobiography, *My Life and Medicine*:

> In October I reported to Dr. Thomas Lewis for work. He stopped for a brief moment to greet me, as he stood in his cutaway morning coat at the operating table in his laboratory, massaging the heart of a dog with one hand while the other hand held his top hat and dress gloves. Impatiently he gave directions to his "diener" [laboratory assistant] as to what to do in his absence while he was attending some official luncheon. After a short greeting my new chief paid no more attention to me or to three other [students] . . .

After two months of treating White as an ignoramus "very evidently in the way," Lewis abruptly asked him to help with experiments—and then White's position changed to being a "devoted slave of the master" involved in experiment after experiment of great importance (for instance, an epochal series of experiments on dogs which defined the sinoatrial node as the origin of the heartbeat), and eventually to being a close friend.

Despite Harold's initial torment, after several months of diligent work he, too, was admitted to the inner circle and helped conduct some of Lewis's classic experiments. They represented the last, remarkable phase of Lewis's cardiology research. The work revolved around the subject of "atrial flutter"—a very rapid abnormal heart rhythm (300–500 beats per minute) that starts in the atria, the upper chambers of the heart. A patient in flutter commonly suffers from lightheadedness, palpitations, and rapid changes of heart rate, and is in danger of developing even more life-threatening arrhythmias. In 1919, there were two major theories of the cause of atrial flutter: first, that the sinoatrial node, which originates the normal heartbeat, was firing far too quickly; and, second, that some abnormal process of excitation began—and was perpetuated—in the atria themselves, outside the normal conduction pathways.

To answer this question, Lewis and his two assistants, Harold Feil and a Dr. W. D. Stroud of Philadelphia, did some ingenious experiments. Using dogs, they were able to create an artificial state of atrial flutter, and then to track it closely by attaching EKG leads directly to the heart's surface. What they discovered is still being investigated today, albeit with 150 leads instead of three, and with sophisticated computers instead of pen and paper to analyze data. A "circus" phenomenon, a process of circling or reentry, was occurring. After some stimulus set off the abnormal conduction, a rapid circular pattern of contraction, relaxation, and contraction began. The electrical impulse stimulating contraction traveled in a circular fashion around the rim of the great blood vessels that emerge from the heart. By the time the electrical impulse returned to where it began, the heart muscle had left its "refractory state"—the recovery period during which it cannot be stimulated—and was ready to contract again. Unless interrupted, this rapid cycle continued indefinitely. Physiologist A. G. Mayer had produced similar waves of excitation in rings of muscle cut from the bell of the medusa, or jellyfish: once stimulated, the abnormal impulse would pass around the circle of muscle for days or weeks at a time—just like flutter, which could last for months.

It is tempting (though perhaps not wholly sound) to speculate about the connection between the technologies of war and the technologies of healing. After the world war's unprecedented orgy of killing, the British Medical Research Council, in its first sponsorship of medical research, commissioned Thomas Lewis, the outstanding medical scientist of his generation, to study the aberrant rhythms of heart disease. No doubt, societies often compensate for the horrors of war with a postwar burst of healing science. In this case, the goal was to determine how aberrant rhythms, abnormal forces, take over from normal rhythms, and how they are propagated, how they continue week after week, annihilating normality, injuring health, and causing disease, sometimes even death. Is it absurd to see here a metaphor for the madness of war? Certainly for my grandfather, an obscure Midwestern American Jew with an indifferent medical education, these researches were a form of salvation. He yearned for discovery, for a role in scientific progress, however slight, against death, against the disease which had taken his father's life. And he found it in London, in the white-hot center of medical science. He yearned for the opportunity to prove himself, to form alliance with powerful men of science, for fathers who would not fail him. His instincts were impeccable: he could identify genius, even if he did not possess it.

In December, taking a holiday from research work, Harold and Nellie traveled to France, touring through the war-devastated countryside.

Tues. eve.

Dear Aunt Tessie & Uncle Nate:—

While the memory is still fresh I shall talk to you a bit about the war zone we just visited. We left Paris at 8 a.m.—and arrived at Reims at 11—where we immediately repaired to a restaurant for lunch—a good one too. The Cooks Guide said that out of 14,700 houses in Reims—7 were not hit and only 2000 were repairable. The city is one huge pile of devastation—the fragments of walls alone remaining. Here and there as we rode along the habitable places were made use of—and an occasional shop was opened—but for the most part—it was a city of the dead . . .

All we saw was desolation—fragments of walls—barb wire entanglements—several tanks—and just one hole after another. We walked over the fields—saw dug outs—went in one—saw trenches—shell holes—entanglements & a seeming unending lot of barb wire. Everywhere along the roads were to be seen the refuse of war. Piles of unexploded shells—boxes full of ammunition—several tanks—a huge collection of wagons at one place—remains of camouflage (faded canvas, reeds, etc.) fragments of shells—bits of destroyed accoutrements—and even a thigh bone. Above all it was a picture of desolation—on this dull Dec. day—with a flurry of snow. On the way to Reims several cemeteries were seen . . . Reims was under bombardment 4 years & little wonder that it was so completely destroyed . . . But the few people we did see were cheerful & hopeful—

A week later, he was back in the laboratory: "At present Dr Lewis is working on a new method of demonstrating the conduction of the heart contraction wave—mechanically and by the electrocardiograph . . . Nellie & I are both very well. We are looking forward to our new arrival & Nellie is getting along splendidly."

In March, Nellie went into labor and delivered a healthy baby boy, who was named George Herbert Feil. It was a highly symbolic name for a little baby—honoring Harold's late father and Nate and Tessie's late son, not to mention the King of England and the Elizabethan clergyman-poet. As was then the custom, Nellie spent a month in convalescence, staying at the Manor House Nursing Home in Hampstead, before returning to their apartment with the baby. The former home of the actor Sir Charles Wyndham, the Manor House bragged of private rooms and bracingly clean air and absolute quiet, though it was only "five minutes by car" from Harley Street.

In the spring of 1920, Harold left Nellie and the baby and went to St. Andrews, Scotland, to study with Sir James Mackenzie, who taught him the technique of the polygraph and impressed upon him the value of keeping accurate records on one's patients, from which one could hope to derive new information about the prognosis of various heart diseases and the effectiveness of treatments.

Soon enough, the year was up. In October 1920, Harold and Nellie and baby George sailed for the United States aboard the RMS *Adriatic*, leaving from Southampton. Before returning to Cleveland, they stopped at Baltimore, where Harold spent some time in the EKG laboratory at the Johns Hopkins Medical School. Then they came home.

It was peacetime; in the words of fellow Ohioan Warren Harding, a return to "normalcy." Harold and Nellie took an apartment on Kenilworth Road in Cleveland Heights, a quiet, leafy suburb just a few miles from the medical school, and Harold returned to medical practice, declaring himself a "cardiologist." His new private office, no longer shared with Uncle Nate, was now located in a triangular-shaped building in downtown Cleveland. Again he began working at Cleveland City Hospital and Mt. Sinai Hospital, with an appointment as Demonstrator in the Department of Medicine of Western Reserve Medical School. That same year an EKG machine was ordered for City Hospital from the Cambridge Scientific Instrument Company.

Within one year, Harold's professional life had changed dramatically. He had left Cleveland a thirty-year-old general internist with an average American medical education, who had written a few minor medical papers; he returned as a heart specialist, one of two in the entire city. While in London, he had written several classic scientific papers (his work on atrial flutter was published in August 1920 in Lewis's journal, *Heart*); he had gained proficiency as a research physiologist. He had mastered the EKG machine, a state-of-the-art technology that was only beginning to be applied to heart disease. Perhaps fortuitously, he had chosen a specialty that was about to explode with new developments, to be utterly transformed.

The city to which he had returned was now the fifth largest in the country. Its newly consolidated medical school and hospitals were recognized as among the nation's best, and aggressive efforts were being made to develop a medical research center. Instead of a dead-end career as second fiddle to Uncle Nate, an entire new world had opened to Harold. In his year abroad, he had made his best efforts to prove himself in science. In contrast to his stepfather Gustave, his uncle Nate, and even his famous great-uncle Marcus, Harold was now a full-fledged clinician-scientist, capable not only of clinical work but of original scientific investigation.

Perhaps the clearest earnest of future success came in a

letter Harold received soon after his return to America, from the man he had looked to as a model both as doctor and as scientist, and in whose company he had suffered and learned so much.

Oct. 9, 1920

My dear Feil,

This evening a parcel awaits me from Messrs. Laekendorf & I cannot tell you how delighted I was to find inside it, the "Mechanism" in its very proud new clothes ... You will be glad to hear that our latest experiments have gone well ... so all our spirits are in the ascendant.

We all have very pleasant memories of your visit & miss you a lot in the laboratory.

I trust that you and Mrs. Feil will have had a pleasant crossing, & that your child will have traveled comfortably to his fatherland ...

Kindest regards & renewed thanks
Very sincerely yours
Thomas Lewis

4

READING SHADOWS:
THE YEARS BETWEEN
THE WARS

MR. Edward J. Moore, a sixty-year-old widower with two grown children, had come to Dr. Harold Feil's EKG laboratory for evaluation of chest pain. A crushing, squeezing pain that left him breathless and shaking, it characteristically began beneath the sternum and spread across his chest, up to his left shoulder. Mr. Moore smoked eight cigars and many pipesful per day, but had no other illnesses or vices. At first the pain was occasional, the result of effort or excitement; then it became more frequent. Finally it came on ten to fifteen times a day, and Mr. Moore was forced to take premature retirement as a mechanical engineer involved in the production of foundry equipment.

It was October 1926. After his return to Ohio six years before, my grandfather had established a successful cardiology practice. Over the past twenty-five years, deaths from infectious disease had dramatically decreased, mostly as a result of better public-health measures. Cleveland's typhoid-fever epidemics, for instance, ended for good after the city's drinking water was chlorinated in 1925. The average lifespan in the United States increased greatly, from forty-two years in 1890 to fifty-six years in 1921, and fifty-nine years by 1929. As people lived longer, there were more deaths from illnesses such as heart disease and cancer.

From a relatively rare cause of death in 1890, probably less than one percent, by 1920 heart disease accounted for one out of fifteen deaths.

Furthermore, Cleveland had rapidly become industrialized, spurred by the war, which employed 175,000 workers in the city. Immigrants by the tens of thousands came from Europe and the South and the surrounding countryside to find work in steel mills and brassworks and automobile plants and railroad yards. Increasingly, men operated heavy machinery and vehicles and poured molten metal: should their hearts give out, dozens, even hundreds, might die. Then, too, there was the new class of business executives, desk-bound and highly stressed: after a heart attack, could they return to their pressure-cooker lives?

Since Harold Feil was one of only two cardiologists in the city, his practice had grown rapidly. Besides his private practice in downtown Cleveland, he ran the EKG lab at Mt. Sinai Hospital, and did rounds at Cleveland City Hospital. At Western Reserve's Medical School, he was collaborating with other professors in physiology and cardiology research.

Hardly recognized as a legitimate field a dozen years before, by the mid-1920s cardiology was making enormous strides. By applying the EKG and other new instruments that monitored pressure and flow in the heart's chambers, an elite group of researchers and practitioners were redefining the way the heart functioned both in health and in disease. There were major research centers in Boston, Chicago, Baltimore—and Cleveland. In a few short years, Cleveland had risen to prominence as a center of cardiac research, and by 1940 it was perhaps the world's leading center. Under the leadership of Carl J. Wiggers, director of Western Reserve's Department of Physiology, tremendous advances were being made in understanding heart physiology.

These advances were not yet matched, however, by effective treatments. With few exceptions, treatment had hardly improved in over a century. In the early 1800s, heart failure and high blood pressure were treated by bleeding; angina pectoris by application of magnets to the chest; as well as the old standbys of opium and brandy for the intractable pain of heart attacks. Digitalis, extracted from the leaf of the foxglove plant, had been described in 1785 by William Withering for treatment of dropsy, or fluid retention—he ground dried foxglove leaves into a powder, then made an extract with alcohol, which patients drank. By causing the heart to contract more vigorously, this extract rid their bodies of excess fluid. Then it was forgotten. It was only in the 1890s that Dr. James Mackenzie correctly used "tincture of digitalis" for treatment of atrial fibrillation and heart failure. Some diuretic medications, which help patients with high blood pressure or heart failure to urinate away excess fluid, were available, including various mercury salts, but they were highly toxic. One early advance was nitrate medications: amyl nitrite, an inhalant, was introduced in 1867, and brought relief from angina by dilating the blood vessels and decreasing arterial pressure; nitroglycerine, which had similar effects, and is placed under the tongue, was first used in 1879.

In 1926, though, medical treatment offered little for Mr. Moore and other patients with coronary-artery disease except symptomatic relief. Little progress had been made since Harold's father, George Cohen, had died of a heart attack thirty years before; in reality, not much had changed since 1800, when British doctor William Heberden wrote: "The termination of the angina pectoris is remarkable. For if no accidents intervene, but the disease goes on to its height, the patients all suddenly fall down, and perish almost immediately. Of which indeed their frequent faintness, and sensations as if all the powers of life were failing, afford no obscure intimation." The average survival of a patient who developed anginal pain was still only five years—and indeed Mr. Moore survived only two more years after his 1926 visit to Dr. Feil.

After a heart attack, there was nothing to do but let nature have its way. The recommended treatment was weeks or months of bed rest—and then retirement from active life. Except for those patients foolish or brave enough to defy doctors' orders, surviving a heart attack meant becoming an invalid.

On that October day in 1926, Harold Feil examined Mr. Moore. He felt his pulse, took his blood pressure, and inspected his arms and legs for signs of deficient circulation, such as edema, cool temperature, or distended veins. He listened carefully for heart murmurs. He took samples for a blood count, and a Wassermann test (the patient had contracted syphilis many years before). Then Mr. Moore was readied for the EKG machine. A technician vigorously cleansed areas of his arms and his right leg with alcohol to ensure optimal electrical contact. Silver electrodes, smeared with electrode jelly, were tightly attached with rubber straps. The EKG's magnet was switched on, and it was laboriously calibrated, so that a one-millivolt signal caused the beam of light—which passed through the galvanometer—to move one centimeter. A strip of photographic paper moved across the camera, a big metal box, a rotating spoke marking intervals of time. The EKG strip could measure as much as thirty feet in length, coiling down into a large metal cassette.

Before you could see a tracing of the heart's rhythm, the paper had to be developed in the darkroom, so the only way to know what was happening during the EKG was by watching the shadow of the galvanometer's string—by becoming expert at reading the shuddering and twitching movements of a shadow.

From observing these movements—a regular rhythm, with the three bumps of the heart's P, QRS, and T waves— Harold concluded that Mr. Moore's EKG was essentially normal.

By chance, when the electrodes were still attached and the beam was still on, Mr. Moore began to develop angina: breathlessness, sweating, pain in the middle of his chest which radiated toward his left shoulder. While an assistant went for nitroglycerin, Harold took another EKG tracing.

After Mr. Moore was given a tablet of nitroglycerin, his attack began to abate. Several minutes later Harold obtained a third record.

I can imagine my grandfather's anticipation as he took the large metal canister containing the EKG to the dark-room and drew the long strip of paper through the smelly developer and fixer solutions in large metal tanks, and his excitement as he emerged from the amberlit room with bits of the still-damp paper, which confirmed what his eyes, trained by watching hundreds of tremulous shadows, had discerned: abnormalities in the ST segment, the portion of the EKG following the heart's contraction, when the muscle is "repolarizing" (returning to its baseline electrical state), awaiting the next beat. Three months later, on a return visit, Harold provoked another attack by asking Mr. Moore to climb a flight of stairs. Again the EKG showed these same findings.

What Harold had recorded that October day was a rarity—a transient, ephemeral event. Only two other cardi-ologists had reported EKGs taken during angina, and their findings had been inconclusive. With Mr. Moore's and three other patients' EKGs (two showed similar findings), my grandfather and his co-worker Dr. Mortimer Siegel proved that angina pectoris caused temporary changes on the EKG.

The angina attack caused both pain *and* EKG changes. It caused abnormal conduction of the heart's electrical impulses and impaired muscle functioning.

With publication of this study, Harold surpassed the work of his mentor Thomas Lewis. Despite his scientific eminence, Lewis held some strange beliefs about heart disease. Although he was a highly skilled clinician, Lewis did not recognize the importance of the heart attack, the myocardial infarction; and he barely addressed the topic of angina pectoris. In Lewis's mind, anatomical abnormalities of the heart were insignificant compared to physiological ones; he thought of the narrowing of coronary arteries in ischemic heart disease, as well as the pain of angina, and the heart attack itself, as important only to the degree they gave evidence of the heart's electrical exhaustion. Even more baffling, in 1922, declaring "The cream is off," Thomas Lewis had abandoned cardiology entirely, to study pain and the peripheral circulation.

Nothing, however, could have been further from the truth. Within only a few years, it had become clear that in coronary-artery disease there was a crucial common pathway of illness. In an obscure 1912 paper, Chicagoan Dr. James Herrick had first clearly described the symptoms of the heart attack, and in 1919 he stated that the heart attack was due to thrombosis (or clotting) of the coronary arteries, the vessels providing oxygen to the heart muscle itself. In the 1920s, cardiologists began to accept Herrick's radical view. Atherosclerosis caused narrowing of these arteries, and narrowed vessels were more likely to clot. Because part of its muscle had died, the heart often could not pump effectively, and a patient could develop congestive heart failure, and even die. In this scenario, angina pectoris might be critically important. If the EKG showed changes during angina, this implied that angina was a symptom of physiological danger, of inadequate blood flow. Furthermore, it was possible that injury might be detected before it was irreversible. Perhaps the EKG could be used in patients with chest pain to determine which cases involved angina, reflecting heart disease, and which chest pain resulted from other causes, such as gallstones, an excess of stomach acid, or anxiety.

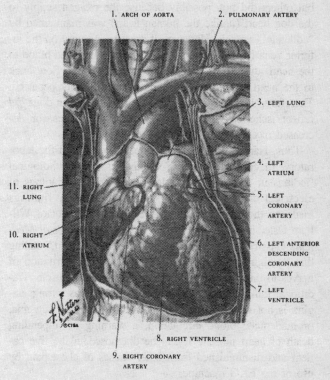

FIG. 1. EXPOSURE OF THE HEART

As one of the new breed of clinician-scientists, my grandfather was in a unique position to explore this question. After his work with Dr. Siegel, Harold went to the dog laboratory to confirm and expand his findings. There, working with Louis N. Katz, a talented young cardiologist born in Pinsk, Russia, who had studied in London with Thomas Lewis and with Nobel laureate Archibald Hill, he experimentally tied off branches of the coronary arteries in dogs. Some dogs had EKG changes like those found in patients—but others did not, possibly because the oxygen supply to the dog heart (unlike the human heart) was maintained by "collateral" vessels. However, if pressure was put on the inferior vena cava, the large vein returning circulated blood to the heart, thereby dramatically decreasing blood flow back to the heart, then such EKG changes invariably occurred. Therefore, the changes observed in humans and in dogs *did* reflect ischemia—they were convincing evidence for decreased oxygen supply to the heart muscle.

Thus, Harold was able to connect the clinic to the laboratory, to correlate patients' symptoms with pathological findings in laboratory animals. He linked new findings of electrical conduction abnormalities with older findings made on the autopsy table. In 1892, the great doctor William Osler in his textbook *Principles and Practice of Medicine* classified angina under "neuroses of the heart," stating that it might be caused by "neuralgia," or an irritation of nerves to the heart, or by a cramp of the heart muscle. Traditional thinking, as summarized by Osler, was wrong: angina is not neuralgia or a cramp. It is a sign of ischemia, or inadequate blood circulation, a warning of impending death of heart muscle. It can be diagnosed in the live patient and distinguished from other causes of chest pain by use of the EKG machine.

Finally—mentioned in passing in their report—was the innovative method by which Feil and Siegel had produced angina in two of the four patients: by having them exercise, climb stairs or do sit-ups against resistance. Dr. Arthur M.

Master and other researchers later systematized this approach into "exercise testing," using a step test (1929), treadmill, or bicycle ergometer (in the 1950s) to provoke angina. Feil and Seigel's ad hoc method of producing angina in Mr. Moore was to be turned into a systematic means of exploring the level of activity a heart patient could withstand—and therefore how incapacitating his heart disease might be.

The year Harold had spent in England studying cardiology changed not only his professional career but also his personal life. A lifelong outsider who had spent his childhood dependent on the goodwill of aunts and uncles, a Midwestern general practitioner whose education and career had been cramped by financial circumstances, Harold had returned to the United States in many respects an English gentleman.

That he had been abroad only a year was immaterial: the transformation was lasting and complete. He had picked up British tastes: he began collecting old medical books and ancient botanical prints, and smoking fine cigars. In 1924, when he and Nellie built their house on a broad street in the new suburb of Cleveland Heights, it was a solid Tudor with two maid's rooms, a wood-paneled study, and pear and apple trees in the backyard. The centerpiece of its living room was a stone fireplace with a curved iron canopy, modeled after one in the Old George Inn at Salisbury, England.

More important was something else less dependent on material artifacts. What had coalesced during Harold's year abroad was a mode of being, a habitual approach to life that could only be described as gentlemanly, based on the Edwardian model. A gentleman scientist, who was also a proper personal physician, adhered to a certain code. He did not trumpet his accomplishments, or unduly push his cause. He served his community selflessly while maintaining an elegant style of living. In dealing with enemies, it was best to raise, not lower, the level of discourse. If possible, disarm them with cordiality; if not, protect yourself with an air of bemusement. Appeal to their sense of justice and fair play, and should they choose lesser tactics, it would be obvious who held the higher ground. If thwarted or injured, never let your pain and humiliation show.

And there was no shortage of pain and humiliation. In the years between the wars, a new wave of anti-Semitism was apparent not only in Ohio but across the country and the world. Henry Ford's Michigan newspaper, *The Dearborn Independent,* reprinted the slanderous *Protocols of the Elders of Zion;* the Ku Klux Klan attracted record support, electing governors in Oregon, Oklahoma, and Indiana; and the rabble-rousing radio broadcasts of Father Coughlin, over the Shrine of the Little Flower Radio Station coming from Royal Oak, Michigan, aroused hatred and nativist bigotry, especially after the banks closed in March 1933 and the Depression truly began.

More painful, prejudice came from the very colleagues whose acceptance Harold so yearned for—his fellow doctors. Part of a largely Anglo-Saxon gentry who had established the city's schools and hospitals, museums and libraries, banks and businesses—not to mention the green suburbs on the city's eastern edge—his colleagues felt little compunction in openly using bigotry to protect what they had. Tycoons O. P. and M. J. Van Sweringen, eccentric brothers who owned a vast railroad empire, developed the suburb Shaker Heights following World War I, and they put ninety-nine-year "deed restrictions" on resale of houses, ensuring against the encroachments of Jews, blacks, and Catholics. In the professions, newly enacted quotas stemmed the flood of outsiders. (Yale adopted a quota for Jews in 1920, Harvard in 1922; at Columbia University's College of Physicians and Surgeons, a quota decreased the number of Jews per class from fourteen percent in 1920 to four percent in 1948.) At Western Reserve, as at other medical schools across the country, Jews were limited to four or five percent of each medical-school class, even though they might constitute as many as sixty percent of applicants.

Against these defenses of "gentlemen," Harold's strategy of being a better gentleman gave only partial protection. There was some advantage in camouflage: the newly arrived Russians and Poles coming into Ohio via the Lower East Side of New York, who now comprised 85,000 of the 90,000 Jews in the city, were stereotyped as being loud, and pushy, and anarchistic. Many of them were active in socialist organizations and labor unions. Feil was none of these things. He was no leftist; he was a solid Republican. You could trust him completely.

Accommodation had its costs, however. Once, at a medical-school faculty meeting, a certain Freddy Waite, Ph.D., professor of histology, went into a diatribe about how disgraceful it was that the school was admitting Jews—next thing you knew, they'd be letting in "niggers." Hearing this, Harold lost his temper, blurted out that what he was hearing was inexcusable, reprehensible, and he stormed out of the room. The dean, aghast, called Harold into his office. He was shocked—such outbursts weren't to be tolerated. Unless Feil apologized publicly at the next faculty meeting, he would be fired.

Astonished and enraged, Harold left the dean's office. At home that night, he and Nellie discussed what to do. There was in fact no recourse. If anyone would lose his job, if anyone would have his career ruined, it was Feil.

Harold spoke up at the next faculty meeting, and delivered the required apology. He chose his words carefully. He regretted deeply having lost his temper, in a way unbecoming a gentleman. There was no apology for what he said.

The nicety of such distinctions was likely lost on his fellow doctors: they had heard vicious slurs, and an apology. Feil was apologizing, rather than being apologized to.

The greatest danger, though, was not the pain one silently endured: it was more subtle, a kind of confusion, a diffusion of who you were. It wasn't just that the Feil children were named for British royalty, or that the family had Christmas trees, which they festooned with beautiful German crystal ornaments, or that their synagogue had organ music, not a cantor, and Sunday, not Saturday, services. It was that by mimicking the forms of a culture which despised you, you risked becoming utterly confused. At worst, hating yourself; at best, always uncertain where your heart lay, whether in the scrupulously genteel surface or in the suppressed passion of your instincts, always alert to the slights you had endured yet powerless to seek justice.

For the most part, for Harold and his family, the genteel surface held sway; only occasionally was there any hint of frustration. In 1932, at age forty-three, Harold was the nationally known author of many classic medical papers, yet he had not even been promoted to assistant professor at Western Reserve University—he still held the lowly title of Demonstrator of Medicine. He gave an address at his synagogue to the League of Jewish Youth, entitled "Medicine as a Career." With typical understatement, in speaking of the opportunities for Jews in medical research, he said: "Unfortunately, anti-Semitism places difficulties in their path and the aspirant, who may be gifted both in mind and personality, often finds the reward solely in intellectual achievement and advancement slow."

Despite its frustrations, the doctor's life and the practice of medicine gave unity and meaning to the lives of Harold and his family. A biased promotions committee, or the nasty asides of colleagues, could not take away the enormous gratifications of being a doctor, of advancing medical knowledge, of healing and caring for the sick. Illness itself transformed, erased social distinctions, allowed—even if briefly—the veneer of class hatred and exclusion to crack, and common humanity to emerge.

There were three children by this time. George, born in England in 1920, had been followed by Mary, my mother, in 1922, and Edward in 1924. As parents, Harold and Nellie were loving to the point of indulgence. The Feil children were known to be wild and mischievous; they shocked their second cousins by climbing on furniture when they visited, something no well-bred 1920s child would do. After one of Harold and Nellie's dinner parties, the children poured water from a second-floor window onto the heads of departing guests. Camp counselors wrote letters home and teachers called Harold and Nellie in for conferences, complaining that the three Feil children talked back, were fresh, and would not sit still in class. Yet in other aspects of life Harold and Nellie were very strict. In intellectual matters, Harold was demanding and hard to please, and George— more interested in football and girls than in studying— never achieved the grades his father expected. There were frequent conferences, discussions, demands, apologies, letters full of anguish and promises.

Harold and Nellie had long planned to send the two boys to Yale, from which George Cohen, Harold's father, had graduated. Nellie attended Smith College, and when Mary was still in elementary school a place at Smith was reserved for her. Just as his English Tudor house gave the impression of an ancestral home, solid and well polished, so, too, would the tradition of Feil children attending certain colleges—and if they showed the requisite intelligence and stamina, the tradition of becoming doctors as well.

From an early age, Harold took the children down to his office, and took them in his black Plymouth sedan on house calls. In 1932, Harold got one of the earliest "portable"

EKG machines—its three parts weighing a total of 150 pounds. George would often help lug the heavy wet-cell batteries and the string galvanometer into a patient's house, and then would wait in the living room while Harold examined his patient in an upstairs bedroom. Afterward, George fetched the instruments and carried them back to the car. Sometimes little Mary accompanied them on the house call as well. As the children got older, the plan gradually emerged that they would become doctors. Assuming George was able to get into medical school, he would finish medical training and then join Harold as a partner in private practice. Mary also showed a talent for science, and there was no reason why she should not go to medical school, too: indeed, when Mary was in the sixth grade and developed a sore throat, fever, and a bright-colored rash, she realized that her symptoms matched those of Beth in *Little Women* and she went to her father, saying, "I think I have scarlet fever"—her first medical diagnosis. There were several women doctors on the staff at Western Reserve, friends of Harold and Nellie. Aunt Tessie had been a suffragist, Nellie and her mother both completed college—so there was precedent for Mary to have a career. Perhaps Edward, too, would enter medicine, though he was fascinated by a different technology—the motion-picture camera, not the EKG machine, and showed little inclination toward science.

Tradition established identity; it protected against the vicissitudes of economic uncertainty and social ostracism; it soothed sad memories. It also provided a solid foundation for the daring leaps of one's scientific investigations.

Much to my surprise, as I discovered in reviewing my grandfather's medical reports, his thinking traversed a daring path between the wars. A cardiologist friend of mine, trained at the Texas Heart Institute under Dr. Denton Cooley, was astonished to see a bound volume of these papers that I brought back from a visit home. "It's amazing what your grandfather was doing back then!" he said. "Measuring portal pressures in 1922! The dynamics of mitral insufficiency! Working with Wiggers and Katz—the giants!"

I'd never known Papa as a pioneer: as a kid, I'd always seen the cigar-smoking gentleman, quiet, unassuming, and bookish. I'd mistaken the mask for the man. But here was incontrovertible proof.

The daring was this: in moving from description to vigorous investigation, from pathology to physiology. And then, taking risky leaps into the next phase: treatment. He was not alone, of course, in investigation; but he took real risks in treatment.

Shortly after his return from England, Harold had begun working as a volunteer in the laboratory of Carl J. Wiggers, Thomas Lewis introducing Feil as "a young man in whom I have detected a talent for research." Wiggers was America's greatest physiologist. A fellow Midwesterner, Wiggers grew up in Davenport, Iowa, and began practicing medicine in Michigan before training in research at New York Hospital and studying with the physiologist Otto Frank in Munich in 1912. Wiggers had come to Western Reserve University in 1918 as director of physiology. He was particularly interested in heart physiology, in "hemodynamics"—the study of the dynamic forces of blood circulation. He studied the relation between electrical and mechanical events in the heart, and how these are affected by disease.

Especially important was an instrument that became known as Wiggers's optical manometer, an adaptation of a pressure-measuring device used by Otto Frank in Germany. (Wiggers visited Frank's laboratory in 1912. A suspicious and secretive man, Frank refused to give him a copy of his manometer, so Wiggers secretly bribed Frank's technician to build him one.) The manometer Wiggers had copied and later improved was essentially a hollow metal tube with a thin membrane at one end, to which a mirror was attached. A bright beam of light reflected off the mirror and—like the EKG—was focused onto a moving strip of photographic paper. The other end of the tube was connected to a funnel which could be placed against the surface of a blood vessel. When pressures changed within the vessel, the mirror was displaced, moving the beam of light. With exquisite sensitivity and a high "frequency response," the manometer was a dramatic improvement over previous devices. Pressures in various chambers of the heart and in the great vessels could be closely correlated with the EKG and heart sounds—relating electrical and mechanical events in the heart to clinical data. For forty years, Wiggers and his students used such instruments to investigate heart function. While this work had no immediate application, it later became the essential basis of cardiac catheterization. It was crucial in understanding the effects of cardiac medications, and in designing better ones.

Wiggers, a big man with a cherubic face, who enjoyed cigars and whiskey, was a generous and often inspiring teacher. Dozens of his students became important researchers in their own right; his physiology textbook was a classic. Having practiced medicine in his early years, he had a great interest in clinical problems, and unlike many of his colleagues, he was free of anti-Semitism.

Harold worked both with Wiggers and with his students. In 1922, he and Wiggers did dog experiments describing the abnormal pressure curves in the heart's chambers in mitral insufficiency—a disease where the mitral valve cannot close completely, so that when the ventricle contracts, blood gushes back through the valve into the left atrium and the lungs. Commonly seen following rheumatic fever, mitral insufficiency leads to fatigue, weakness, shortness of breath, and often to early death. In the 1920s, no treatment was available. The normal mitral valve is held in place—like a sail—by tendon-like cords. If the cords are torn, the valve leaflets flap free, and blood flows backward when the heart contracts. Using a plunger to tear the cords, they created mitral insufficiency in dogs, and investigated abnormalities in pressure curves and heart function.

Harold was equally innovative in his clinical work. In 1923 he described using epinephrine to treat Stokes-Adams syndrome. In Stokes-Adams, or complete heart block, the electrical impulses, beginning in the sinoatrial node in the upper heart, are blocked from reaching the ventricles. The heart rate slows dramatically, and a patient often loses consciousness and is at risk for ventricular tachycardia or fibrillation, and sudden death. This condition is now treated with a pacemaker or with "beta-adrenergic stimulant" drugs, but then it was untreatable. Harold turned to epinephrine in an attempt to stimulate the heartbeat and overcome the block—and his work was successful.

In other studies, Harold used the new technologies to investigate various heart diseases. With Louis N. Katz, he applied the optical manometer to patients with aortic stenosis (narrowing of the aortic valve, leading to impaired blood flow from the heart), and atrial fibrillation, and aortic insufficiency. In 1924, they investigated the dynamic findings in "hypertension," or high blood pressure, which was only beginning to be described as a disease. They investigated normal heart function as well, for it is useless to investigate disease without understanding normality.

His greatest interest remained the heart attack, the end result of coronary-artery disease. In 1920, Dr. H.E.B. Pardee had demonstrated that in patients who later died of heart attacks the EKG had shown significant abnormalities. In 1928, Dr. Joseph T. Wearn proved that, by looking for characteristic EKG changes, one could make a diagnosis of myocardial infarction during life. In a 1938 paper, Harold showed that one could now confidently make this diagnosis. Especially if one used several EKG leads attached to the chest wall, as Wolferth and Wood described in 1932, instead of the usual three-lead technique (with electrodes attached only to the legs and both arms), and combined this with various clinical signs—then it was possible correctly to diagnose myocardial infarction in over eighty percent of heart patients. Given that this disease had been clearly described only twenty-five years earlier, this gave dramatic evidence of the rapid progress of medical science.

Harold's most daring work dated from the mid-1930s, when he began working with the pioneering heart surgeon Dr. Claude S. Beck. A coalminer's son from Shamokin, Pennsylvania, Beck had originally been trained as a neurosurgeon, doing research at Johns Hopkins and with Dr. Harvey Cushing in Boston, before determining that his real interest lay with the heart. In 1923, while at Harvard, Beck had assisted Dr. Elliot Cutler in the first successful surgery to widen the scarred heart valve in mitral stenosis, surgery that had been proposed by Cutler and Dr. Samuel Levine.

In 1925, Beck set up an animal laboratory at Western Reserve University to practice heart-surgery techniques on dogs. It was perhaps the first such laboratory in the world. He began doing research on pericarditis, the inflammation of the fibrous sac around the heart that occurs as a result of illnesses such as tuberculosis and rheumatic heart disease, and developed an operation to cure this. When he audaciously determined to pursue heart surgery on humans, the dean of the Western Reserve Medical School, Joseph T. Wearn—who perceived Beck as a radical, a wild man—refused to submit his grant applications, and, when he persisted, sent distinguished physicians to demand that Beck stop operating. (The National Institute of Health sent a special committee to review this highly unusual situation, and in a packed amphitheater with a kangaroo-court atmosphere, one professor after another, including Carl Wiggers, spoke about the dangers of heart surgery. Eventually, Wearn was overruled, and Beck was exonerated and allowed to submit his grant applications.) In the 1950s, when Beck advocated open-heart defibrillation of heart-attack victims, the dean said he was "not a safe man to have on the faculty" and tried to have him fired. Becoming associated with Harold Feil, a well-established practicing cardiologist, as well as an expert in heart monitoring, gave Beck an important element of respectability in the 1930s and 1940s—and also made him an important scientific and medical ally.

Beck's surgical work, though primitive, was a great and daring step forward in the treatment of coronary-artery disease—a leap from investigation to treatment. Once a doctor could reliably diagnose myocardial infarction during life, and once it was proven that angina was a sign of serious narrowing of coronary arteries, the next logical step was to try to prevent heart attacks by surgically improving circulation—to "revascularize" the heart. In view of the state of medical technology in the 1930s, Beck's decision to attempt this surgery was heroic. (By our current standards of medical ethics, it was also shocking, in that Beck, like other researchers of that era, routinely performed dangerous experimental treatments on patients who had not given "informed consent"—who had no clear idea of the risks or benefits of treatment.) Not until the mid-1950s, after the development of a pump oxygenator which allowed the heart to be bypassed, would *open*-heart surgery be possible. And only after the development of selective coronary arteriography by Dr. F. Mason Sones, Jr., at the Cleveland Clinic in 1960, could doctors see individual lesions of the coronary arteries, making possible the coronary-artery bypass grafting operation (developed by the Cleveland Clinic's Dr. René Favaloro) that is so common today.

Beck's 1935 "closed-heart" operation was crude, even grotesque, by today's standards. The patient's chest wall was opened widely by cutting both sides of the sternum or breastbone and removing much of the cartilage connecting it to the ribs. The pericardium was cut away. Once the heart was exposed, its epicardium, or external layer, was scraped off. Then a graft of muscle from the chest was sewn onto the surface of the heart. In addition, powdered beef bone (and later talcum powder and even asbestos!) was placed in the pericardial cavity, the area between the outside of the heart and the pericardial sac, in order to "produce a low-grade inflammatory reaction" and stimulate the growth of blood vessels. Then the chest was closed.

Beck's theory was that new "collateral" vessels would grow between the chest muscle and the heart, providing better blood supply to the heart muscle. Of the first twenty patients treated with this technique (all of whom had severe heart disease), eight died in surgery or shortly afterward; but several survivors reported marked improvement in the angina, and some were even able to return to work. In their 1937 paper describing this procedure, Beck and Feil conclude: "At the present time we can scarcely make a statement concerning the future of this operation . . . This work offers the beginning of a new method of approach in the treatment of a serious disease."

Beck later modified the operation, turning the coronary circulation in reverse by sewing the aorta to the coronary sinus, the vein that drains blood from the heart muscle. The operation remained controversial, even though the mortality rate dropped to fifteen percent. While these operations were eventually superseded by more effective techniques, they opened up new frontiers in medicine. First and foremost, they proved that surgery to revascularize the heart was possible. Beyond that, they opened frontiers in the surgical management of the cardiac patient. In the process of scraping the heart and attaching the skeletal muscle grafts, the heart was handled roughly and many patients developed arrhythmias, the most serious of which was then-universally-fatal ventricular fibrillation. In 1938, Harold Feil and a resident, Dr. Phillip Rossman, wrote perhaps the first paper about the EKG effects of cardiac surgery.

The concept of following the EKG during surgery, particularly during surgery on the heart itself, was a dramatic culmination of several decades of expanding the boundaries of measurement. The EKG had left the laboratory for the hospital and the clinic—it was now entering the operating room. Beginning in the late 1920s and early 1930s, cardiologists had begun monitoring the EKG during general surgical operations; but Harold Feil was the first routinely to monitor the EKG during cardiac surgery.

In the 1930s, the operating room was almost blind to the patient's cardiac status. Anesthesia was administered by the "drop-ether" method, by a nurse anesthetist, not a physician anesthesiologist. A bottle with a wick was placed against a cone on the patient's face; when the bottle was inverted, drops of ether soaked a cloth within the cone. During surgery, the patient's breathing was maintained by squeezing a bellows-like bag. Pre-operatively, few blood tests were available: sodium and potassium levels were determined by the laborious method of flame photometry; hemoglobin levels and blood counts were done as a matter of course. The intern routinely did blood typing for transfusion—but this was often moot, since there was no ready source of blood: blood banking was not established until 1937, by Chicagoan Bernard Fantus.

Once surgery began, the only way to monitor heart function was by following the patient's heart rate and blood pressure, and by the color of blood in the operative field. If the blood turned blue (and it often did during the Beck procedure, because the lungs were compressed in order to better expose the heart), the surgeon would scream to pump more air to the lungs.

Following the EKG in the operating room was not so simple as placing a small machine at the bedside and watching a neat paper tape emerge: for one thing, drop ether was highly volatile, and the bright lamp inside the EKG's galvanometer created an intolerable risk of explosion. Furthermore, technology had not yet advanced to the point of being able to produce a moment-by-moment tracing of the EKG.

It was necessary to place the galvanometer in the hallway. Electrodes were connected to the patient, and a long cable passed through a hole in the operating-room door. Beck (who bore more than a passing physical resemblance to W. C. Fields) conducted surgery in a solemn, cathedral-like atmosphere. Though his hands were massive, his little fingers as thick as thumbs, he handled tissues with slow, meticulous movements, with unusual delicacy and sensitivity. During operations, Harold Feil, wearing a surgical gown, would stand in the hallway, closely watching the moving shadow of the galvanometer's string. If there was any evidence of a serious arrhythmia, he could step into the operating room to see what the surgeon was doing, and tell the nurse anesthetist to improve aeration, or advise which drugs to administer: procaine spray to the surface of the heart to decrease irritability, quinidine for ventricular tachycardia, epinephrine for inadequate contraction. Following surgery, the patient was put under an oxygen tent, and since there were no antibiotics, and no mechanism for resuscitation, the most one could do besides attentive nursing was to hope and pray.

In the years between the wars, there were other shadows to watch besides those of moving strings. After the banks closed in 1933, money became tight. In 1929 Harold had moved to new offices in the Republic Building in downtown Cleveland, near the van Sweringens' massive new Terminal Tower, the tallest building west of the Alleghenies. Times were hard. Many patients could not pay their bills; others paid in groceries instead of cash. The Feils were better off than many families, especially after *The Omaha Bee* was sold to the Hearst newspaper chain in 1928 and Nellie inherited a share of Edward Rosewater's fortune. But it was necessary to conserve electricity and heat and food. George was set to work washing Harold's car or mowing the lawn to earn his allowance; and Mary once made the mistake of coming into her parents' room without knocking and discovered Harold sitting on the bed, counting the family's savings—flustered, he yelled at her to get out.

Then, too, there were the shadows of political forces. Sunday night was radio night, and the family would sit in the living room listening to Ed Wynn and Eddie Cantor, and Burns and Allen, and Jimmy Durante. There was a switch by the telephone to turn off the radio if a call came in for Harold. In addition to comedy, the radio also brought frightening news from Europe. And at the movies, at the Alhambra Theatre or Keith's 105th Street Cinema, between the Buck Rogers serial and the main feature, the Pathé World News newsreel showed Adolf Hitler gesticulating, and huge crowds responding *"Sieg Heil!"* and marching Brownshirts, and camps for Aryan girls, *Deutsches Mädchen*, recruited to make babies for the Fatherland. In the late 1930s, refugee professors arrived at the university. Dozens of German Jewish boys came to stay at the orphanage on Fairmount Road, formerly known as the Cleveland Jewish Orphan Asylum, now called Bellefaire.

It was a time of great fear and instability, great social unrest, and great opportunity as well. In the depths of the Depression, Harold finally began to receive some of the professional recognition he deserved. In 1933, at the age of forty-four, he was named assistant professor. And when Dr.

Horace Korns, head of the EKG lab at Western Reserve, left for a job in Iowa, Harold was invited to take it over, and to be physician-in-charge of the medical clinic. Due to the Depression, as the official notice of his promotion stated, however, "the promotion for this coming year involves no increase in salary."

As head of the EKG lab, and as a Western Reserve Medical School professor, Harold entered a new stage in his career. As a reflection of the increasing importance of heart disease as an occupational hazard in industry, he became a consultant to the Erie Railroad, evaluating railroad workers who had survived heart attacks and their fitness to go back to work. In November of 1936, he was asked to participate in the autopsy of O. P. Van Sweringen, the fifty-seven-year-old railroad magnate, builder of the Terminal Tower and developer of Shaker Heights, who had died mysteriously in his private Pullman car, his personal fortune of $120 million having dissolved into $70 million in debts and a host of lawsuits from enraged bondholders.

As health care became more effective and more expensive, there was concern as to how to make adequate medical care available to the indigent. In 1937, Harold was one of 430 prominent American doctors who joined in a national "medical revolt," demanding that the federal government recognize that "the health of the people is a direct concern of the government," and that it formulate a "national health policy directed toward all groups of the population." Public funds should be made available for adequate medical care for the medically indigent, these doctors argued, as well as to support medical education and medical research. The American Medical Association bitterly opposed this resolution, fearing the incursion of socialized medicine.

But Harold's greatest influence—like Marcus Rosenwasser's before him—was on a generation of young doctors going through training. In 1931, Lakeside Hospital, the new hospital for Western Reserve University, had been completed. The building was wired so that EKGs could be done from the patient's bed on the ward, rather than sending the patient down to the EKG laboratory—but this arrangement was quickly supplanted by the portable EKG machine, which could be wheeled from room to room. Harold's routine, which he continued for the next twenty-five years, was to read EKGs from 7:30 to 10:00 every morning at the hospital. Sometimes he read alone, but increasingly he was accompanied by young doctors eager to interpret these records, which few doctors understood.

Harold was beloved by students for his kindly manner and the breadth of his knowledge, which ranged from physiology to medical history to botany to cardiac rehabilitation. The other cardiologist on staff at Western Reserve was the irascible Roy Scott, who was also a professor of medicine at Cleveland City Hospital and had been president of the American Heart Association. Scott would often tell a patient referred to him from some small town in southern Ohio, "Your arteries are like rusty pipes—they can blow at any minute and you will die." In contrast, Harold would speak gently, advising the patient about the risks he faced and his prognosis. He encouraged the more talented students to do research, and to specialize in cardiology. With his guidance and encouragement, two students, Reginald Shipley and William Hallaran, wrote a classic paper on the variants of the normal EKG, something that, paradoxically, had never been studied.

His influence was especially strong with Jewish students. There were three or four other Jewish doctors on staff at the medical center, including the great Harry Goldblatt, who had discovered in 1934 that one form of severe hypertension was caused by narrowing of the "renal artery," a vessel supplying blood to the kidneys, proving the importance of the kidneys (and the renin-angiotensin system) in the regulation of blood pressure. But Feil had the greatest impact on young Jewish doctors.

In the late 1930s, despite the frightening events in Western Europe, it was not at all clear to a Midwestern family that war would break out, or, even if it did, that America would be brought in. Though Adolf Hitler presented his "plan for conquest" to his generals in 1937, British Prime Minister Neville Chamberlain visited Hitler three times in September 1938 and returned to London confident that there would be "peace in our time." True, Hitler annexed Austria in March 1938 and the Sudetenland later that year, bringing ten million Austrians under his rule. And in the spring the German Army marched into Prague, dividing Czechoslovakia into satellite states. Yet each time it seemed possible that Hitler might stop, that he might be satisfied with bloodless occupation.

Mary was to begin her freshman year at Smith College in September 1939. Beforehand, with Harold and Nellie's encouragement, she and her older brother, George, a junior at Yale, decided to go on a summer Youth Hostel bicycle trip through Europe. Starting in Scotland, they planned to bicycle through the Lake Country and south to London, and then cross to the Continent, through Amsterdam and Rotterdam and Bruges and Brussels, and end up in Paris. (On one of my visits home, I discovered the brochure for his trip. A piece of orange paper stuck into the brochure described "unpredictable conditions in Western Europe" but expressed confidence in peace, and a belief that the Continent was just going through "temporary adjustments.")

Earlier that spring, Mary had accompanied her mother to Northampton, Massachusetts, for her twenty-fifth college reunion. Concerned about events in Europe, Nellie asked Dr. Hans Kohn, a professor of modern European history at

Smith, and a Viennese refugee, whether he thought they would be safe.

"Where are they going? And when are they coming back?" asked Dr. Kohn.

Nellie described the planned itinerary.

"Stay in Western Europe," Kohn replied. "Come back before the harvest, because if there is war, it will start after that."

Mary and George had a fascinating time in Europe. In England, they saw soldiers marching at railroad stations. Gas masks were being handed out to civilians, to prepare for poison-gas attacks. In Scotland, they slept in ancient castles. On the Continent, they bicycled through the flat Netherlands, sleeping in barns on beds of straw, and showering in a former dungeon. In Paris, they stayed in a *pension* and went to the Moulin Rouge. They could not see the Rose Window at Notre Dame, because it had been removed in fear of war. The Continent was exhilarating, the people edgy, more excited than fearful.

They returned to the United States aboard the SS *Volendam*, arriving in New York Harbor on August 23, 1939. That same day, Hitler and Stalin signed a non-aggression pact, secretly partitioning Poland. Mary and George had wonderful photographs of their trip, and one of Harold's patients took the negatives to his basement darkroom and blew up huge photos of the two of them standing with their Raleigh bicycles in front of Buckingham Palace. On September 1, Hitler invaded Poland, and two days later England and France declared war. The Feils were relieved that Mary and George had escaped; some members of the group had continued on to Greece and were trapped there for months.

In November 1939, Stalin's troops invaded Finland, which surrendered in March 1940. He next invaded Estonia, Latvia, and Lithuania. Hitler's troops overran Denmark, then

Norway. In May 1940, Germany invaded Belgium and neutral Holland. The French Maginot Line collapsed. The British retreated, withdrawing nearly 400,000 troops across the English Channel from Dunkirk. On June 15, Paris fell. The Luftwaffe began bombing England nightly, causing great destruction and thousands of casualties in London and Birmingham and Coventry. The United States remained neutral.

In December 1940, Harold received a letter from Thomas Lewis, his former professor. Harold had offered to provide refuge for Lewis's daughter.

> Clearburn, Loudwater,
> Rickmansworth
> Dec. 7, 1940

My Dear Feil

It gave me pleasure to get your letter; it was 4 weeks on its way; & I am most grateful for your offer to help our young daughter. I trust however that the occasion may not arise. We shall fight on. There is indeed no option for us. But if we fight on alone the chances of us winning are not 100% by any means. We are indeed fighting the war for America as well as for ourselves; I shall personally be grievously disappointed if you do not join with us in the spring.

It is pitiable to see London practically crumbling though I do not think it can be brought down by aeroplanes.

It is win the war or it is the end of everything in regard to civilization. We shall fight in this crusade for decency & freedom even if you still stand watching; but I am sure that win or lose you would never forgive yourselves in times to come if you do not come in actively.

> Best wishes & renewed thanks
> Yours very sincerely,
> Thomas Lewis

A month later Harold received another letter, stating that Lewis's daughter had gone to stay in Boston with Paul Dudley White and his family:

Jan. 7, 1941

Miss is all in the hands of PDW til the war ends & I must settle up with him then. When the war ends—who knows when that will be! . . . This country cannot alone police Europe. We have a terrific time in front of us; our fighting has not really started yet & no one can see the end.

II

THE GOLDEN AGE

5

CLASS OF '41

ONE of Harold Feil's best students was Herman K. Hellerstein, a Clevelander, the son of Russian immigrants, who had begun medical school in 1937. He came from Dillonvale, Ohio, a rough small town in coal-mining country, near the bend of the Ohio River, on the border of Pennsylvania and West Virginia. There, on June 6, 1916, my father was born, the fourth surviving child and first surviving son to Samuel and Cecelia (or Tzivia) Hellerstein.

Both Samuel and Cecelia were natives of Brest-Litovsk, Russia, near the Polish border. Samuel was the son of a family in the Perve Gilde Kupetz, a bonded guild of merchants who were free to travel beyond the limits of the Jewish Pale of Settlement, and Cecelia was descended on her mother's side from the Soloveitchiks, a prominent rabbinical family.

After Cecelia's mother, Rebecca, died, her father married a young girl who was Cecelia's classmate at school. Cecelia was outraged, and even more furious when her new stepmother influenced her father to cut off her *yerusha*, or inheritance. As a result, Cecelia left Brest-Litovsk in about 1901, age eighteen or nineteen, and arrived in New York, where she worked in a garment factory. A few years later, Samuel came to the United States to avoid a military draft

that would have condemned him to twenty-five years in the
Russian Army. The plan was that he would become a doctor. From New York, he headed for Pittsburgh, to the home
of an uncle who had promised to put him through university and medical school. However, his uncle had remarried
after the death of his first wife, and this second wife vetoed
the plan, asking Samuel, only a few days after his arrival,
"So, when are you going to start paying rent?"

Samuel had no choice but to acquire a horse and buggy
and begin traveling through Pennsylvania and the Ohio Valley as a peddler, selling "notions." In 1903 Samuel married
Cecelia and moved to Dillonvale, where he was taken into
partnership by an elderly store owner named Finkelstein. In
front of their store hung a large sign with the motto:
FINKELSTEIN AND HELLERSTEIN: OUTFITTERS FROM HEAD TO
FOOT. It was said that you could walk into the store naked
and, assuming that you were carrying enough money, could
walk out a while later fully clothed.

In Dillonvale, a land of rolling hills and blossoming trees
and cruelly fought miners' strikes, everything had a mythic
cast—the eternity and finitude of village life. There was a
bank, a courthouse, a hardware store, a brickyard, a two-
engine firehouse, a hanging bridge over a creek fouled with
tailings from coal mines in the hills above. Near the bank
was the office of Dr. William Mercer, the country doctor,
and owner of the town pharmacy as well; he delivered all
six of Cecelia's children, and cared for her oldest son,
Louis, who died of infantile diarrhea at the age of one year.

Dillonvale was a shopping area for people from surrounding villages, and on a busy day ten thousand people
might come from Jug Run, Mingo Junction, and Adena.
One-legged Mr. Henry, maimed by a locomotive, stood out
at the railroad junction holding a sign to stop traffic when
each of the eight daily trains to Cleveland came through.
One day, little Tom Henry, his son, darted in front of a

passing train and had his leg cut off, too. The coal miners, emigrants from Czechoslovakia or Poland or West Virginia, lived in tiny, company-owned houses along the creek and were paid in company scrip, and fell victim to malnutrition and TB and mining injuries and black lung.

Once Herman saw a Tin Lizzie careen down Dillonvale's Main Street, carrying two union organizers, and in pursuit a huge, powerful Stutz with big side wheels and flashing spokes; as they rounded a curve, gunshots rang out, and the Tin Lizzie swerved off the road into a tree. The Stutz roared off. The two union men, agitators for the great John L. Lewis and the United Mine Workers, were slumped over. They had been shot dead by hoodlums hired by the mine owners, the wealthy Hanna family.

The Hellersteins lived first in a house on the hill, and in later, more prosperous times, in a house downtown on Main Street, near the town lawyer, the banker, and Dr. Mercer. The house on the hill was two hundred steps up from the road leading out of town. From those steps, surrounded by lilac bushes, one could see the entire valley: the scaffolding around the coal mines, the tailings of rubble, the trains as they passed through town, the church and the football field. They had a wonderful view of Dillonvale High School the night in 1923 that it burned to its foundations.

One day, when my father was four years old, Cecelia said to him: "Herman, go to Dr. Mercer. Tell him I need him right away."

My father ran down the two hundred steps and down the street to Dr. Mercer's office, where he entered the waiting room and politely took a seat. Fifteen or twenty minutes later, Dr. Mercer—a large, full-bodied man in a vest and suit coat—poked his head out.

"What!" he said gruffly, upon seeing the small boy. "Why were you waiting?" He grabbed his medical bag and rushed down the street, leaving Herman behind, and climbed hurriedly up the two hundred steps to the Hellerstein house. Within a few hours he delivered a baby boy who was named Earl.

When Herman was five or six, his oldest sister, Rebecca, a high-school senior, took ill. She was tall, a redhead, and vivacious, the best student in her class and a passionate basketball player. Tired of small-town life, she was eager to go on to college. Suddenly she had fevers, chills, a rapid pulse; she became weak and breathless. She couldn't even do her homework. In desperation, Samuel sent her to a "diagnostician" in Wheeling, West Virginia. The expert examined Rebecca, holding his stethoscope to her chest to listen for heart murmurs, feeling her swollen joints, scanning her freckled skin for a tell-tale rash. He made his diagnosis: rheumatic fever.

In 1922, despite the great progress in British cardiology, despite the development of the EKG machine and the advances in physiology research, there was no treatment for rheumatic fever—just nutrition, isolation, and bed rest. For the whole of her senior year, Rebecca lay in bed, barely able to move. Rumors in town were that she was pregnant. The likely father, townspeople thought, was a cousin, Ralph Coff, who lived in Adena and came to visit every weekend, bringing a dozen fresh eggs. My father knew only that something was wrong with his sister's heart—that there was something important about the heart. By spring Rebecca, who continued to study with a tutor, had recovered enough to deliver the valedictory address.

Beyond that were the experiences of illness and injury of Dillonvale townspeople. When there was a cave-in at one of the mines on the opposite hill, the Hellersteins would hear underground explosions, and then the wailing of emergency sirens, and would see the miners' wives gathering at the entrance of the mines, and rescuers rushing in; they saw, too, as miners were pulled out, their arms or legs broken, chests crushed, bodies limp from poison gas.

And then there was the example of Cecelia, their mother, whose charity extended to giving money to a priest to open a storefront church, and who was always sponsoring relatives from foreign countries, or sending clothing to the poor in Europe. She brought chicken soup or food to the miners' families who lived near the brickyard, and extended credit at the store during strikes. The local minister called her "the best Christian in town." There were continual reminders of hunger, poverty, oppression, and disease—and, from Cecelia, the saving value of compassion.

In July 1929, the family moved north to Cleveland. They rented a house on Milverton Road in Shaker Heights, a brand-new white clapboard house on a suburban street. By this time, Samuel was a prosperous businessman, owning clothing stores in Wheeling, West Virginia, and Adena, Ohio, and a confectionery in Steubenville, in addition to his original store in Dillonvale. Along with Cecelia's brother, Alex Zeiger, he was co-owner of an apartment building in New York in which a hundred people lived. Without working, he had an income of $20–30,000 a year, a large sum in those days. No longer tied to daily work, Samuel was free to give his children a "modern education."

In my father's eyes, the Milverton Road house was miraculous; it had bathrooms with flush toilets and running water; it had central heating. No more midnight trips across a snowy field to the three-seater outhouse; no wood or coal to fetch on icy February mornings for fireplace and stove. And instead of a kitchen pump connected to a cistern full of rainwater or an outdoor pump to hard groundwater, in Shaker Heights there was a faucet that one turned on for an infinite supply of water that was clear and cold.

Only three months after their move, the Great Depression began. While the children adjusted to suburban life, Samuel felt at loose ends. Accustomed to uninterrupted hard work ever since his arrival in America, he found himself at age fifty idle and without direction; furthermore, as economic conditions worsened, the rents from his New York property fell, so that they scarcely covered his costs. In the early 1930s he opened a shoe store; and a few years later, as the United States government began mobilizing for the coming war, he took two partners and opened a trouser-manufacturing shop in downtown Cleveland, called Star Trouser Manufacturing Co. Soon there was work to keep fifty, sixty, seventy-five, a hundred sewing-machine operators active. They opened an outlet store on the first floor of their factory building, and sent salesmen through Ohio, Indiana, West Virginia, Pennsylvania, and Michigan.

Unlike Earl, who had radical, perhaps even Communist, inclinations as a teenager, and despised his capitalistic father for having betrayed his socialist ideals, Herman spent evenings and weekends helping Samuel do the factory payroll. He accompanied Samuel to New York's garment district to buy bolts of cloth, and on sales trips through the Great Lakes states, where Herman would drive his father's charcoal-gray Peerless sedan at season's end to help clear merchandise.

Samuel offered to send Herman to the Wharton School of Finance if he would agree to become a partner at Star Trouser. But my father had other ideas: he had decided to become a doctor. Very possibly, to some degree, he was living out Samuel's blighted dream, and his interest perhaps was kindled by Rebecca's illness and by the example of Dr. Mercer and the suffering and injustice he had seen in Dillonvale. In any case, his interests were further piqued by his studies of chemistry and biology and physics at Western Reserve's Adelbert College, and as senior year approached, he prepared to apply to medical school.

On presenting his application to the Dean of Admissions

at Western Reserve, he had a rude shock, a foretaste of what was to come.

"You'll be considered under the quota," he was told.

He asked the dean what she meant.

"You're a Jew," she said. There were only five spaces for Jewish students in a class of eighty-two. Perhaps he should not complain: Negroes were not admitted at all; and there were only two spaces for women.

He submitted his application and was relieved to be accepted into the class of 1941. Classes began in the fall of 1937.

It was a bitter experience, a first taste of what doctoring had become in America. At the same time that American medicine was on its way to becoming the world's greatest, the new American medical-education system had become increasingly discriminatory and cruel. It was founded on intimidation, humiliation, and ruthless competition—indeed, a grotesque caricature of the intent of the reforms that had been instituted thirty years before with the publication of the Flexner Report.

Even for the elect, medical education was cruel, bordering on sadistic. On the first day of medical school, as was customary, Herman's class was told: "Look at the man to your left and the man to your right; at the end of this year, one of you will not be here." Perhaps a third of the initial eighty-two students would be summarily expelled before graduation.

As far as anti-Semitism went, it did not help that many of the faculty members were German, and some were overtly Nazi sympathizers. A famous pediatrics professor, active in a local German language club, would invite members into his study after dinner, to play war games with toy Nazi soldiers. During World War II, a professor in the pathology department at City Hospital, Dr. Herbert Reichle, had to flee to Mexico to avoid being arrested as a German spy.

While in college, my father (who had shot up to six feet in height, though he weighed no more than 135 pounds, and had an intense nervous energy that is apparent even in photos of that era) had been editor of the yearbook, a member of the debating team, and a member of the Interfraternity Council, and had engendered controversy by founding the local chapter of an anti-war organization called Veterans of Future Wars, and in all had an intellectually stimulating and enjoyable education. In medical school, though, he found himself in continual confrontations, in painful, no-win situations. Unlike some of the older Jewish doctors, who had learned to tolerate or ignore such slights, Herman, as a result of his natural strongmindedness (if not at times arrogance), fought back. Showing up his tormentors by making the correct diagnosis, by discovering the hidden lesion, disregarding oppressive authority for the higher cause of pursuing truth, enduring humiliations and setbacks in the hope of eventual triumph by the rightings of wrongs—these are the themes of his medical-school stories. Above all, he wished to avoid being the "subservient Jew," outwardly accommodating and genteel, who inwardly burned with rage and humiliation.

During this time, Samuel began to suffer mysterious pains. He would become short of breath while at the factory, would feel pain in his chest, which inexplicably traveled down his arm. About 1935, he went to cardiologist Dr. Roy Scott, who did a physical examination, took his blood pressure and an EKG, and declared that his symptoms were merely the result of an overactive imagination.

For my father, Samuel's pains (which now would be understood as classical symptoms of angina pectoris, and which culminated in a heart attack ten years later) further spurred his interest in the rapidly advancing field of cardiology. With a Western Reserve professor, Dr. Howard Karsner, as his advisor, Herman began to spend free hours in the Institute of Pathology, working on a massive project, an analysis of two thousand autopsies of the heart. Professor Karsner, a classical pedagogue, precise in expression and manner, and an elegant dresser (reputedly the only man in Cleveland to wear cuffless trousers), was one of the great pathologists of his day. In 1923, when he was thirty-five years old, he was given $750,000 by the Rockefeller Foundation to establish an Institute of Pathology at Western Reserve University, only the second such institute in the United States. Research at this institute, especially in pathology, microanatomy, and anatomy, in combination with Dr. Carl J. Wiggers's physiology laboratory, had made Western Reserve Medical School one of the most prominent medical research centers in the country.

In his second year of medical school, convinced that war with Germany was inevitable—and just—my father joined the medical ROTC. He began training at Carlisle Barracks in Pennsylvania on weekends and vacations. After the ominous 1939 German-Russian non-aggression pact and the invasion of Poland and France, a military unit of doctors and nurses from Western Reserve was formed, the elite Fourth General Hospital unit, ready to go overseas at a moment's notice.

Since he might be drafted before finishing even a year of internship, Herman decided to take a position that would give him the widest and best practical experience as a doctor—a rotating internship at Philadelphia General Hospital, starting July 1941. Unable to finish his paper on the two thousand autopsies, he left the data with Dr. Harold Feil, one of his professors, promising to return and finish it, even if it had to wait until after the war.

In Philadelphia, it was possible to plunge into medicine,

to try to forget the danger that lay ahead, to forget President Roosevelt's proclamation of national emergency, to forget that the Japanese had invaded China and were poised to occupy French Indochina, and to forget that Hitler—astonishingly—had just turned against his ally, Joseph Stalin, and was beginning to attack Russia. The world was mad: through medicine, through the rituals of healing, one could find some kind of order. Despite the demanding schedule (every second night on call, only one afternoon off every two weeks), the meager pay (a grand total of $50 salary for the entire year, $25 of which was deducted for laundry, and the other $25 for membership in an honorary medical society), and the Spartan accommodations (a six-by-eight-foot room), Herman felt the relief of total dedication.

Only a month into his internship, he received the results of his performance on the Ohio medical exams: he had scored first in the state. The July 23, 1941, issue of the *Cleveland News* reporting this ran his photograph on the front page, with a banner headline: CLEVELANDER GETS TOP GRADE IN STATE MEDICAL EXAM. The next column, headed SCORES DIE IN RAID ON MOSCOW, began: "German bombers left scores killed and wounded in Moscow today and reported that 'vast flaming seas' engulfed the Soviet capital while on the fighting front Adolf Hitler's high command declared Russian troops were suffering 'extraordinarily sanguinary losses' everywhere." And the largest headline on page 1 read:

FEAR NEW JAP WAR MOVE IN WEEK

Foreign military quarters in Shanghai, noting an ominous series of Japanese war preparations, declared today that Japan was girding to invade French Indo-China within a week. Both Washington and London anxiously watched the mounting crisis, with authoritative British quarters predicting a quick break in developments.

In December came Pearl Harbor. Congress declared a state of war with Japan, and Germany and Italy declared war on the United States. Millions of men were drafted, including twenty-five thousand doctors. Herman's own prospects soon were clear. In a January 1942 letter to his sister Esther in Collinsville, Illinois, Herman wrote: "I will probably be in the army in several months. All the 2nd year men who are in the reserves have been called up to active duty. So I will be glad to finish up one year. Till then I will try to pick up as much as possible. Knowledge, you know." During his previous rotation on the TB ward, he had cared for seventy-five patients. Now he was working on the "Anesthesia, Ambulance and Receiving Ward"—already in twelve days having given anesthesia to one hundred patients, as well as admitting new patients, a busy job in a 1,200-bed hospital.

Here we get the first crack at diagnosis. I have been very happy in doing this work, differential diagnosis being one opportunity where one's real knowledge can be put to practical use. With my past experience in pathology and current literature contacts, I have been able to recognize several interesting cases that may have gone undiagnosed ... For example, the other day I diagnosed an early case of adult Vitamin C deficiency ... As you can see, I am thriving (my ego) on this type of work. There are many days I go back to my room, inspired to read more to improve myself ... there being such a perplexity of material which confronts one in the receiving ward and which cases we often dismiss with the diagnosis of crock, or psychoneurotic. Pelvic inflammatory disease, ectopics, hot bellies, fractures, knife wounds, rabies infections, pneumonias, gall bladders, strokes, psychotics, all these are bread and butter cases which we soon become proficient in recognizing.

A tremendous irony: as the world was sinking into a global war that would take more than fifty million lives, medicine was actually capable of curing disease. Since the 1920s, when Banting and Best had discovered insulin, diabetics could be successfully treated. Subtle vitamin deficiencies could be identified and remedied—pellagra with niacin, pernicious anemia with raw liver, which contains vitamin B12. Surgery of the abdomen and chest and even the brain had become safe and almost routine. Most amazingly, over the past three or four years, the new miracle sulfa drugs (developed by the German pharmaceutical industry) had turned previously incurable diseases into child's play. Pneumonia, once a dreadful disease that required months of hospitalization and had a death rate of twenty to thirty percent, now could be treated with sulfapyridine or sulfathiazole or sulfadiazine. Within three days the fever would be gone; in ten days, the patient could go home. The story was similar for bacterial meningitis, and gonorrhea, and streptococcal wound infections, and dysentery and cholera and typhoid fever, and a dozen other diseases. Everywhere one looked, previously incurable disease was falling before the advance of science.

In June of 1942, Herman was called to active duty and assigned to the Medical Field Officers' School at Carlisle Barracks, near Harrisburg, Pennsylvania, as one of five hundred doctors undergoing military training and learning battlefield medicine. The course completed, transfers began. Herman was sent to Fort Smith, Arkansas, where he was assigned to be a commander of a medical company, helping activate the 14th Armored Division for the June 1944 invasion of Europe. As commander of a company, he would run a mobile hospital. For months they engaged in simulated combat in the rough mountains and valleys of Arkansas.

Early in 1944, much to his distress, he was transferred to the 7th Armored Division at Fort Benning, Georgia, where, under the direction of Colonel Boland, young medical officers were being mobilized into medical detachments. In contrast to medical companies, which operated mobile hospitals at a distance from the line of combat, medical detachments were attached to individual combat units, on the front lines. Each detachment included a doctor as its captain, and a MAC, medical administrative corps officer, some T3s, staff sergeants, and several technicians; they amounted to twenty-three men in all, riding in half a dozen jeeps and several ambulances. Exercises at Fort Benning included opening equipment, using IVs, and practicing combat-medicine techniques under blackout conditions. It was no coincidence that the doctors in the front-line medical detachments were named Hellerstein, Friedman, and Cohen, whereas those in the medical company (which would be at the rear base camps) were named O'Reilley and Ferguson.

In May of that year, while he was back in Cleveland on furlough, his friend Austin Weisberger, also a recent medical-school graduate, set him up on a blind date with Mary Feil, Dr. Harold Feil's daughter. When he drove over to the Feils' house to pick her up, however, Herman was met at the door by Mrs. Feil, who told him that Mary had a strep throat, and the date was cancelled. Mary looked out her bedroom window as Herman left, getting only a glimpse of a tall young man in an officer's uniform. A few months later, when he was again back in Cleveland, they had a date, going downtown to see a movie at the Palace Theatre.

Afterward, Herman told his older sister, Rebecca, that he had found the girl he wanted to marry; not that he would have any opportunity to do so in the foreseeable future, however. One spring day, Herman telephoned Mary to say that he would be in New York City for one afternoon before being sent overseas. Could she meet him there? Mary took a train to New York and stayed with a college friend, Mary Blumberg, a Viennese refugee; the next day the three of them had a date at Rockefeller Center, eating a leisurely lunch and watching skaters glide around the unseasonable ice.

Barely a week later, the 7th Armored Division boarded the *Queen Mary* in Boston, heading for Europe. It was June 6, 1944: D day, the day of the invasion of Normandy. The ship's gyroscope had been turned off to avoid giving signals to enemy submarines, so they pitched and rolled in heavy ocean swells. Three days out of port, a twenty-seven-year-old sergeant died suddenly, and my father was called on to do the autopsy. The man had been considered a "goldbricker" because he had complained of chest pain and was unable to do five-mile training runs in full combat gear. Autopsy proved that there had been real disease: an obstruction of one of the main coronary arteries, the left anterior descending branch, which supplies oxygen to the left ventricle.

The 7th Armored Division disembarked at Greenock, Scotland, and went by train through beautiful, desolate heath to Tidworth Barracks, Salisbury, England, not far from Stonehenge. Then, in the beginning of August, they assembled on the south shore of England, preparing to cross the English Channel. Hundreds of airplanes roared overhead as the entire division of 30,000 men stood in an open field—before them, on a high podium, General George Patton. Microphones amplified his voice, and the sun glinted off his helmet, which was rumored to have thirty-two layers of shellac, as he welcomed them to a historic battle.

"Just remember, men," he called out. "A hero is not a man who dies for his country. A hero is a man who makes another man die for *his* country!"

By dawn, the division had crossed the English Channel in flat-bottomed landing craft, which disgorged jeeps and other vehicles in five-foot-deep water. Intake and exhaust pipes had been specially modified so engines wouldn't die in the water. Though two months had passed since D day, defenses were still significant. The landing troops drove onto Omaha Beach, facing heavy enemy fire.

Regrouping, they headed pell-mell east toward Germany, liberating France. They moved so fast they were strafed by American airplanes, and when they began running out of fuel, they had to cannibalize their own vehicles. Over the next month, they took LeMans, Chartres, Château-Thierry, and Reims, facing a chaotic army of advancing Germans and retreating Germans and lost Germans and black-uniformed SS troops; they freed Verdun in a day, fighting on a landscape still scarred by trenches and shell craters from World War I. They roared across France until they were stopped dead at the city of Metz, a maze of old concrete forts, interconnecting underground passages, and blasting artillery.

It was there that he almost died.

It was September 6, 1944, and he was twenty-eight years old, commander of a medical detachment of twenty-three men assigned to the 40th Tank Battalion of the 7th Armored Division of General Patton's Third Army, stationed on the front lines in the town of Ste-Marie-aux-Chênes, France.

They had set up a temporary aid station in the cellar and first floor of a wrecked farmhouse. Across the stone floors lay American tank soldiers and infantrymen on stretchers, thirty of them, their bodies torn by shrapnel and gunshot, by mortar fire and deep burns. Abdominal contents spilled out of open flesh; a thigh, half a face were missing.

I can just imagine my father working among them: dulling pain with morphine, staunching bleeding with tourniquets and crude bandages, making sure bottles of plasma dripped in faster than blood oozed out. I can see the set of his jaw, his intent expression, the force of every gesture, and I can hear his voice angrily barking orders to the medics, and turning soothing and reassuring as he spoke to the wounded.

Then, momentarily calm, he radioed the net control station which transmitted messages to and from the front lines: "Faro-niner, faro-niner"—his code name—"message for you, faro-niner. Send vehicles to transport wounded."

He waited as the message was relayed to the collecting point, five miles to the rear. Then he received the laconic response: "Follow S.O.P."

Standard Operating Procedure. According to protocol, it was *his* responsibility to evacuate the wounded from the aid station back to the collecting point; the collecting point was responsible only for transporting them farther back to the field hospital.

And then I can see him—utterly enraged—hopping into his jeep, roaring along five miles of dusty roads back to the collecting point, and jumping out, heading for the cluster of trees where a group of medical officers sat playing cards before several empty ambulances.

To the commanding officer, also a captain, he said: "I need four ambulances to bring back wounded."

"Doctor, don't you know protocol?" sardonically, from the medical officer. "That's *your* job."

Upon which my father went back to his jeep, reached under the seat, and pulled out an empty German P-38 pistol, which he pointed at the captain's head. "Tell me," he demanded. "Am I going to shoot you dead—or are you coming now?"

A column of ambulances followed his jeep to the aid station, where the American wounded lay.

An hour later came a call from Colonel Boland, division surgeon of the 7th Armored Division, a courtly, silver-haired Chicagoan who rarely ventured up to the front lines.

"Captain Hellerstein, are you cracking up?" asked the colonel.

"Before you say that," my father responded, "spend one day with me."

Boland came up the next day.

It just so happened that six 76-mm Sherman tanks had been waylaid in a valley near the town of St-Privat, a few miles away from the heavily fortified city of Metz. They sat in an open field, burning. From their position on the rim of the valley, the Germans had an open line of fire to the twenty or more wounded soldiers lying on the ground nearby.

A medical jeep coming for the wounded was pinned down by heavy machine-gun and mortar fire. A second medical jeep went forward, and then a third—they were pinned down as well.

Colonel Boland stood beside the captain, trembling at the nearness of gunfire.

Finally, knowing that what he was doing was crazy, Herman radioed the net control station: "Faro-niner, faro-niner . . . I'm going down, give me cover."

And he and his driver, Sid Diamond, hopped into their jeep and started down across the rocky slope.

Descending into the bright midday, they were relieved to see tracer bullets coming directly at them, wobbling in the heat: relieved because, if you could see them, you were not dead.

"Turn left! Turn right!" he shouted.

Dodging fire, they veered wildly across the hillside, approaching the tanks in the open field. They jumped from the jeep and began to attend to the wounded. Inside one tank they found a soldier with a neck wound, George Hook, heir to the American Rolling Company steel fortune, who had been "the point"—the leading tank for the entire Third Army from the moment the campaign began at Omaha Beach six hundred miles back.

If Hook was pulled out headfirst, my father realized, his spinal cord could be severed. So, sending his driver, Sid, down into the turret, he stood atop the tank, ignoring the artillery and rifle fire, and began lifting the wounded soldier out by his ankles.

They lowered Hook on the side of the tank away from Nazi fire, and immobilized his neck with blankets and put him on a litter. They wrapped up the other wounded GIs in blankets, and put four litters on their jeep and drove back up the hill to where Colonel Boland—white-faced, his fists clenched, elbows drawn in close to his chest—stood murmuring, "Oh my God, oh my God!"

Then, followed by two other jeeps, they headed back into the valley. Soon twenty wounded lay on stretchers around the colonel.

"Why don't you evacuate them?" Boland asked.

"Because all the ambulances are at the rear," my father responded.

After that, protocol was changed. After that, there were always enough ambulances.

From this story and its variants (sometimes it is the other captain, not Colonel Boland, who asks, "Hellerstein, are you cracking up?") comes the image that haunted me as a child; indeed, one that haunts me even now: my father, the young doctor, the young soldier, standing atop a crippled tank, carefully hauling a wounded soldier feet-first into smoke and gunfire on a European battlefield. As a kid, when my friend Jimmy Baumann would come over to spend the night at our house, we would drag my father's army uniforms out of the attic closet and lay out his collection of German bayonets. Then we would find him downstairs and insist that he tell his war stories once again.

This was our favorite. There was the heroism, even foolhardiness of this act, my father's total disregard for personal safety possibly endangering the entire company, not to mention dozens of other wounded soldiers. There was the intimidation of myth, the implicit challenge of impossible comparison—for what could we ever do in the peaceful green Ohio suburbs to match this? And there was the panicky thrill of realizing that only one bullet, one piece of shrapnel, one German with good aim or good luck, and I wouldn't have been there to listen; none of us six children would have been born.

Twenty-five years later—nearly half a century after the war—prodding my father to tell his war stories again to put the past to rest, I heard other things. Many things.

And with them came the realization that moments mattered. Artillery and shrapnel could kill, but by World War II—as my father so viscerally, so passionately knew—medicine could save lives. Never before in warfare had time mattered to any degree. During the Civil War, the wounded often lay for days on the battlefield before being evacuated; tourniquets and amputation and cautery might prevent a man from bleeding to death, but infection culled all but the hardiest. By World War I, horse-drawn or motorized ambulances could evacuate the wounded, but the man who survived acute wounds was likely to die of shock or blood poisoning or pneumonia.

But now many of the wounded could be saved. The war gave dramatic evidence of medical progress over two decades. There were great advances in treatment. Shock could often be prevented by administration of fluids, especially plasma, which was brought to the front lines in powdered form and reconstituted with sterile water. Pain could be relieved rapidly, with the medics' "syrettes" of morphine, little toothpaste-tube-like containers with a needle under the cap, which was opened and jabbed into a soldier's arm or leg. Infection could be prevented by cleaning wounds with iodine, and by packing them with anti-bacterial powders, such as sulfanilamide. The first true antibiotics had become available in 1937—so, on the front lines they had a number of sulfa drugs, and at the base hospitals farther back, the earliest shipments of the miracle drug, penicillin. The Germans had devastated Allied troops during World War I with mustard gas and phosgene attacks; but by World War II, American doctors had learned how to treat gas injuries, and gas masks were available; perhaps as a result, gas was never used.

The greatest advances leading to better survival of soldiers came from prevention, not treatment. The American army in World War II was healthier than any army in history. Certainly, the troops were better fed. The K ration was developed by Minnesota nutritionist Ancel Keys to contain all nutrients and vitamins necessary for a day's survival. American soldiers also had improved water supplies. Because the tank required vast quantities of gasoline to keep running, supply lines had to be maintained at all costs—resulting in fresher supplies of water as well. Thus, typhoid, cholera, and dysentery were almost entirely prevented.

Immunization also prevented illness and death. Diphtheria, tetanus, and smallpox, all important causes of death in earlier wars, were hardly threats anymore. Then there were the sexually transmitted diseases. VD was well controlled, in contrast to World War I, when 250,000 soldiers were hospitalized for an average of sixteen days for gonorrhea. Not only did the army have education programs for soldiers, and distribute prophylactic kits, but there were crude but effective forms of treatment: iodine preparations injected into the urethra to kill gonorrhea, arsenical compounds or penicillin for syphilis.

Furthermore, the nature of war had changed. It had become mobile, rapid, fought from a distance. In the trench warfare of World War I, soldiers were in trenches for months at a time and developed highly debilitating infections such as trench foot, and often suffered grievous wounds in hand-to-hand combat; by the 1940s, war was increasingly fought in jeeps and tanks and airplanes. There were mobile operating rooms, and evacuation ambulance airplanes, and motorized laboratories, and cross-country ambulances, and most of all there was the medical jeep, which carried well-trained medics with a supply of emergency medical equipment, and could evacuate four soldiers—two litters on the front hood, two on the rear.

As the 7th Armored Division roared east, spearheading the American drive that was liberating France by as much as sixty miles a day, they suffered enormous casualties. Yet their death rate from wounds was remarkably low. If a wounded soldier was located and attended to by a medic, only one or two in a hundred would die. George Hook's case was not unusual, then: after being medically stabilized on the battlefield and transferred to a field hospital, he was evacuated to a hospital in England, where he convalesced for several months, his neck immobilized by a cast. He recovered totally. He is retired and lives near Paris today. In any prior war, he would have died of his wounds.

They were saving lives by the hundreds; what more could any young doctor ask? And so, despite the horrors and deprivations, these were—as my father often said—the greatest moments of his life.

* * *

In December they entered Germany. At St-Vith they withstood a ferocious German attack, holding back more than a hundred thousand Germans in Field Marshal von Rundstedt's winter offensive, what became known as the Battle of the Bulge; they finally retreated, and a month later took St-Vith again. Then in the spring of 1945 the "Lucky 7th" crossed the Rhine River, taking thousands of German prisoners and freeing tens of thousands of POWs.

As captain of a medical detachment, my father was responsible for the health of about a thousand men. When they were not in combat, this consisted of treating colds, anxiety, and a little gonorrhea. Of primary importance was prevention: keeping the soldiers healthy—the main risk being "combat exhaustion," in which combat soldiers would be disabled by utter fatigue and anxiety; for instance, one soldier had had three tanks shot out from under him. In combat, the medics would ride in the third or fourth vehicle from the lead, behind the first tanks, which would wind down narrow roads, with a front-row view of the battle. When they met the enemy, they would spread out, seeking cover.

On one occasion, in the Black Forest, my father traded seats with his driver, who was tired. He was going through the forest when their jeep hit a land mine and was destroyed. His driver was killed instantly, and my father, thrown out of the jeep, fractured the spurs of several vertebrae in his neck. He cut a six-inch strip off a GI blanket and wrapped it around his neck; thus, he was able to continue in active duty.

In the frigid Battle of the Bulge, a new problem emerged; so-called cold injury—ground type. Medics would discover soldiers crouched in foxholes, virtually frozen in position, and suffering from hypothermia and severe frostbite; they needed to be carefully thawed out.

Of the twenty-three men in my father's medical detachment, none was killed or seriously wounded until one day in the fourth campaign, when the 7th Armored Division was in northern Germany. The land was utterly flat, and the Americans could see trains coming from a great distance, bringing German troops from Denmark to defend a village the Americans were attacking. It was a beautiful spring day, the sun shining over a pastoral landscape: ahead they could see the village, and farmhouses with barns attached to them, and shimmering fields of wheat and oats. From their aid station in an abandoned farmhouse, the fighting seemed distant, almost unreal.

A group of German sharpshooters began aiming directly at the red crosses on the army jeeps and at the red crosses displayed on either side of the medics' helmets and on the sleeves of their uniforms and on their hips. Shooting medics, unarmed men, is a violation of the Geneva Convention, against all rules of war.

Within a few hours, six medics had been killed.

When the firing died down, six litters holding the dead men, men from North Carolina, Georgia, South Carolina, friends and colleagues, lay in the courtyard of the farmhouse, surrounded by mowers, farm wagons, tractors.

Later that day, the German sharpshooters were flushed out by light tanks and captured. They were young men, newly inducted, on their shoulders the lightning insignia of SS troops. Handsome youths with blue eyes and blond hair, they were lined up opposite the litters of the dead American medics. The American commanding officer said to my father, "We're going to kill these SOBs." (Or, in some versions of the story, "It's up to you to decide—should we kill these SOBs?") Walking down their ranks, my father asked them, in German, "Are you ready to die?" One after another, they began to whine and cry: to proclaim their innocence; they knew nothing of what had happened, they said.

Finally, my father turned to the American officer. "They're prisoners," he said. "Don't kill them."

On April 15, 1945, the 7th Armored Division, in support of the British Army, entered the Bergen-Belsen concentration camp, which had been captured only hours before. The troops had smelled death from twenty-five miles away. Over the front gate was a legend: *Arbeit Macht Frei*— WORK MAKES YOU FREE.

Inside were sights beyond even a soldier's capacity for horror. There were bodies everywhere, emaciated bodies, filling mass graves, bodies piled like cordwood. Shocked beyond anger, Herman took photographs, dozens of them, which were developed later as tiny postage-stamp-sized pictures, and which he sent to Mary in Cleveland, writing on the back in pencil: HOW? HOW? And: THIS CAN NEVER BE FORGIVEN. In a barracks room that would hold a hundred people, a thousand or more lay on cribs or shelves, some living, some dead. Moaning, cachectic, stinking of vomit and incontinence, the living literally had to be pulled out from between the dead. English Quakers had come as volunteers to help the survivors; and women from nearby villages were recruited to assist them. After doing triage— who might live, who would die—they set up tables to begin to bathe the survivors with soap and water, and delouse them, and feed them.

My father, facing these Giacometti-like figures, asked in broken Yiddish, and in the German he had learned in college: *"Warum sind Sie hier? Why are you here?"*

"Bin jurist. Ich bin Jude," might be the answer. I am a lawyer, a grade-A Jew, my mother was half Jewish. Or: I am a Hungarian, or a Lithuanian, my grandfather was a Jew.

One inmate, a skeletal sixteen-year-old Polish boy, answered: I am a Polish Jew.

I am a Jew, also.

"Nein, 's iz nisht meyglich," the boy said. That is impossible.

My father asked why.

"Di bist Offigier" was the boy's reply. You are an officer, how can you be a Jew?

When my father translated this response, the other American officers began to cry.

Other inmates held a rag with a roughly drawn Star of David. *"Wi zenen di shifn?"* they asked. Where are the ships? They had been told there were ships to take them to Palestine.

There were hideous sights: a lamp made from a human chest wall, on which one could make out a gypsy's tattoos. Vases and urns filled with gold teeth. Massive containers full of human hair. Form letters, which were sent to family members of inmates ("Your family member is doing well here, could you send money for extra things . . ."). And evidence of horrifying means of mass killing: furnaces, crematoria, shower rooms whose faucets dispensed poison gas. And tales of how German doctors had performed gruesome experiments on inmates and had discovered that injections of four milliliters—about a teaspoon—of petrol were the simplest, cheapest way to end human life. Only a decade earlier, German medical science had been known as the world's greatest; under Nazi ideology, it had degenerated into this.

Meticulous German records showed that over thirty thousand people, mostly Jews, had died at Bergen-Belsen between 1943 and 1945. Despite British rescue attempts, nine thousand more were to die by the end of April, and four thousand more by the end of June, of typhus and diphtheria and starvation. The camp, a health menace, was soon burned by the British.

The 7th Armored Division did not stay at Bergen-Belsen; it continued eastward, in pursuit of fleeing Germans. In the town of Friedeberg, the medical company examined wounded Germans left behind in the hospital by fleeing troops. Here were other signs of the desperate state of German medicine—soldiers' limbs had been amputated at the least sign of infection because of the shortage of antibiotics; and their foul, infected bandages were regularly washed to reclaim rare iodine.

Reaching Köthen, on the Elbe River, the 7th waited. The medics processed people who were crossing the river, checking for contagious diseases, trying to prevent epidemics of cholera and typhoid. A small military detachment raced east toward the Baltic Sea. On May 3, 1945, they met the Russians—troops composed of elderly men, adolescents, the one-eyed, the wounded and infirm.

The war in Europe was winding down. The 7th had traveled 2,260 miles from Normandy to the shores of the Baltic; the division of 31,000 men had suffered 6,150 battle casualties, with about a thousand killed in battle; they had taken 113,000 prisoners. Of the twenty-three members of my father's medical detachment, eight had been killed; two or three others had been seriously wounded and died after the war.

After the German surrender in May, General McConnell, who had been impressed by the courage of the 7th Armored Division, put in a tracer to regroup the 7th in Antwerp. It was to be renamed the 409th Amphibious Tractor Battalion and assigned to the Japanese front, to travel to the Pacific via the Suez Canal. My father prepared himself for yet another campaign.

Before the 409th could be sent across the Pacific, though, the atomic bomb was dropped on Hiroshima, and the Japanese surrendered.

In August, the troops of the 7th returned to the United States on a ship renamed the *George Washington*. They landed at Fort Dix, New Jersey, and soon my father was demobilized. He hitched a ride with another soldier going to Cleveland, and moved back into his parents' house on Lee Road. The war was over. Millions of veterans were returning, among them tens of thousands of doctors whose training had been accelerated and interrupted by the war, who were hardened and outspoken yet had not finished their medical training. For years, hospitals had been short-staffed, pressing into service older private practitioners and medical researchers; medical schools had been opened to women. At Western Reserve, a number of young doctors had managed to avoid military service by getting themselves declared essential to hospital operations; they were comfortably settled in, and had advanced their careers, while most of their contemporaries were overseas. The white-shoe boys at the hospital, the elite Fourth General Hospital unit, had spent the war in Australia, at base hospitals far from combat; their biggest complaint was that Down Under, the beer was warm.

The returning veterans, war heroes though they might be, did not fit easily into a system that had become accustomed to their absence. As my father puts it, "They had absolutely no idea what to do with us."

6

SECRET REBELS:
THE WOMEN OF '49

NOR did the system know what to do with the women
of the class of '49.

In September 1945, just a month after horrific atomic explosions over Hiroshima and Nagasaki put an end to World
War II, Mary Feil, Harold's second child and only daughter,
started medical school. The war was over, but without a
doubt, Mary was there because of opportunities it had created. During the 1930s, only one or two women had been
admitted in each class at Western Reserve Medical
School—but in the class of '49, along with a host of returning soldiers fresh from Europe or the Pacific Theater who
were on the GI Bill, ten of seventy students were women.

In some ways, Mary's whole life had been a preparation
for medicine. Her parents held her to the same high educational standards as they held her brothers George and
Edward. As a little girl, her father brought her along on
hospital rounds, and she assisted in doing EKGs during
house calls. Harold admired Dr. Helen Taussig, the Johns
Hopkins pediatrician who collaborated with Dr. Alfred
Blalock in devising operations for "blue babies," children
with congenital heart defects, surgery first successfully performed in 1944. He was friendly with several young
woman physicians at Western Reserve as well, residents or

144

fellows or doctors in early practice. Furthermore, there was a long history of educated women in Mary's family; both her grandmother and her mother had gone to college, and her mother, Nellie, was a writer for magazines and newspapers.

Yet, if not for the war, it is doubtful that her background would have led to anything more than membership in a women's charitable auxiliary, or a few hours each week of hospital volunteer work.

Mary's first two years at Smith College had the idyllic flavor that Nellie remembered from thirty years before—an education for a life of feminine gentility. There were dances at Yale and Dartmouth and Harvard, and ski trips to Vermont, and visits to theaters and museums in Manhattan. To get to school, Mary would travel to New York by rail, and spend the day with cousins Kay and Jo Stein, or her friend Martha "Hoppy" Hopkinson, before continuing on to Northampton. Twice a month she would send her laundry home in a large box held shut with canvas straps; it was returned a week later, the laundry starched and ironed, along with a package of homemade brownies.

After Pearl Harbor and the declaration of a state of war with Japan and Germany, life changed dramatically. Victory gardens were planted, gasoline and meat were rationed, cans and tinfoil and chewing-gum wrappers were collected to be turned into shell casings and airplane fuselages. Day and night, warplanes roared overhead from the Air Force base at Westover Field, near Northampton. One day, Mary heard over the radio that a plane had crashed, killing its pilot, the fiancé of her classmate Dixie Byerly. Mary heard this before Dixie was notified, and agonized whether to tell her. A few weeks later, another young man, engaged to her friend Izzy Dunn, was traveling to Europe with Canadian troops when his ship was hit by a German torpedo, and he was killed.

One by one, Mary's male friends were drafted or volunteered: one went to Quantico with the Marines; another joined the Air Force to become a pilot. Her older brother, George, age twenty, a senior at Yale, became a chemical-warfare officer with the 76th Infantry Division. Her younger brother, Ed, age eighteen, was drafted in 1942 and was a PFC in an artillery battalion; while his convoy was crossing from England to northern France, one of the ships was torpedoed in the English Channel and for a time the Feils feared that he had been killed. After Mary's young doctor friend Herman Hellerstein went overseas, she worried that he would be killed in action. Her anxiety was hardly allayed by his letters—hard-edged, unromantic descriptions of tank battles and medical-aid stations in abandoned farmhouses, and later on, of the rescue of Jews from the Bergen-Belsen concentration camp. Twice, Herman was reported missing in action, only to turn up unharmed.

Mary was twenty-two years old, vivacious and pretty. She was tall and had blue eyes and curly brown hair, and she was as passionate about science as Herman was about medicine. The war had interrupted Herman's medical education and had called away Mary's two brothers, but for Mary it had provided new opportunities. With the men gone, women were called to take their places in factories and offices—and hospitals, too.

After graduating from Smith College, Mary moved back home. She enrolled in a master's program in chemistry and began working in the laboratory of Ralph Dorfman, Ph.D., an endocrinologist who had fled Hitler and who later became famous as co-inventor of the birth-control pill, working in the 1950s and 1960s in Worcester, Massachusetts, at the Sandoz Corporation, with Dr. Gregory Pincus.

Using extracts from the adrenal glands, Dr. Dorfman was investigating how hormones could help rats cope with stress and cold—his eventual goal to prolong a soldier's life in combat and to help pilots deal better with high-altitude flying. Her father Harold Feil's EKG lab was across the hall, and a few doors away, Hans Hirschmann, Ph.D., another German refugee, a biochemist, was collecting and boiling pregnant women's urine to get various hormonal extracts. Mary saw remarkable evidence of medical progress. In one case, a patient with Addison's disease, a heretofore universally fatal illness caused by failure of the adrenal glands, was treated with adrenocortical extract produced in Dr. Dorfman's laboratory: month after month, the patient continued to thrive.

Mary loved the excitement of laboratory work. She envisioned for herself a life modeled on that of Madame Marie Sklodowska Curie, the Polish chemist and physicist who had won two Nobel Prizes for her discoveries of radium and polonium, who had done research side by side with her husband, Pierre, and who had also raised two happy children.

Mostly, it was women doing science. There was Dr. Dorfman's wife, Adeline, and Sarah Schiller, a researcher crippled by polio, and Betty Rubin, who was working on a Ph.D., and several female lab technicians. There was a wonderful camaraderie among the lab workers, a coming together of passionate minds and new ideas that was invigorating. Mary became one of the first researchers to use radioactive potassium. Using rats that had had their adrenal glands removed, she developed an assay that could gauge the effects of various hormonal extracts—a widely used process known as the Feil-Dorfman test.

But after two years of research, of boiling urine to extract hormones, of struggling to write up her findings, Mary came to a painful realization: she was no Madame Curie. She did not have the indomitable dedication necessary for basic science, and she missed the patients, the consultations and examinations and prescriptions that were so familiar from her childhood observations of her father. She decided not to go on for a Ph.D., but instead to apply to nursing school.

One night—as she tells it—one of her father's colleagues, Dr. John Toomey, professor of pediatrics and infectious diseases, came to dinner at the Feils' house. On hearing Mary's plans, he suggested that she apply to medical school instead. Her father, Harold, agreed.

And so, after some thought, she did.

Would the opportunity have been there had her father not been a medical-school professor? Perhaps not. Mary was not adventurous or rebellious by nature; she had never lived on her own or supported herself. Was she once again just being the good daughter, complying with her father's wishes? Or perhaps—and I have never been able to determine with certainty—was my mother a rebel in disguise, a women in whom fierce determination and independence of mind were masked by a mild demeanor?

I tend to think it was the latter. After all, as a little girl, Mary had been a fearless tomboy—tagging along after her older brother, George, and joining in his baseball games, and kick the can, and touch football. Rather than dress-up or tea parties, her favorite pastime was playing office. Her friend Marjorie Gunderson, who lived down the street, had a miniature rolltop desk and a little telephone and a pretend cigar, and Mary and Marjorie would spend hours making imaginary business deals. As a young adult, like other women of her generation, Mary tended to ask "permission" from men to do what she wanted, especially men in positions of authority, and to attribute her success to others, often these same men. Not so much a conscious strategy, it simply evolved into a habit of being.

Whether obedient daughter or secret rebel, in September 1945, barely a month after the *Enola Gay* dropped the first atomic bomb over Hiroshima, Mary Feil began medical school at Western Reserve University. The other women in her class had had similar pre-medical experiences. There was Sarah Luse, who had been a technician in an electroencephalography (EEG) laboratory at the Mayo Clinic from 1940 to 1945; and Myra Johnson, whose father was a general practitioner in southern Ohio, and who had been a biology professor at Smith College; and Anne Jan Tausch, who had worked in a diabetes laboratory; and Nanette Dice, and Mary Staley, and half a dozen others. Most of them, like Mary, had been through graduate school, and most had worked in laboratories, doing essential research during the war. Most of them had long hoped to become physicians. Their fiancés and husbands had come back from Europe with medals and wounds and war trophies, evidences of heroism. In an unobtrusive way, the experiences of Mary and her female classmates were heroic, too. They were pushing against barriers of gender, struggling to make the most of their opportunities without the benefit of rhetoric or a feminist political movement or general social acceptance of women having careers. They were ahead of their time—and destined to be isolated by a resurgence of traditionalism in the Eisenhower years, by the following generation of women, who mutely obeyed society's command to stay home; it would be thirty years before their example would be widely followed.

Their courage is especially apparent given the medical profession's traditional attitude toward women. For centuries women have played a large support role in medicine—founding and organizing hospitals, donating money, doing volunteer work, sewing bandages and surgical dressings (as Mary's mother, Nellie, had done during World War I). Florence Nightingale's work in the Crimean War had created the profession of nursing—but women were almost always barred from enrolling in medical schools and becoming physicians.

The first American woman doctor, Elizabeth Blackwell, got her M.D. degree from Geneva Medical Institute in January 1849 after a prolonged struggle. That she was there at all was a fluke: the student body had been allowed to decide whether she should be admitted, and they unanimously voted in favor of admission as a joke on their professors! In Cleveland, a liberal outpost of New England's "Western Reserve," there was somewhat more than average acceptance of women in medicine, and as early as 1850, several women attended the Cleveland Medical College, the precursor of Western Reserve University Medical School. The second American woman to get an M.D. was a Nancy E. Talbot Clark, who earned her degree from Cleveland Medical College in 1852. The next American woman M.D. was Emily Blackwell, Elizabeth Blackwell's younger sister, who had been expelled without cause from Rush Medical College in Chicago after one semester. She graduated from Cleveland Medical College in 1854, and after further training in Europe, she moved to New York, where she and her sister Elizabeth co-founded the New York Infirmary for Women and Children, the first hospital for women in America. (The building at Beth Israel Medical Center where I work is on this exact site, at the edge of Stuyvesant Park.) In the late 1850s, the Cleveland Medical College's policy allowing admission of women was rescinded. It was only in the 1880s that a few more women were able to graduate from Western Reserve University School of Medicine, the successor of the Cleveland Medical College. Steady enrollment of women at Western Reserve did not occur until after World War I, and then in small numbers—fewer than five percent in a class—until the Second World War.

The surge of women admitted to Western Reserve University Medical School after World War II reflected a na-

A FAMILY OF DOCTORS

DR. MARCUS ROSENWASSER, obstetrician-gynecologist, 1890s, Cleveland, Ohio.

THE TEN ROSEWATER/ROSENWASSER siblings, Omaha, Nebraska, 1904. *Front*: Sarah Rosewater Kohn, Dr. Marcus Rosenwasser, Grace Rosewater Singer. *Standing*: Dr. Nathan, Dr. Charles, Frank, Andrew, and Joseph Rosewater. *Insets*: Elizabeth Rosewater Feil (mother of Dr. Gustave Feil), Edward Rosewater.

DR. GUSTAVE FEIL, approximately 1900.

DR. HAROLD FEIL (left), in 1911, upon graduation from medical school.

DR. HAROLD FEIL (right), cardiologist, age fifty-eight, reading EKGs at Western Reserve University Hospital, Cleveland, in 1947.

THE HELLERSTEIN FAMILY, about 1919, Dillonvale, Ohio. *Top*: Samuel, Cecelia Hellerstein. *Middle*: Ralph Coff (a cousin), Rebecca. *Front*: Herman, Velma, Esther.

DR. HERMAN AND Dr. Mary Feil Hellerstein with Kathryn, 1952, Cleveland.

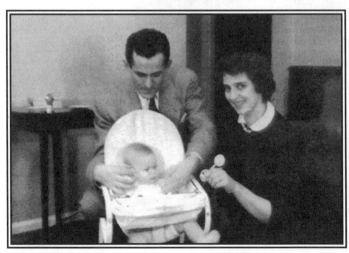

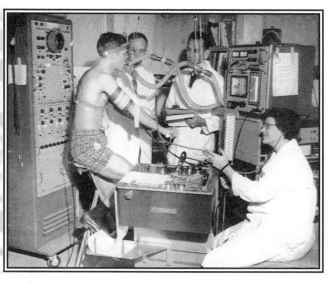

DR. HERMAN HELLERSTEIN, cardiologist (*third from left*), in an exercise testing laboratory at Case Western Reserve University Hospital, Cleveland, in 1967.

THE HELLERSTEIN FAMILY on bicycles in Cleveland Heights, Ohio, 1966. *From front*: Herman, Elizabeth, Daniel, Susan, Kathryn, David, Jonathan, and Mary.

DR. HERMAN HELLERSTEIN, lecturing at CWRU Medical School, approximately 1988.

DR. MARY HELLERSTEIN, pediatrician, with patients at Metzenbaum Children's Center Clinic, Cleveland, early 1980s.

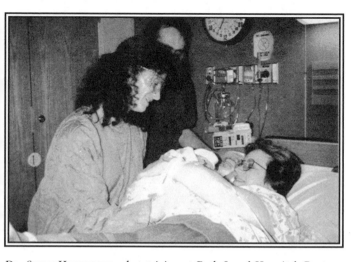

DR. SUSAN HELLERSTEIN, obstetrician at Beth Israel Hospital, Boston, presents baby to mother moments after performing a delivery, 1992.

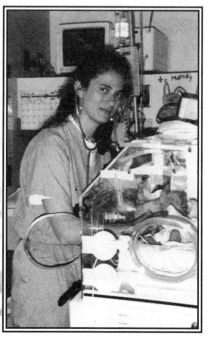

DR. ELIZABETH HELLERSTEIN, pediatrics resident at CWRU Rainbow Hospital, Cleveland, with infant in Neonatal Intensive Care Unit, 1992.

Dr. David Hellerstein, psychiatrist at Beth Israel Medical Center, New York, leading a conference at which new clinic cases are presented, 1992.

Dr. Daniel Hellerstein, urologist at Mayo Clinic, Jacksonville, Florida, performing a urological procedure, 1992.

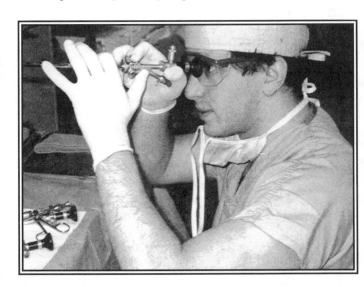

tional trend: the number admitted to medical school increased from 4.5 percent in 1941 to ten percent in 1945. It was a short-lived gain, for between 1950 and 1965 the average decreased to five percent. It was not until 1970 that women again comprised ten percent or more of medical-school classes, and then there was a dramatic increase, to 23.7 percent in 1975, to more than forty percent today.

Discrimination against women did not end with admission to medical school, of course, and beginning in the 1850s and 1860s, more than fifteen all-women's medical schools were founded in America. First was the Female Medical College of Pennsylvania (later known as the Women's Medical College of Pennsylvania), and soon there were women's medical schools in New York, Boston, Baltimore, Cleveland, and other cities. All but two closed, however, within six years of the publication of the Flexner Report [1910]. Numerous women's hospitals were founded as well, because of the difficulty that women graduates had in getting further training and in being permitted to admit patients to established hospitals. Antipathy toward women doctors ran deep—so much so that the American Medical Association did not grant women full membership until 1915.

Mary Feil and her women classmates were so relieved to have been admitted at all that the discrimination they faced, whether subtle or flagrant, hardly fazed them. In urology, the women students were not permitted to attend clinics where the male patients were examined—though men, of course, attended the gynecology clinic. Women were not allowed to learn to catheterize male patients—the idea of a young woman threading a catheter into a man's penis was inconceivable. In orthopedics, the professor called Mary Staley, one of their classmates, to the front of the lecture hall to show how high heels threw off the alignment of the vertebral column. Once they began taking call at night, staying overnight in the hospital to take care of patients, as third-year medical students, the inequalities became more blatant: women had to sleep at Robb House, a dormitory far from the hospital, whereas men had comfortable rooms and a lounge upstairs in the hospital itself.

But they had been admitted—and were virtually certain to be able to complete their education and become practicing physicians. They were in. In comparison to other groups, the discrimination they faced seemed minor. Blacks were entirely excluded from the hospital's professional staff until the middle of World War II, when staffing problems prompted the hospital for the first time to accept "colored student nurses" and "colored dietitian aides." (The nursing shortage became so acute that two Japanese-American nurses were hired in 1945!) During Mary's internship year at City Hospital she had one black classmate—Creed Ward, a former social worker. On completing his internship, he decided to become a pediatrician, but was unable to get a position at Western Reserve, because there was "nowhere for him to sleep" at the pediatrics hospital, Rainbow Babies and Childrens Hospital—it was forbidden for him to be housed with the white men! Ward finally stayed at City Hospital and eventually set up a practice in Cleveland.

Mary and Herman were engaged in the fall of 1946, and after a fellowship year at Michael Reese Hospital in Chicago, Herman returned to Cleveland in July of 1947. That November, Mary's junior year of medical school, Mary and Herman were married in a quiet ceremony at the Feils' house. It was Thanksgiving. They left on a snowy evening, driving to a hotel in Uniontown, Pennsylvania, for their honeymoon; they were back by the following Monday, so Mary would not miss medical-school classes.

Her professors were not sure whether a married woman

was up to the rigors of medicine. When Mary applied for an internship at City Hospital, the three distinguished professors interviewing her stated: "We don't know if you can do an internship. What will your husband think about you being away every second night?" Mary responded that she thought she could handle it; during a "practice" internship period at Rainbow Hospital, she had no problem taking call every other night.

In July 1949, she began a "rotating" internship at City Hospital. She spent months doing surgery, obstetrics-gynecology, dermatology, pediatrics, psychiatry, and contagious diseases, leaving behind the protected suburban world in which she had grown up. It was hard work, with little supervision. The patients were poor, an endless stream of Hungarians and Yugoslavians and Poles and Czechs, and Southern blacks. On surgery, there were patients with gruesome leg ulcers which needed to be debrided, or scraped, and which never seemed to get better. On the "contag" or contagious diseases service, she saw almost every disease in the raw, as it ran its course. The antibiotic era had begun, but you wouldn't have known it from the cases at City Hospital. She saw meningitis and tuberculosis, whooping cough and measles, encephalitis, chicken pox, mumps, and the dreaded disease poliomyelitis. Polio was treated with hot packs and isolation, and when the polio virus attacked the brain's respiratory center, the patient was kept alive in an "iron lung." Out at Sunny Acres, the tuberculosis sanatorium where she had worked as a medical student, the major treatments were still rest and nutrition, along with pneumothorax, or deflation of the infected lung, which killed the tubercle bacillus, and the occasional draining of abscesses. Mary caught so many strep infections from her patients during internship that she developed an abscessed tonsil, which had to be taken out.

It was hectic being married and doing medical training;

she left their small apartment near Shaker Square before dawn and took the streetcar down to City Hospital. Late at night, Herman picked her up, and they drove back home for a quick dinner. Then she went back to studying. She felt guilty, dragging Herman through medical school for a second time, and her mother cringed when hearing of the meals she served. However, there was no doubt she could do it—just like the other nine women in her class, all of whom had completed medical school, though some a year late.

Mary had decided to become a pediatrician. Residency began. She worked at Babies and Childrens Hospital, taking call every second night for her first year, hardly leaving the hospital. It was a busy, wonderful time. She and her women classmates were pioneering; so, too, the field she had chosen, pediatrics, was breaking new ground in the medical profession. Like changes in the treatment of heart disease, so familiar from her father's stories around the dinner table, progress in pediatrics represented a remarkable triumph of scientific medicine.

In Colonial America, as Dr. Thomas Cone describes vividly in his classic *History of American Pediatrics*, childhood was a time of extreme peril. Common diseases included convulsions, worm infestations (roundworms, tapeworms, and pinworms were ubiquitous), and a variety of infections that were attributed to problems in teething. Fevers in childhood, divided into "intermittent" types (such as malaria), "continued" (such as typhoid), and "hectic" (such as tuberculosis), were frequently fatal. Most diseases were believed to be caused by "fermenting corruption" (that is, by decaying vegetable and animal matter, or, alternately, by meteor showers, volcanic eruptions, and earthquakes) and were believed to be spread through the night air. Witchcraft was often suspected as a cause.

Through the eighteenth century, women delivered babies and provided medical care for young infants, but gradually so-called man midwives became active in childbirth. By the mid-nineteenth century, male obstetricians (like Marcus Rosenwasser) began to do many deliveries, relegating women to the sidelines. Obstetricians focused the bulk of their energy on the mother, and often paid little attention to the health of newborns and infants. Older children were traditionally cared for by physicians, not midwives or obstetricians, and were subject to the same regimens of bleeding, purging, and ineffective, toxic medications as adults.

By 1850, child health conditions in America were in a critical state. It was a time of enormous population growth. The census went from 5 million in 1800 to 23 million in 1850, and by 1900 there would be 76 million Americans, a third of whom were less than fifteen years of age. Furthermore, the rapid industrialization and urbanization of America led to unprecedented crowding and filth, to contaminated milk and water supplies, to chronic malnutrition and poor hygiene, conditions perfect for the breeding of infection. In such environments, cholera, diphtheria, scarlet fever, cerebrospinal meningitis, and typhus flourished, and death rates soared. Epidemics of smallpox and "summer diarrhea" (violent attacks of diarrhea and vomiting, believed to result from teething, worms, or summer fruits) carried off the young by the hundred. Contaminated milk—often from diseased cows fed swill from neighborhood breweries—led to infection of entire neighborhoods. In virtually every American city, fully one third of all children died before the age of five!

Yet there were virtually no specialized treatment facilities for children. Unwanted, sick, or destitute children were routinely sent to almshouses, or placed in indentured servitude. Around mid-century, orphanages began to be established for sick and unwanted children, as humane alternatives to the poorhouse or jail. Only gradually were orphanages replaced by children's hospitals. In 1848 a hospital for children opened in Boston, but closed three years later for lack of funds. In 1887, the New York Babies Hospital became the first hospital in the United States that exclusively cared for infants.

Change in American pediatrics, as in general medicine, came from abroad, from the enormous advances in European medicine. The greatest advance was Pasteur's discovery in the 1860s of bacteria as a cause of disease. Only then did treatment and prevention undergo radical reevaluation. Americans gradually learned to recognize the need for greatly improved hygiene, for the purification of food and water supplies, better sewage systems, and cleaner streets, and the pasteurization of milk.

A dozen other advances between 1850 and 1920 led to a revolutionary new understanding of childhood diseases. The development of cellular pathology in the second half of the nineteenth century made possible the precise classification of diseases. New instruments such as the thermometer (introduced in 1870) allowed for monitoring of the child's illness. Roentgenology (1895) permitted visualization of fractures and localization of infection. Diphtheria antitoxin (1895) allowed successful treatment of what had been mainly a fatal disease, and soon other contagious illnesses began to yield to scientific medicine. The famed Berlin Pediatric Clinic, directed by Dr. Eduard Henoch from 1872 to 1893, treated sick children and also educated doctors. This innovative model spread to other cities, encouraging the systematic discovery and transmission of new knowledge. Child-welfare laws were passed—regulations which, ironically, were derived from regulations that prevented cruelty to animals. And milk stations, at which families could get supplies of non-infected milk, sprang up in most cities in the first decade of the twentieth century.

The most prominent early American pediatrician, Dr. Abraham Jacobi, a student of Henoch's, fled Germany in 1853, after being jailed for two years for involvement in the revolution of 1848. In 1860 he established the first American children's clinic in Manhattan's New York Medical College, and he became professor of "infantile pathology and therapeutics." He later established children's clinics at University Medical College in New York, and, in conjunction with his wife, Dr. Mary Putnam Jacobi, also a pediatrician, at Mt. Sinai Hospital in New York. Both were tireless advocates for children's health.

The development of pediatrics in Cleveland in many ways mirrored trends in the rest of the nation. There, as in other cities, the death rate of young children was very high. The city's first facility for the treatment of children was founded in 1887 and opened in 1891; named Rainbow Cottage, it was established by a women's charitable organization with the purpose of caring for crippled and malnourished children so they could recover in comfortable surroundings, with healthy food and fresh air. Although the death rate had decreased from thirty-three percent in 1880 to twenty percent by 1900, children still commonly suffered the effects of poor nutrition, contaminated food, and tuberculosis-infected milk. In 1907, Dr. Edward Cushing (brother of Dr. Harvey Cushing, the famous neurosurgeon) founded the Babies' Dispensary and Hospital. According to Mark Gottlieb, author of a history of University Hospitals of Cleveland, the Babies' Dispensary became the first in America "to provide medical advice to parents of well children—in effect, practicing preventive medicine even before the term was coined." In addition, the clinic hired visiting nurses to travel to slum neighborhoods and teach immigrant mothers how to care for and feed their babies, and produced instructional brochures on infant care in German, Italian, Slovak, and Yiddish, as well as English.

By 1925, when a new Maternity and Babies and Childrens Hospital opened, with 150 beds, infant mortality had dropped to 6.6 percent. The Depression led to the drastic curtailment of medical services; jobs were cut, salaries decreased, and wards closed. In 1932 the entire Babies and Childrens Hospital and the maternity hospital were closed, not to reopen until 1935.

By the time Mary began her residency in 1949, a new set of difficulties had arisen—essentially, the consequences of success. The return of millions of GIs who married and started families led to an unprecedented flood of obstetrical patients, what became known as the "baby boom." Obstetrical wards were overcrowded, and hospitals delivered thousands more infants per year than ever before. Hospital maternity stays, once lasting a month or more, had decreased to two weeks before the war. In 1946 they were cut back to eight days to make room for more patients. The pediatrics wards, previously filled with chronically ill children who remained for weeks or even months, saw more patients than ever—children who could be treated with new antibiotics, especially streptomycin and penicillin, and sent home in a matter of days. Premature babies could be treated and saved. In 1948, the Babies and Childrens Hospital opened a "premature infant suite" of six six-bed wards.

These changes led to a further decrease in infant mortality from 4.7 percent in 1940 to 2.9 percent in 1950, and as a result, dramatically altered the relation between parent and child. In the old days, when a third of all children died before entering school, there was every reason not to become too emotionally involved with any one child, and it made sense to have as many children as possible, to beat the odds. Now that any infant born was likely to grow to adulthood, there was every reason to make childhood close to ideal. Pediatricians were the logical candidates to make this happen, to educate parents to raise children in the best possible way, both physically and mentally.

Mary took call every second night during her first year of residency, and then only every third night in her last year. By mid-year, the end of 1952, she was pregnant, and the last few months she was unable to take call because of her difficulty in getting around. Her training was completed on July 1, 1952; on July 27, she gave birth to her first child, my older sister Kathryn.

By fall, Mary was back at work. She took a job at the Pediatric Family Clinic, a new clinic located in the basement of the pediatric building. It had been founded as part of the New Curriculum, organized in 1952 by Dr. Joseph T. Wearn, dean of the Western Reserve Medical School. This innovative curriculum—which was copied by Harvard Medical School in the 1980s—strove to break down the increasingly rigid divisions between medical specialties in order to keep doctors' attention focused on the patient as an individual human being, not a collection of organs and physiological processes, as modern medicine was increasingly wont to do. Philosophically, it was of great importance—a strong statement that medicine's central purpose was not only to study and treat isolated organ systems but to care for patients.

The Family Clinic was central to the New Curriculum. It introduced medical students to patients from their first days of school, rather than having them first endure two "preclinical" years of dry booklearning. Each student worked with a pregnant woman, followed her through pregnancy and delivery, and then watched as the infant developed. Medical students would also attend multidisciplinary meetings of nurses and social workers and pediatricians and psychiatrists, to learn how best to plan treatment, not just medically but psychologically and socially as well. The Family Clinic was headed by Dr. John Kennell, later to become well known for research with Dr. Marshall Klaus on mother-child bonding, demonstrating the importance of contact between the mother and the newborn baby for its development and survival, and the benefits of allowing parents to touch and hold premature babies in the plastic incubators of intensive-care units.

Mary spent one afternoon each week at Family Clinic, teaching and supervising medical students. One of her colleagues there was a towering, gentle man, Dr. Benjamin Spock. A pediatrician who was also trained in psychiatry, Spock had been a member of the Yale crew, and looked the part. He was lanky and aristocratic, but he had a gentle manner, and a good sense of humor, and he was a passionate amateur figure skater. While in the army, he had written *The Common Sense Book of Baby and Child Care*, which was published in 1946 and sold four million copies in its first six years. Mary always joked with him that she would like to write footnotes for his book, all the things about child-raising that he had left out, but of course Spock's book was not meant to answer every question, but essentially to teach parents how to think about their children. Indeed, his book exemplified the nation's newfound concern for children, and further stimulated its interest in understanding the child's psychological as well as physical development.

The Family Clinic was crowded, and despite the fact that it was moved several times, it always ended up in an out-of-the-way location, usually a basement. Over the years its director had to defend its existence, to prove that it was worthwhile. Forty years later, it still exists—and my mother still works there. Both the New Curriculum and the Family Clinic have been copied widely, though with variations in some countries: for instance, in Thailand, medical students are assigned to an underserved village to provide health care that would not otherwise be available. The New Curriculum's emphasis on continuity of care, on what is known as horizontal, not vertical, teaching, has remained a basic principle, a medical ideal.

Pediatrics in general, and the Family Clinic in particular, gave Mary a place in medicine; but, unquestionably, her professional choices were limited from the beginning. In the 1950s, women did not go into surgery or radiology or ophthalmology, as men could; they tended to go into general practice, pediatrics, psychiatry, or internal medicine. Mary's options were further limited by her decision to have children—one after another, until there were six of us. In those years, of course, husbands were not expected to sacrifice their careers for the family. If Mary wanted to work, it was she who had to adapt; she was the one expected to make compromises. She never established her own practice or opened her own office.

Instead, she worked in the Family Clinic on a part-time basis, and as we kids got older, she also began to work in various other clinics and children's homes, and to cover other pediatricians' practices when they were sick or at a conference or on vacation. Often, she covered for Dr. Beulah Wells and Dr. Betty Patterson and Dr. Arthur Burns, whose practices were in the inner city, working in their offices and making house calls in run-down factory neighborhoods. When going to a particularly dangerous area, she would call the local precinct house and have a police officer meet her near her destination and escort her to the child's home. Her friend (and her own children's pediatrician) Dr. Henry Saunders advised her on the technique for house calls: Always get a strong lamp, and bring it into the kitchen. Beds are no good for examinations—they are too low and too soft. Instead, clear off the kitchen table and lay the child there. She would do so, and then she would peer into red throats, and infected ears, and would palpate swollen glands and tender bellies. In the summer of 1966, when all of urban America seemed to be exploding in rage and violence, she was covering Dr. Zoltan Klein's practice at Chester and 107th Street, only a block from the ghetto. Rioting broke out in Cleveland's Hough neighborhood. She was working alone in the office, without a secretary or receptionist. She could hear gunfire and sirens, and see the sky filling with smoke. The radio told of men driving around the city, throwing Molotov cocktails out car windows. Herman phoned to urge her to go home; she went on working.

After our first child was born in 1987, my wife, Lisa, and I were struck by the enormous difficulty of taking care of a baby while we were both working, and many times we discussed my mother's example. It was hard enough for Lisa to take care of one child and have any sort of professional life outside the home; how was Mom able to do that with six kids, much less keep her sanity?

"How did you do it?" Lisa asked on innumerable occasions, but Mom's answers were always less than illuminating.

"We just did it," she responded. Or: "We managed."

The costs of pioneering seemed more apparent in the lives of her female classmates. For some, the choice seemed to be between work and a personal life. Dr. Sarah Luse, who had been an EEG technician and later became a prominent neuropathologist at the Washington University School of Medicine, and then at Columbia Presbyterian Medical Center, never married. Neither did Dr. Myra Johnson, who had been a biology professor at Smith College—she returned to her hometown of Wooster, Ohio, lived in her family home, and set up a practice of internal medicine. Other classmates did marry, but the happy combination of work and family life was elusive. Several were later divorced. One woman's husband died young; another's husband was in and out of mental hospitals. One classmate became embroiled in medical-legal problems and even got a law degree to protect herself.

Some friends, though, had happy lives, more similar to her own. Dr. Virginia (Ginny) Owen Packer, who graduated with the Western Reserve University Medical School's class of 1950, also became a pediatrician. Ginny was on the board of Women's General Hospital, and active in the Women's Medical Society of Cleveland. She worked together with Mom at the pediatric clinic at the Metzenbaum Center, with foster children, wards of the county; they did physical exams prior to placement of the children in foster homes, and treated everything from earaches to sexual abuse. Like Mom, she married a doctor and had one child after another—five in all. The oldest, Geoff, was my best friend in junior high school; he and I spent innumerable afternoons as twelve-year-olds shooting baskets on the asphalt court at Roxboro Junior High.

In 1990, on a visit home to do research on the family's history, I went to see Mom's office. On the East Side of Cleveland, near Cleveland State University, the Bessie Benner Metzenbaum Center is a modern brick, concrete, and glass building shaped like an octagon. It stands, I realized, a quarter mile from the site of the Cleveland Jewish Orphan Asylum—now a weed-covered field behind a chain-link fence—where Marcus Rosenwasser cared for hundreds of orphans more than a century ago.

I parked and went into the Center, a cheerful, well-maintained place, filled with plants. My mother introduced me to the director, and I followed her down half a flight of steps and along a corridor to her office. It was telling that I had never been there before, in contrast to the hundreds of times I had been to Dad's laboratory and office. It was a reflection of how she has always done things—quietly and without a fuss—as well as how I had always unquestioningly accepted this.

She explained that her job involved examining all new admissions to the Center, as well as caring for children who got sick. Since there was a chicken pox epidemic at the time of my visit, the Center was closed to new admissions, and its census had fallen from its usual forty to twenty-eight. That afternoon she would be going to two foster homes where there were nine babies to examine, five in Mrs. Zernito's home on West 25th Street, near the Zoo, and four at Mrs. White's house in Oakwood Village, twenty miles farther away. There were four homes altogether. She went to examine the infants, to immunize them and measure and plot their growth and development. She also lent an ear to the women who struggled to care for so many infants, all of whom would be removed to more permanent homes as soon as possible.

The problems she saw reflected new urban plagues. As the cost of medical care rose from 5.2 percent of the GNP in 1960 to 11.6 percent by 1989, life expectancy increased to over seventy years, and infant mortality continued to drop. From 2.9 percent in 1950, the death rate in the first year of life dropped to 2.6 percent in 1960, and to only 1.0 percent in 1987. The death rate among black babies remained twice as high as among whites. No more did whooping cough or polio or summer diarrhea or cholera kill thousands of babies each year—instead, babies were born addicted to heroin, or with their brains scarred by alcohol or cocaine. Cocaine-addicted mothers who had received no prenatal care and who were overwhelmed by caring for four or five children already would abandon their new babies. Now ninety to a hundred percent of the babies at Mrs. Zernito's had cocaine in their bloodstreams at birth, compared to almost none a decade before. Emergency rooms filled with young victims of random gunfire. And, increasingly, my mother and her colleagues treated young children who had been sexually abused, though it was not clear whether abuse itself was increasing or whether doctors were just more capable of recognizing it.

One baby boy at Mrs. Zernito's home, with fetal alcohol syndrome, needed surgery for crossed eyes and clubfeet. His mother's drinking had most likely left him mentally retarded as well. Mrs. White had two "cocaine babies"—both born with vascular rings, or abnormal development of the great vessels in the chest, which compressed their tracheas and led to difficulty in breathing. Once the foster-care system had three to five pediatricians, but now my mother was the only one, and she worked long hours.

When we kids were young, Mom worked as little as half a day a week, but by my 1990 visit Mom, at the age of sixty-eight, worked nearly fifty hours a week. She spent three-quarters of her time at the Metzenbaum Center alone. Friday afternoons were still reserved for teaching medical students at the Family Clinic. She also managed occasional clinics in Cleveland Heights and East Cleveland, examining children for school. A typical day started with an 8:00 a.m. continuing-medical-education conference at St. Luke's Hospital; then she traveled to a Well Child Clinic in Cleveland Heights, where she examined a mixed population of middle-class children. There were many Orthodox Jewish families with anywhere from five to twelve children, as well as black, white, and Hispanic families. In the afternoon she went to the Metzenbaum Center, and then to the infant homes. On Saturdays about once a month, she worked at the Hough-Norwood Walk-In Clinic, from 10 a.m. to 4 p.m., in one of the poorest black areas of the city, seeing anywhere from five to twenty children and counseling their mothers about nutrition and vaccines and ear infections.

During our childhood, Dad's example of doctoring always seemed to be the modern one, contributing to the progress of medicine through scientific research. Yet, after listening to Mom discussing her day, I realized now that, if anything, *her* career was just as paradigmatic for modern medicine; not necessarily what medicine is, but what it should be.

For one thing, there was her quiet dedication to patients, her willingness to treat those cast off by society and abandoned by their parents, and her indifference to the patients' ability to pay.

Then there was the non-traditional pattern of her own career. For perhaps fifteen years after she completed her residency, her doctoring was something that flickered, that waxed and waned, and yet did not disappear. She claimed that she kept working because it was a way to get out of the house, away from the six of us when we drove her crazy, that it was better than tennis lessons or a bridge game—but we knew that wasn't the whole story. Some years she worked only a few hours a week; other years, two or three days a week. By the 1980s, when most of her male contemporaries were retired and sitting on a beach in Florida, we could hardly get her to take a day off. She insisted that there was no one to cover for her at work; but we all knew that it was really that she loved the practice of medicine.

My women friends always want to know how she did it—and I suppose her example does have a particular relevance to feminism. Certainly, for my three sisters, her example made the idea of having a career almost a matter of course, and gave them confidence that they could do whatever we boys did, if not more. They knew that somehow things would work out, whether it was doing research, writing papers or books, or traveling around the world.

More than that, her career reflects a step forward in a larger context; that is, the redefining of opportunities for many different groups, not just women, and a rethinking of the boundaries of proper social roles, not only of privilege but of responsibility. The Flexner Report, published as long ago as 1910, was intended to shut down marginal medical schools, the proprietary degree mills that sent out legions of poorly trained doctors. Its goal was to foster reforms in American medical education. It did these things, but it also had the unanticipated, and probably unintended, effect of virtually eliminating opportunities for women and minorities—because the lesser medical schools did not discriminate so systematically against these groups. For more than fifty years, doctoring became a white man's game. It took decades to even begin to reverse that. The women of the class of '49 took one of the first steps.

Beyond that, there is the issue of the redistribution of wealth. A lifelong Republican, my mother has never reconciled her political philosophy with her daily work; yet she has outlasted several generations of social activists in working in the ghetto. The redistribution is that of knowledge, of health, and ultimately, of life. In the classic fashion of medicine, it occurs not in the street or the courthouse or the newspapers. It occurs in the privacy of the office or in the clinic or behind a curtain in a hospital room, doctor to patient, one human being to another. What caring doctors have always known, of course, is that the giving goes both ways.

7

SCIENTIFIC MEDICINE: 1946–1960

The patient, a boy of 14, was being operated upon to relieve extreme sternal depression [a sunken breastbone]. While the wound was being closed the heart suddenly stopped. The patient was apparently dead. The wound was reopened and cardiac massage started. Digitalis and epinephrine were given, without any effect. The mechanical respirator was attached to the intratracheal tube and cardiac massage was continued for thirty-five minutes, at the end of which time the electrocardiogram showed ventricular fibrillation. Another record taken ten minutes later likewise showed ventricular fibrillation. The first electrical shock did not cause any change in mechanism. Procaine hydrochloride (two percent) was injected into the right auricle and the heart was massaged. A second series of electric shock was given, producing complete cardiac standstill. Almost immediately, however, feeble cardiac contractions were observed, and the massage was continued for five minutes more, at which time it was obvious that contractions were coordinated and fairly vigorous, though still fast ... From this point on, the heart gradually increased in vigor ... After the coordinated heart beat had been established for twenty minutes, the wound in the chest was closed. Within ten minutes after closure of the wound the intratracheal tube was removed and spontaneous respirations were resumed ... Three hours after defibrillation of the ventricles, the patient responded rationally to questioning, and by eight hours he was fairly alert in spite of his stormy operative course.

A historic moment in medicine: the first human being ever successfully resuscitated from ventricular fibrillation by the use of cardiac massage and electric defibrillation. The 1947 case of fourteen-year-old Richard Heyward, whose heart returned to normal beating and who spent seventeen days at Western Reserve University Hospital, to be discharged with "no signs or symptoms indicative of injury to the brain," is significant not only as a culmination of several lines of research; it also testifies to the power of modern medical treatment. By the late 1940s, medicine was increasingly able to cheat death, to reverse the course of fatal illness.

A mythic case, too, for our family. This patient was saved by Dr. Claude Beck, Dr. Harold Feil, and Dr. Walter Pritchard. The quote comes from a 1949 paper written by both Harold Feil, our grandfather, and Herman Hellerstein, our father, an article summarizing resuscitation efforts as of 1950. Thus, it represents communication from one generation of doctors to the next, at once both a gift and a challenge.

The resuscitation technique described here is crude, requiring open-chest heart massage and alternating electrical current, which was soon replaced by more powerful and effective direct current. Yet this case became a prototype of the tens of thousands of resuscitations attempted in operating rooms and emergency rooms and on city streets each year, the passionate efforts of doctors and nurses and emergency medical technicians to jump-start the heart. As a result, the mode of human death has entirely changed. The contemplativeness of a quiet hospital room, the billowing of breeze through curtains, the faint sounds of voices in hallways, the gradual slipping away of life, have been replaced by the loud beeping of monitors, the urgent conversation of the Code Team, the infusions of epinephrine and lidocaine, the whirl of EKG tape onto the floor, the thump of electricity through stainless-steel paddles: attempts to replicate the success of this first case.

It was a great moment, the conjunction of unusual circumstances. Dr. Claude Beck, the surgeon who had begun the world's first experimental heart-surgery research laboratory in 1925, was perfectly teamed with Dr. Harold Feil. Both had done research with Dr. Carl J. Wiggers, the eminent physiologist who had studied ventricular fibrillation in dogs for more than a decade, producing it by electrical currents and by tying off coronary arteries, and who had determined that 999 out of a thousand dogs could be rescued from fibrillation if their hearts were shocked with 110 volts before irreversible muscle damage occurred. The third doctor present was Dr. Walter Pritchard, an energetic young resident who would later become head of the department of cardiology and then chief executive officer for Western Reserve University Hospitals. All three were exquisitely aware of the problem of ventricular fibrillation, and the theoretical possibility of reversing fibrillation once it began; they knew not only Wiggers's studies but also those of William Kouwenhoven, an engineering professor at Johns Hopkins University who had been commissioned by Consolidated Edison of New York City to study ways of preventing workmen's death by accidental electrocution.

It was fortuitous that three uniquely able doctors were present that day in 1947, and that an EKG machine was attached and running, permitting proper diagnosis and documentation of fibrillation. Further, a defibrillator was at hand in the operating room. For a decade, at Beck's insistence, defibrillators had been placed in the hospital's emergency room and various operating rooms. Over that time there had been only two attempted resuscitations, in 1938 and 1939, and both patients had died. The odds against the conjunction of these events must be astronomical, and indeed it was 1955 before another life was saved by defibrillation—a sixty-five-year-old physician, Dr. Albert T. Ransome, who had a heart attack in the parking lot outside Western Reserve University Hospital's emergency room and who was revived, to become the world's first heart-attack victim to be successfully defibrillated. He lived for another twenty-eight years.

Eventually, Beck's open-heart massage became outmoded, replaced by closed-heart resuscitation, by a thump to the chest followed by pressure from the heels of the hands, along with artificial respiration, buying time until the 440-volt direct-current defibrillator arrived to produce its solid life-renewing jolt: by 1960, Kouwenhoven and Dr. James Jude from Johns Hopkins reported that fourteen of twenty patients treated with the closed-chest method survived.

When this paper was published, Harold was sixty years old, a senior professor of medicine. He was in the latter part of his career, seeing private patients in an elegant office in the downtown Republic Building, and working out of a tiny medical-school office, running the EKG service, and teaching, and collaborating in clinical research. At the age of thirty-three, Herman, his son-in-law, was just beginning his career. After coming back from Europe following World War II, Herman had completed three years of fellowship in Chicago and Cleveland; he then became an instructor of medicine at Western Reserve University School of Medicine. He was trying to make a place for himself—at the hospital and in the medical profession.

The relationship between Feil and Hellerstein, father-in-law and son-in-law, was complex. In addition to being related by marriage, they were in the same specialty, cardiology, and worked at the same hospital. Both had experienced anti-Semitism, and both were passionate about science. They at once collaborated and feuded with each other. My father saw Feil as obsequious, overpolite, a bit of a dilettante; Feil saw my father as abrasive, rude, impolitic. They worked together, and wrote papers together, and they admired each other's intellectual powers and moral integrity. Yet they could not seem to come to terms on simple things.

For instance, the matter of private practice. Soon after Herman and Mary's marriage in 1947, Harold made an offer to Herman, or rather presented him with a plan: Herman would share Harold's medical office at the Republic Building, seeing patients two afternoons a week. They could share expenses, and provide coverage for each other's patients; eventually, when Harold retired, Herman could take over his practice. Unexpectedly, Herman refused. He told Harold that he wanted to be a full-time faculty member of the university hospital, and to see his patients there; he did not want to follow Harold's footsteps as a part-time professor, a volunteer researcher. It was not entirely a consequence, but when Herman became a full-fledged member of the division of cardiology, working under Harold, a fairly clear pattern of negative nepotism emerged: any honor or promotion Herman could reasonably expect took about twice as long as it should to be given.

The issue was more than personal, more than the prickly relationship between two men who loved the same woman, or who practiced the same profession: it was also generational. Harold had come of age early in the century, when medicine was just beginning to be scientific, and when careers in research were practically nonexistent. Now, as the war had shown—with the triumphs of battlefield medics—medicine was often curative. Just thirty years earlier, when Dr. Claude Beck was a Fellow at Johns Hopkins, working with the great surgeon Dr. William Halsted, a child began to develop a dangerous irregularity of cardiac rhythm; Dr. Halsted had walked down the hall and asked to have the Fire Department called, since firefighters alone knew how to perform resuscitation!

Forty years later, interviewing my father in the backyard in Cleveland, on the beach at Fire Island, at a farm in Vermont, on a Florida barrier island, and many nights over the phone as babies cried in the background, I got glimpses of the young man transformed by opportunity. His energy, pent-up from army years, was finally loosed.

It was the era of Truman and Eisenhower, a time of complacency and comfort in American society, of two-martini lunches and fat-marbled steaks and bacon and egg breakfasts, of Scotch on the rocks, and Lucky Strikes (a generation of GIs addicted to tobacco by free cigarettes in their K rations). For Dad and his colleagues in "scientific medicine," however, it was anything but a complacent time.

The gauntlet had been thrown. Medicine could—no, *must*—now intervene in disease. Not only could it reverse the course of illness; it could bring patients back from the brink of death. New technologies—the defibrillator, the blood transfusion, amazing drugs like penicillin, and a hundred other advances—made the unprecedented almost routine.

The question for Herman Hellerstein, and for other doctors of the World War II generation, was this: What could *they* do to bring this promise to fruition? Previous generations had laid the groundwork; now it was up to them.

Their answer could be summed up in two words: "scientific medicine."

Indeed, their work in a golden age would lead to unprecedented medical advances—and to unforeseen problems and complications. My father's career in many ways typified those of his generation. Like thousands of ex-GIs, Herman Hellerstein had been demobilized rapidly, returning to a prosperous country. The 1944 GI Bill of Rights offered full scholarships for up to four years to every honorably discharged member of the Armed Forces who applied. The National Institutes of Health were being formed, and there was increasing government support for research. It was a time of enormous optimism—the country that had helped to defeat Hitler and had stopped Japan with atomic bombs over Hiroshima and Nagasaki, and then brought a measure of stability to Europe with the Marshall Plan, could bring not only prosperity to all but health and longevity as well. Over the next quarter century, along with several thousand like-minded ex–army doctors turned medical professors, Herman Hellerstein plunged into a frenzy of medical practice and medical science, exploring in the laboratory and the hospital and the clinic.

One consequence of America's prosperity and good health, and the diminishing threat of infectious diseases, was the continued skyrocketing incidence of heart disease. Americans lived longer—average life expectancy increased from fifty-four years in 1920 to sixty-eight years by 1950—and they were more likely to die from heart disease. Deaths from heart disease increased from 7.9 percent of all deaths in 1900 to 12.2 percent in 1920, and 26.5 percent in 1940—and to 38 percent by 1970. The vast majority of deaths were from "ischemic heart disease," or blockage of the arteries supplying blood to the heart. The pathology study that Herman began at Western Reserve University

Medical School, and completed when the war was over, showed that in two thousand consecutive autopsies almost half (49.2 percent) of all patients had significant heart disease. Often it was undiagnosed by doctors, but had contributed to their final illness.

One major question was how to increase survival after heart attacks. In 1946, at Michael Reese Hospital in Chicago, Herman had completed another analysis of data from the autopsy series. Of 166 patients with heart attacks, 44 percent developed "mural thrombi," clots on the wall of their injured hearts. Pieces of these clots could break off and "embolize" to the brain, spleen, kidneys, or other organs, causing serious injury, even death. Nearly a third of these patients had emboli in their lungs at autopsy. Because patients were kept in bed for an average of six weeks after a heart attack, as many as twenty percent of all survivors developed these complications.

In Chicago, he had been involved in a study of the use of the anticoagulant Coumadin, one of the first large multicentered, randomized, double-blind studies in American medicine. Decreasing the blood's ability to form clots might lessen the formation of mural thrombi, resulting in fewer emboli, and thus a lower death rate. The "randomized double-blind placebo-controlled" design was a new, rigorous method for clinical research in which the effect of medication is compared to a placebo, without patient or doctor knowing which treatment the patient is receiving. In this way, false responses can be eliminated. Every morning at 7 a.m. Herman would make the rounds of patients being studied. He palpated the patient's abdomen to make sure the spleen was not enlarged, listened to the lungs (to rule out pulmonary embolism), and then drew blood samples to measure prothrombin time and accelerated prothrombin time, to determine the blood's ability to form clots. Results of this study showed that use of anticoagulants decreased mortality to approximately twelve to fifteen percent, compared to the twenty-five percent mortality in untreated patients.

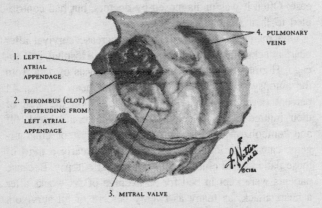

1. LEFT ATRIAL APPENDAGE

2. THROMBUS (CLOT) PROTRUDING FROM LEFT ATRIAL APPENDAGE

3. MITRAL VALVE

4. PULMONARY VEINS

FIG. 2. RHEUMATIC HEART DISEASE:
Thromboembolic Complications of Mitral Stenosis
(interior of left atrium, viewed from above)

There were two sources of clots—legs and the heart itself. After a heart attack, and in rheumatic heart disease, patients often developed clots inside the heart's left atrium, or upper chamber. Anticoagulants were one way to prevent this complication; surgery was another, more aggressive way. The soldier's impulse is to strike, to remove the enemy, and Herman and Dr. Edward Sinaiko, a heart surgeon, working in Dr. Katz's laboratory in Chicago, resolved to enter the heart itself. They developed an open-heart operation on dogs, to prove it was possible to remove thrombi from the heart before they could travel to the lungs. They cut into the atrial appendage, a thin-walled out-pouching of muscle in the upper chamber of the heart; thus, it was possible to remove the large clot. They demonstrated that this could be done in dogs without decreasing survival. Rheumatic-heart-disease patients often developed atrial fibrillation, and large clots in the atrial appendage. In such patients, this operation theoretically would improve chances for survival.

In July 1947, Herman returned to Cleveland as a Fellow in Pathology. He continued his studies in the dog laboratory. By entering the heart through the atrial appendage, he was now able to open up the narrowed mitral valve in mitral stenosis—to approach the valve from above, rather than as heart surgeons then did, through the thick muscle of the ventricle below. He also investigated the origin of the EKG's T wave, and looked at the effects of heat and cold on the EKG, and the impact of tying off various coronary arteries. In one study he showed that by tying off the left circumflex artery, one could produce a state of "electrical alternans," which was related to fatal arrhythmias of the heart—a study reproduced in a 1991 paper by a young researcher using 350 electrodes and complex computer models.

He was searching for a place for himself, expending vast energies to make his scientific mark. Strictly speaking, his dog experiments were "illegal," done on Saturdays and Sundays in another doctor's laboratory where human subjects were normally studied; not only did he have to wheel the dogs down darkened corridors on a shrouded gurney, but also scrub the laboratory after the experiments were done.

He tried to convince Dr. Claude Beck to perform the new atrial approach on humans suffering from mitral stenosis, dangerous narrowing of the mitral valve. Beck refused, saying the heart was too fragile to approach that way. A few years later, in 1948, other surgeons did operate from above in mitral stenosis. They tore open the narrowed mitral valve with the push of a finger, a crude but effective technique. Beck came to Herman with tears in his eyes, saying, "Herman, I missed it again."

What Herman really wanted to do in the late 1940s was to try a new invasive procedure on humans: "catheterization," introduced by Dr. André Cournand from New York's Bellevue Hospital in 1941. A catheter, a thin flexible tube, was threaded through vessels in the arm, and then up to the heart. Radioopaque dye could be injected into the circulatory system, and a fluoroscope (X-ray motion pictures) allowed doctors to see how well the heart muscle and valves were functioning. Through the catheter, physicians also could take blood samples from different chambers of the heart to determine how much oxygen was present in each chamber, and thus to what degree the heart was impaired. Just as in 1910 the EKG combined electricity and photography, the catheterization procedure combined technologies of its day: the fluoroscope, along with the radioopaque contrast agent, the flexible catheter, and other technologies.

However, Dr. Joseph T. Wearn, dean of the medical school, opposed the use of catheterization in humans, and it was not until Drs. André Cournand, Dickinson Richards, and Werner Forssmann won the Nobel Prize for the introduction of catheterization of the right side of the heart in 1956 that Wearn relented and allowed Herman to begin catheterizing humans. Dr. Walter Pritchard was the nominal head of this new laboratory, but Herman did the procedures. He obtained an old fluoroscope, and with the assistance of Hazel Clark, a nurse who earlier in life had spent twenty-five years in bed as a result of rheumatic fever, he began catheterizing humans. He studied patients with congenital heart disease, and people who had just had heart attacks, evaluating their "cardiac output." He even took EKGs within the heart's chambers—publishing one of the first papers in the world on "intracavitary" EKGs. It was daring work, done without benefit of research grants or the formality of informed consent. But he persisted, and eventually did more than two thousand catheterizations.

In another line of work, Herman had begun collaborating with Dr. Toyomo Sano, a Japanese doctor who had been sent to the United States in 1948, in one of the first post–World War II international exchange agreements. Sano stayed for three years. Together they developed a "vectorcardiograph machine"—a way of showing the movement of electricity through the heart. Using a primitive analog computer, they were able to amplify the EKG's faint signal, and perform calculations to produce a three-dimensional picture of the EKG.

In the early 1950s, working together with Dr. Edward Jaruszewski and Harold Feil, he began to use the EKG in the operating room. Feil had pioneered this work nearly twenty years earlier, placing the old string galvanometer in the hallway outside the operating room, and watching the shadow of a moving string to monitor the heart's abnormalities during surgery. Because of technological advances, EKGs now could be monitored directly, and displayed on the screen of a cathode-ray oscilloscope. However, because gases then used for anesthesia were highly flammable, the oscilloscope's electric circuits had to be isolated from the operating-room air. Their solution—a symbolic one for a nation returning from war—was to enclose the sensitive circuitry in an old cannon barrel, and to keep the air inside at "positive pressure"—that is, higher barometric pressure than the operating-room air, so anesthetic gases could not enter. Despite these precautions, the nurse anesthetists were still fearful of an explosion.

After publishing their work on direct monitoring of the EKG during surgery, they met with the president of the Cambridge Company, the major manufacturer of EKG machines, to discuss their findings. During surgery, virtually all patients had abnormal rhythms, or arrhythmias, and it was difficult to know which ones were significant. It would be wonderful if anesthetists and surgeons could know what was happening to *every* patient's EKG during surgery. They recommended that every operating room have a direct-writing EKG machine, as should every emergency room—and even every ambulance.

"Hellerstein, you *are* a dreamer," said the company president.

"Old men have dreams, young men have visions," my father responded, quoting the Bible.

Indeed, it was a vision for which Herman was searching in the 1950s. For in all his scientific and medical work to date, constituting nearly a hundred medical papers in less than ten years, there was no obvious unified thrust or vision, despite its value to the profession; there were no astounding breakthroughs. This burned inside him.

In all eras of science, medicine being no exception, certain major discoveries are waiting to be made. Prefigured by decades of work, made possible by technological innovations, their discovery awaits the individual or individuals with the right combination of talent, luck, and vision. Beck, Pritchard, and Feil's rescue of Richard Heyward, the world's first successful defibrillation, was such a moment of breakthrough—almost. It lacked only the final important insight, that defibrillation did not require opening the chest or laying hands on the naked, beating heart. *That* insight a few years later led to the great practical advances of CPR and closed-chest countershock. But it came close.

The idea of amputating the atrial appendage to prevent emboli in rheumatic heart disease, the idea of entering the heart from above to repair a damaged mitral valve—these, too, were near-breakthroughs. Beck, the radical heart surgeon, had experimented in so many other ways on the human heart—if only this time he had been a bit more daring!

Of Herman's other work—his afternoons in the outpatient department studying atherosclerosis in diabetics, his use of the EKG to monitor patients in surgery, his energetic participation in Beck's annual course of teaching open-heart defibrillation, attended by hundreds of doctors, his evaluations of Beck's later heart operations, and the rest—of all this, catheterization held the most promise. Here the major advance was to lie unsuspected by him and by other investigators for another decade. It was not until one day in 1958, while doing a catheterization on a young Israeli boy, that the Cleveland Clinic's Dr. F. Mason Sones, Jr., accidentally jabbed a catheter into the boy's right coronary artery, a small vessel supplying the heart itself with blood. On the fluoroscope, it appeared that the catheter tip was in the left ventricle, but when dye was injected, it filled the coronary arteries instead, producing a beautifully outlined moving picture of the tree of coronary circulation. The patient had no ill-effects such as arrhythmias or chest pain, and Sones's advance soon lit up the world, showing the cardiologist and surgeon for the very first time the exact locations of coronary artery narrowing. Disease might not involve the entire heart, just a few small segments of one artery. Ischemic heart disease had always been a vaguely defined dysfunction in the patient, diagnosed only with certainty at autopsy. Now the doctor could see all the roadblocks—and maybe someday could bypass them surgically.

Herman and Mary entered into family life with the same profusive energy they brought to their work. Soon after marrying in 1947, they moved into an apartment on Fairhill Road in Shaker Heights, a second-floor garden apartment in a low redbrick building with a large central courtyard. While Herman worked in the research laboratory, Mary continued in medical school, and then internship and residency in pediatrics; and in the final year of training, she became pregnant. After my older sister, Kathryn, was born, they moved to a larger, two-bedroom apartment, and then a year later Mary was pregnant again. I was born at the end of 1953, and soon the apartment was too small, and they bought a house in Cleveland Heights. Less than two miles from the hospital, it was a three-story white clapboard house with seven bedrooms and a two-story garage, and a backyard filled with apple and cherry and quince trees. When I was a year old, my mother was pregnant again. And then again. Within seven years, she had five children, two girls and three boys, and three years later she had another daughter.

Six children—three girls and three boys. Kathryn, Susan, Elizabeth; David, Jonathan, Daniel. A symmetrical profusion. The same size as Herman's own family would have been, the same number of boys and girls, had not his oldest brother, Louis, died in infancy. Though he was no Cabalist, it was a symbolic number for a man who had seen Bergen-Belsen full of the dying and dead. "One for each million," he said.

To some degree, "one for each million" was a figure of speech during our childhood. To a large degree, it was not; and to that degree, his fury to cure, to find a way to defeat disease and forestall death, came from the same anxious urgency of survival, a recognition of fate's random cruelty.

Doctors often state that they learn most not from books but from patients. This is rarely the case: otherwise, medicine would have begun curing disease centuries ago. Only occasionally does a sick person actually cause a doctor to put aside prejudices and preconceptions learned during years of medical education and fraternizing with other doctors. Far more often, doctors fit patients into fixed medical categories, and should a particular disease or the outcome of treatment not fit the norm, then the doctor recalls it as the exception that proves the rule.

The case of Richard Heyward taught the world that fibrillation is reversible, but would have taught nothing had Dr. Pritchard's prejudice held sway: several months after the boy's resuscitation, he had not written an account of the case, as Dr. Feil had requested. "Why are you waiting?" my grandfather asked. "For more cases," Pritchard replied. After all, the individual is just a "case study"; scientific proof requires reproducibility. "Write it up!" said my grandfather, who did learn from his patients. "There are some situations where one case is enough." Indeed, one case changed the world.

Similarly, though less dramatically, the case of Sid Meadow changed the world. Not only did he provide my father with the vision that a decade of medical training and research had not; he provided a model for the tens of thousands of runners and swimmers and bicyclists who fill our country's parks and roadways, who attempt to push back mortality, and buy longevity, through diet and exercise. Thereby, illness was transformed from passive suffering to an aggressive battle against disease. The goal became not survival but rehabilitation, not accommodation to an inevitable progression, but a conviction of the need to arrest, even reverse, disease.

Sid Meadow was in his sixties, a machinist, entrepreneur, and businessman. In the mid-1950s, heart disease left him with disturbed conduction in his heart, what is called "left bundle branch block." Like all heart patients of that time, he was advised to stop work and drastically limit his activity. Life was effectively over. He should remain in bed for months. Thereafter, he should avoid all exertion or excitement, whether work or play or sex. At any moment his heart might give out.

Instead of obeying doctor's orders, Meadow began to

run. With Bill Cumler, a staff member of the Lakewood, Ohio, YMCA, he organized a group of middle-aged men interested in running, and installed a wooden track on the roof of the downtown YMCA. One day, when Herman was giving a speech at the Odd Fellows Hall on East 30th Street and Euclid Avenue, Sid Meadow approached and told him about Cumler's program, Run for Your Life. Meadow was interested in participating in a study Herman was conducting on polyunsaturated fats, an idea that originated with Herman's Chicago mentor, Dr. Louis N. Katz, who believed that some dietary fats were healthful, in particular the "unsaturated" fats found in safflower and other vegetable oils. (Fats are defined as saturated if the bonds between carbon atoms in fatty acids are "single bonds"; unsaturated if there are "double bonds"; polyunsaturated if there are many double bonds; unsaturated fats are able to absorb more hydrogen atoms.) Increasing dietary unsaturated fats might raise the ratio of unsaturated to saturated fats in the bloodstream, and decrease the tendency to develop atherosclerosis.

Sid Meadow was enthusiastic and volunteered to become part of the safflower study. He also invited Herman to visit him at the YMCA and observe the program. There Herman found a group of middle-aged businessmen who were exercising without medical supervision or monitoring, but who seemed to be thriving. Meadow himself ran every day on the wooden track, stressing his heart far beyond what any responsible doctor would recommend. He had lost weight, and lowered his cholesterol, and looked unusually vigorous for a sixty-five-year-old with significant heart disease.

Not only did Meadow participate in the safflower-oil study; he convinced Cumler to allow Herman to study runners in the YMCA program. In 1960, with the assistance of several medical students and with simple equipment—an EKG machine, a two-step barrier (a patient would repeatedly climb up and over and down the steps for one and a half minutes, the total number of steps to be made determined by age, weight, and gender)—they examined each man in the exercise class, monitoring their vital signs and EKGs as they exercised. These studies revealed that nearly half the middle-aged men had undiagnosed heart disease. They next tested those with heart disease by monitoring their EKGs as they ran around the track. Since there was no radiotransmitter version of the EKG, Herman and his team improvised with a twenty-foot-long cable; they attached electrodes to a runner's chest and connected them to the cable. After the runner circled the track, they plugged the cable in and took an EKG.

Later, when Herman developed an exercise rehabilitation program at the Jewish Community Center, Meadow was always available to help—to be interviewed by the newspapers, to take EKGs. Like any paradigm, especially a living, eager one, he was at times an inspiration, at other times something of a nuisance.

In 1949, Robert White, a vice president of Republic Steel, himself a heart-attack survivor, gave a contribution to the local heart society, asking whether any doctor would like to study the problem of cardiacs in industry. Several physicians were approached, and declined, until my father was asked. He agreed—he almost always seemed to find the energy for another commitment—and began to spend a day each week on the project. He traveled around the United States, looking at various rehabilitation projects and interviewing industrial physicians. In Rochester, New York, Eastman Kodak had a program for its workers in which the company would rehire a heart-attack survivor with a heart murmur, but not one with an enlarged heart. He visited a program in Chicago, and several "sheltered workshops" in New York, where the disabled were able to work free of financial pressures. At New York's Bellevue Hospital,

Herman met Dr. Leonard Goldwater; during World War II, because of the urgent need for workers, Goldwater had been sponsored by the War Manpower Commission to begin evaluating cardiac patients to see whether any of them could work. They would be evaluated by a physician, a social worker, and a vocational counselor. Of this medically indigent group of people, twenty to thirty percent had "functional" heart disease caused by anxiety or other nonmedical causes, and they could generally return to work.

After returning to Cleveland, Herman proposed to the board of the Cleveland Area Heart Society that they develop a Work Classification Clinic, a facility available not only to the unemployed and poor but to a broad cross-section of Americans. It was a hotly debated issue, but the board finally agreed to go ahead, with a small annual budget of $2,000.

The next question was where to house the Work Classification Clinic. There was a rehabilitation center on East 55th Street, in a poor downtown neighborhood, run by a Miss Belle Greve, a social worker active in international war relief and with displaced persons; her center specialized in patients with muscular weakness resulting from polio, strokes, and other diseases. She welcomed him, providing space in a rickety old frame house. The equipment was old, and there were only two cramped rooms for physical rehabilitation, but it was a start. He recruited a psychiatric social worker and a vocational counselor, each to work one day a week, and began operations. The beginning was slow. He met with personnel directors from Thompson Products, Cleveland Graphite Bronze, Jones and Laughlin Steel, and other companies. The first two patients were a porter and a company president. Herman would take a medical history and do a physical examination, and the patient would have a two-step exercise test and pulmonary-function testing to determine fitness, and skin-fold measurements to determine the percentage of body fat. The psychiatric social worker, Elaine Goldston, would talk to patients and their families about their adjustment to illness; the vocational counselor would determine the types and levels of work that seemed appropriate to each patient. Daily, after evaluating four or five patients, the team met in roundtable discussion. Over the weekend, Herman would dictate case reports. In general, industrial physicians were receptive to his recommendations, which generally concluded that a patient was capable of going back to work, provided he didn't exceed the energy expenditure his heart could tolerate. However, many private physicians were enraged. "I told this patient to be at absolute rest—he shouldn't bend over to pick up a leaf!" one of them would yell over the telephone. Others would ask: "Why test the patient? We know he has heart disease." Herman began to invite other physicians to the conferences. Some physicians agreed to come, and despite initial hostility, their resistance began to diminish. Eventually, the Work Classification Clinic had more referrals than it could handle.

Using their multidisciplinary approach, evaluating each patient individually, reviewing the demands of specific jobs, they could then match the patient to a suitable job. When they began to analyze outcome, they discovered that about ninety percent of the cardiac patients were able to work, and ninety-five percent of that group could work full-time. Of patients not employed at initial follow-up, sixty percent were working at later follow-up visits. When they reviewed 250 cases, they found that one of the most critical factors in determining ability to work had nothing to do with the heart itself—but with emotional disability, especially depression.

Inadvertently, Herman had discovered the problem of the moment—and his results began to suggest a solution. For the growing ranks of heart-attack survivors, including those rare individuals rescued from fibrillation, the biggest problem was that life after a heart attack was often not worth living. The inactivity and social withdrawal recommended by the doctors to protect them against further heart damage often led to prolonged depression and suffering.

The clearest sign of the success of Herman's program came in 1955, shortly after President Dwight D. Eisenhower suffered a heart attack. Dr. Paul Dudley White, the eminent Harvard cardiologist (who was known for his humanistic management of patients with heart disease, as well as for research describing, among other things, the Wolff-Parkinson-White Syndrome, an arrhythmia resulting from an abnormal conduction pathway in the heart), telephoned Herman to give the details of a case, and to ask, "Herman, what's your experience with high-level executives with heart disease?"

"Those who go back to work," Herman responded, "do better than those with equal heart disease who don't go back to work."

He did not know at the time that White was asking for a curbside consultation about his most famous patient, the President. White later credited Herman and his data with helping make the decision to send Ike back to work, with a prescription of a low-fat, low-salt diet and a regimen of moderate exercise and weight loss.

Later, White invited Herman to present his work at the Massachusetts Medical Society before a distinguished group of Harvard cardiologists. After his talk, Dr. Samuel Levine, another famous Harvard Medical School professor, rose in the audience and began to speak at length about these results, which, he said, represented the most important work being done in cardiology in America.

Gradually, the local heart society grew in size and prestige. When it acquired an old stone mansion on East 116th Street for its headquarters, and moved in, the Work Classification Clinic was given the entire first floor. With Eisenhower's example, heart patients by the thousands began to contemplate returning to work, and the clinic was soon receiving visitors from all over the world—Australia, Brazil, Chile, and dozens of other countries. More than fifty American centers were built and modeled on the WCC.

Despite the clinic's reputation and influence, a nagging question remained: did the research team *really* know their patients' work capabilities? Although the WCC successfully sent workers back to steel mills and foundries, and never had a workmen's compensation claim filed against it, in truth no one even knew the specific cardiac demands of various types of work. Or the relation between an evaluation in a doctor's office and the demands of actual work. Furthermore, they saw patients after heart attacks, when disease processes were advanced, and long after irreversible damage had occurred. Why not intervene sooner?

Clearly, on-the-job studies were required. Using telemetry equipment from the navy, Herman and one of his students, Dr. Amasa B. Ford, went to steel mills, and foundries, and factory floors in the late 1950s and early 1960s. Here is where my memories begin; for I recall Dad's job studies, which extended to lawyers and musicians from the Cleveland Orchestra, and radio disk jockeys, and, especially, sky jumpers.

Dad and Amasa Ford brought the latest technology to these ecological studies. They calculated "heat stress" by a complex formula that included heat produced by effort and heat absorbed from the environment. They collected urine samples to study the production of the "stress hormones" norepinephrine and epinephrine; that is, hormones produced in response to stress. They took blood samples to measure lactic acid, in order to calculate oxygen debt (the amount of oxygen that the body "owes" after intense exercise, and must replace later). Using machinery to measure oxygen uptake (the percentage of oxygen in the bloodstream absorbed by muscles during exercise), they calculated how much oxygen was consumed during various phases of work. They discovered that most factory work was not as physically demanding as had been believed. Using the unit of METS, or metabolic equivalents (the amount of oxygen consumed per minute per kilogram of body weight), they calculated that if climbing two flights of stairs required 7 METS, most factory work required only 2 to 3 METS. If a factory worker who shoveled ashes, a task requiring 5 to 6 METS, did his work in thirty minutes instead of fifteen, he would only expend 2 to 3 METS. Even a person with severe heart disease could often continue doing manual work—if he slowed down enough. As Herman and psychiatrist Dr. Ernest Friedman began to study work physiology and psychology, their impressions from the Work Classification Clinic were confirmed. Using psychological tests, including the MMPI, the Minnesota Multiphasic Personality Inventory, and the Forstman Lindgard Manifest Anxiety Scale, they calculated that approximately sixty percent of what determined return to work wasn't anatomical disease in the heart but the patient's emotional response to the disease. Poor prognosis, while related to the severity of heart disease, and the number of vessels known to be diseased, was more strongly related to inadequate "psychological defenses" against depression, measured by an "F minus K" score on the MMPI, a measure of self-esteem. Interestingly, as physical fitness began to return to the normal range, depression and self-esteem scores improved as well.

Dr. Harold Feil had done work before World War II with the employment of cardiac patients, allowing a locomotive engineer with heart disease to go back to work—moving trains in the rail yard rather than trains filled with passengers. Fifty years before that, Dr. William Osler, in his *Principles and Practice of Medicine,* described European regimens of gradually increasing exercise for patients with heart ailments. As scientists often do, Herman built on the work of earlier researchers, but what was different about his approach was quantification—he measured the amount of disturbance of heart function, the cardiac demands of work, and psychological and physical factors related to the ability to go back to work. From all this, he came to several striking conclusions.

Not only could most heart patients tolerate some degree of exertion, but most work could be adapted so that the exertion required would match a patient's capacity, however limited. Demoralization and depression could be alleviated by increasing activity and fitness. Exercise had been traditionally used in cardiology as a way of **testing** heart impairment, for instance with the two-step test—having patients repeatedly step back and forth over the steps to increase their heart rate, and periodically checking their EKGs for signs of ischemia. It now became clear that exercise might improve heart function in cardiac patients—it could be used as well to **treat** heart disease. Through regular exercise gradually increased in intensity, one could theoretically increase the heart's capacity to tolerate exertion. Exercise might even cause increased "collateral" circulation, growth of blood vessels in the heart bypassing the obstructed coronary arteries.

Exercising heart patients! It was a heretical idea. Although in the late nineteenth century (with the revival of the Olympics and of marathon running) there had been increased interest in the health benefits of exercise, the physicians who advocated exercise were largely regarded as quacks. Furthermore, the clinical entity of "myocardial infarction," or heart attack, was not specifically identified until early in the twentieth century, and many prominent cardiologists were pessimistic about the value of exercise in heart-attack survivors. In 1946, Paul Dudley White, in a paper co-authored with W. W. Jetter Mallory, studied twenty-two mental-hospital patients who had survived heart attacks and who had exerted themselves freely (often in agitated, psychotic states); of these, sixteen had "ruptured" (or broken through) their heart muscle and died. While White had more recently become an advocate of gradually increased activity, the standard treatment of the heart patient for many years had included exercise no more strenuous than walking from the hospital bed to the nearest chair.

Was exercise dangerous? Clearly, overexertion might bring on a heart attack in patients with coronary artery disease. But in small doses, might it be useful as a treatment? The risks seemed overwhelming to many doctors. Nevertheless, there were the individual patients—the Sid Meadows—who had intuitively followed such a course; had they escaped disaster by chance? Or had they stumbled onto something?

By this time the Framingham Study group had begun to publish its early results. Organized in 1949, this epidemiological study of a community in Massachusetts followed 5,200 people prospectively, with twice yearly physical exams, EKGs, X rays, and biochemical measures, with the goal of determining who was at risk for developing heart disease. By the early 1960s, the Framingham Study had shown that several "risk factors" were related to the development of heart disease. The sons or daughters of parents with heart disease had a much higher than average risk of developing it themselves. So did men with muscular, "endomesomorphic," builds, and those with a lot of body hair, and male-pattern baldness. Some of these factors, such as family history, obviously couldn't be changed. But other factors could: high cholesterol, high blood pressure, cigarette smoking, obesity, and poor physical fitness.

The logical thing to do was to test exercise as a way of

treating heart disease—if it was part of a program also related to changed diet and smoking habits.

The YMCA lacked sufficient room for such a study, so when the Jewish Community Center moved from midtown Cleveland to Mayfield Road in Cleveland Heights in 1960, Herman met with their board of directors and got their approval to conduct a study, the Western Reserve Physical Fitness Study of Cardiacs. He set up staff and equipment in an empty basement, and began work. Patients were evaluated with a medical history, family history, psychological tests, measurements of body fat, a multi-stage exercise function test, pulmonary function tests, and blood tests. They were instructed to keep a seven-day diary of everything they ate, so their intake of cholesterol and fats could be estimated. An exercise regimen was begun, to a maximum of seventy to eighty-five percent of each patient's maximal heart rate and blood-pressure level. There would be a period of "walk/run," and thirty minutes of calisthenics, and games such as basketball, and lap swimming. The concept was that exercise—like any drug in the *Physician's Desk Reference*—could be "prescribed," with a certain frequency, dosage, and manner of application. Just like penicillin or insulin, exercise had its indications and contraindications, as well as side effects and toxicities. The most-feared "toxicity" of exercise was cardiac arrest, and to forestall it, a defibrillator was kept in the middle of the gymnasium, and a doctor or physiologist was present at all times. It was needed only once, when an older man, while jogging, was egged on by a younger man, who said, "C'mon, Pops, let's see what you can do!" and exercised himself into asystole, or standstill of the heart. He was successfully revived.

When Herman began to present his results at national and international meetings, the response of other doctors was mixed. While some applauded his efforts, others were harshly critical. Dr. Arthur M. Master, for instance, the New York Mt. Sinai Hospital cardiologist who had introduced the Master two-step test in 1929 as a way of testing heart disease, approached him and said, "What in the world are you *doing*, Herman? It's okay to use exercise to make a diagnosis, but not as a training modality!" The study was open to criticism on scientific grounds: while it eventually enrolled over 650 patients, of whom 250 had had heart attacks and 400 were "coronary prone," it was not a placebo-controlled, randomized study. It was impossible, therefore, to know whether the successes were due to a real effect of exercise—or to chance, charisma, or other causes.

Heart patients who exercised might *feel* better, but did they live longer? Did changes in exercise and diet really reverse, or at least arrest, the disease process in their coronary arteries? That was not easy to prove. The fact that no one dropped dead while exercising at the Center was somewhat reassuring, but it did not provide scientific proof. That would require replication in "multi-center" studies with a randomized, placebo-controlled design.

However, the evidence remained: hundreds of patients whose lives were changed. What was medicine about, if not transformation from suffering to recovery, from despair and hopelessness to purpose and new life? All six of us kids grew up as witnesses to these changes, to the gradual emergence of new concepts which not only affected heart patients and their doctors—but which gradually permeated American society. We saw our father, the doctor, possessed by his vision. The patients we met, whose lives had been changed, gave evidence to this vision, and gave us our first real inkling of the power of healing.

For instance, Mr. Laugesen.

Victor Laugesen was a driven man, publisher of a trade journal for foundries and twist-drill companies. After his heart attack at age fifty-five, doctors told him to sell his business and retire. Naturally, he became depressed. He withdrew to his house, an old place filled with antiques and paintings, on a former farm, located in the semi-rural eastern suburbs of Cleveland. To him, retirement was death.

This was the state of things around 1950 when my father saw Victor Laugesen on a house call. Laugesen was pale, depressed, and withdrawn. My father did a physical exam, and took an EKG, using the "direct-writing" EKG machine, the latest technology. They discussed his diet, typical for successful Americans of that time—steaks, eggs, sweet country butter—and the possibility that he might gradually increase his activity by doing some work on the farm. They walked behind the house to the old barn.

"Do you think it will be okay for me to open the barn door?" Laugesen asked fearfully. My father nodded, and watched him push the heavy door open on its rollers. He felt Laugesen's pulse: nothing of note.

They walked into the barn, past empty stalls.

Dad's prescription was simple: based on a simple on-the-job assessment, Laugesen should change his diet, avoiding fatty foods and cholesterol. He should gradually increase his activities and level of physical exertion.

Mr. Laugesen followed this advice. He sold his trade journals and lost twenty-five or thirty pounds. He began working the farm, buying first one, then two dairy cows, then half a dozen, finally filling his barn. His cows won prizes for their milk, and he bred them, staying up all night to deliver their calves, rubbing newborns awake with handfuls of straw. Years later, when he got tired of raising cows, he began bringing thoroughbred horses up from Florida, keeping them through the Ohio winters to harden them for Northern racetracks. Several times a year throughout the 1960s, on our family's visits to his farm, we would be struck anew by his vigor. We saw evidence of strenuous labor, watched the milking and herding and feeding that had begun before dawn and would end after the sun went down—we witnessed a man's metamorphosis from disease and despair into a new health.

He lived for decades more, into his late eighties. At first he was an anomaly, an unusual case, but he survived until he was ordinary, just one of millions of heart-disease patients who had returned to an active life. By then, the hilly country roads around his house became crowded with joggers and ten-speed bicycles, with people who ate low-cholesterol foods and who had stopped smoking, and were, as my father put it, running for their lives.

III

THE NEW GENERATION

8

SHADOWS IN WHITE COATS

CERTAINLY, for our generation, these examples of healing held enormous power. It is no surprise to me that four of the six children in our family have become doctors, that I went to medical school, that little Daniel grew up to do sex-change operations, that Susie delivered babies in China, that blond baby Beth learned to transplant genes. To Mom and Dad, medicine was not something to be practiced forty hours a week; it was not to be kept within the confines of a private office or the curtains of a hospital bed.

Consequently, in every way, we were different from our neighbors. It was not only that in due course we went down to the hospital to see patients with Dad, six little shadows whose borrowed white coats dragged along the floor as we hurried after him down the long corridors, or accompanied him to the firehouse to see him study cardiovascular responses to stress, or to the Jewish Community Center to watch cardiac patients exercise. And it was not just that we did fancy science projects while our classmates could barely track the readings of a barometer. It was that we lived by the science of medicine.

There was food, for instance. The Collinses across the street ate spareribs and homemade doughnuts deep-fried in lard. The Saffords breakfasted every morning on eggs sunnyside-up, with bacon. Annie Dole's father smoked three packs a day. Tareytons. *We* cooked with safflower oil and spread our bread with paste-like "oleomargarine," and for dessert we had something strange (and not very good) called "ice milk." We had eggs just about never. When Dad ran into people smoking cigarettes at a picnic or party, he never hesitated to lecture them about stopping smoking, and sometimes he would pull the cigarette right out of their mouths.

Most embarrassing of all, Dad believed in something called "aerobic exercise." The sit-ups and chin-ups and calisthenics we learned in gym class might tone your muscles, he told us, but they did nothing for cardiac function. The only good exercise trained the heart. As a consequence, while our peers were watching cartoons on TV on Saturday mornings, all four, five, then six Hellerstein kids would be out back, our bicycles turned wheels-up on the asphalt driveway, dousing sprockets with 3-in-1 oil and adjusting derailleurs. With mist still hanging in the hollows we headed out Fairmount Boulevard, a trail of bicycles weaving toward Squire Valley View ten miles away, Dad in the lead, Mom bringing up the rear. Cars honked and swerved, kids in station wagons leered at us as they roared by. What were we *doing* out there on the long hills, Dad on his Schwinn five-speed, Mom on her 28-inch black Raleigh, countless children on balloon tires, riding past empty fields or toiling uphill, watched by cows?

Didn't we have a car?

It didn't help either that I was inclined to plumpness, a good twenty pounds heavier than the "ideal weight" on the health tables at Dr. Saunders's office, and that I had an incurable urge for cake and doughnuts and cookies, everything bad for the heart. I was not the best advertisement, perhaps, for Dad's theories. All that skim milk, all those cans of chocolate- or strawberry-flavored Metrecal, and still an "endomesomorph." Nevertheless, Dad hadn't given up—I was like an experiment whose results kept going slightly awry, contrary to expectation, yet the scientist kept repeating it, hoping that the next time things would come out right. So he would still ask on a Saturday morning: Did I want to come to the hospital with him? Or: Was I interested in helping test for cardiac-risk factors in junior-high-school kids? Or: There were some extra white mice at the animal lab. If he brought them home, wouldn't I want to do some experiments? Usually I said no, but sometimes I said yes, and then he would take me down to the laboratory and let me choose some surplus equipment, or hook me up on the bicycle ergometer and measure my baseline oxygen consumption and then gradually increase the resistance. Strength, endurance, maximal work output in kilogram meters. At best, I was nearly average.

Then there was the issue of mortality.

"If only we could put my head on your body!" he would say. "When I die, think of all the knowledge that will be lost!"

"What about *my* head?" I would respond.

After a pause, he would answer, "No, I mean, if I could transfer all the *knowledge* from my head into yours, so you didn't have to spend all those years learning."

Still, it seemed I'd end up with a spare head and a spare body, at least one of each. Plus, what about the stuff that was in my head already? Wouldn't it be kind of crowded by the stuff that came from his head?

Sometimes it would have been nice to grow up in a normal family.

In 1967, I was thirteen. Only four years earlier, President Kennedy had been shot, and Mrs. Adams, our principal at Roxboro Elementary, had announced over the loudspeaker that his condition was "grave." The girls in our classroom started crying when Mrs. Adams said he had died, and our teacher started crying, too, and she sent us home early, and we all walked home very quietly. Now Lyndon B. Johnson was President, and we were fighting a war in Vietnam, which Sheila Brown, one of our classmates, before she ran off to San Francisco with her twenty-five-year-old boyfriend, said was immoral; but I wasn't sure yet, because I knew that Communism wasn't so great, either.

We knew it was a historic time. With the Civil Rights Act, and the Freedom Marches, and the Peace Corps. And the space program: One year there was a Space Fair downtown, and we got to touch Mercury, the blackened space capsule in which John Glenn orbited the Earth, the first American to do so, and we saw Mylar, shiny metal like tinfoil, but you could see through it, and they gave us Tang to drink, like the astronauts, and a man from NASA told us that "space ve*HIC*les" would soon be going to the moon, maybe even to Mars.

Everywhere one looked, there was History. Even my room was History. At the age of ten, when my littlest sister, Elizabeth Leah, was born, I moved up to the third floor, to a room that had been Dad's study, with an EKG lamp that glowed a heartbeat across my room (a gift from some of his cardiology fellows), and human hearts preserved in lucite blocks. I slept on a hospital bed, and I could crank up its head to read late at night; my bedside stand was from the hospital, too, and it had a metal circle like a basketball hoop, which held a wastebasket and swung underneath. A door halfway down the room led to the walk-in closet, which had two oval windows, like eyes, looking out on either side of the chimney.

It was there that I found my father's World War II uniforms. And a big heavy white sheepskin coat, fleece turned in, and a matching pair of pants; they came from Siberia, from a Russian soldier, and had kept him from freezing.

Under the arm was a big gash torn by shrapnel. There were pictures, too, from Bergen-Belsen, the concentration camp Dad had helped liberate in 1945—that was *really* History—but then I put them away, and couldn't find them anymore, and neither could Dad, and I could tell he was really upset, but it wasn't my fault. Anyway, I knew they were still around somewhere, because in our house no one threw anything away. There just got to be more and more of everything. That's what History seemed like to me in those days—there would be more and more of everything until the world burst. My father subscribed to *The Bulletin of Atomic Scientists,* and there was a clock on the front cover, its minute hand seven minutes before midnight. When Cuban exiles supplied by the United States attacked the Bay of Pigs in Cuba, the editors had moved the minute hand closer to midnight, and with Vietnam, and everything else—we never knew. Midnight was when the atomic bomb would go off.

Until then, it was best to try to save lives. Being a doctor was a pretty good thing, I believed. Sometimes, though, the prospect of atomic war gave me doubts. If we were all going to die anyway, what was the point of saving lives? Just so more people would be alive to die? Then I thought, well, maybe you'd save the life of someone who would stop the war and save everybody else's life. Or maybe you set a good example, or something. As if God kept score . . .

One night, Dad had me ride with the rescue squad. He was doing a study of firemen, to learn how their hearts responded to stress. The question was, did fighting fires cause heart disease? Could firefighters who had had heart attacks keep working? Dad had some medical students who came to the firehouse for twenty-four hours at a time and followed the firemen. Scotty, his laboratory technician, would drive behind the fire engine, and once at a fire, she would run up almost into the fire with her syringes and rubber-topped tubes, her round face all red, her hair crew-cut, her white coat flapping in the hot wind, and take samples of blood to test levels of epinephrine, which told how the firemen were responding to stress, or to pump up the blood-pressure cuff, or to change the tape on the EKG telemetry machine.

I hadn't really wanted to be involved in Dad's experiment; I would rather have been in my attic room at home, reading *The Tin Drum*, by Günter Grass. It was about this dwarf in World War II, a genius drummer. Jonny was the one who really liked this research stuff. But Dad prodded me. He complained that I was too dreamy, that I could dream my life away. So I came.

Behind us, in a white Oldsmobile convertible, Scotty and my little brother, Jonny, were following at seventy miles per hour, trying to stay close enough to keep the telemetry equipment in range. Scotty's main passions in life were Tennessee walking horses (whose gait was so smooth that a glass full of water held in a rider's hand wouldn't lose a drop at a full trot); and her Harley-Davidson "hog," which she festooned with mirrors, lights, and white fringe. Those days she spent much of her time chasing rescue-squad vehicles and fire engines, capturing heartbeats.

Mostly we waited at the firehouse, though, doing nothing. There were false alarms: trucks would pull out of the firehouse, slow down before they reached the first corner, round the block, then slowly back in. But occasionally there was a real emergency.

Then, sirens wailing, we were roaring through an unfamiliar industrial area; we squealed to a stop in front of a tractor-trailer jackknifed across the road. It had smashed into a warehouse. The firemen jumped out, opened the semi's door, and pulled out a limp, blue-faced man whose head was slumped against the steering wheel; they put him on a stretcher and carefully slid him into the rescue vehicle.

"No heartbeat!" one man shouted. The oscilloscope showed wavy green lines, nothing but static.

We roared toward Metropolitan Hospital, bouncing across potholes; the EMTs pounded on the man's chest, doing their best to get his heart started again. Fatty blue sweaty skin, drool coming out of his limp mouth—he looked dead. Out the back window I could see the Oldsmobile's long hood and fins dipping and rising, Scotty steering with her "suicide knob" as she tried to keep up.

They kept pumping his chest. And squeezing the ambu bag. Nothing.

Then we roared over some railroad tracks, and one of the firemen fell off his seat, landing on the man's chest.

"It's beating!"

And indeed I could see it: irregular, twitchy, but unmistakable. Life. The same P wave of the atria, the QRS of the ventricles' contraction, that I saw every night on the lampshade of my bedside lamp before I went to sleep, the same QRS that twitched across the slippery coils of EKG tape I helped Dad refold late at night on the picnic table in the breakfast room.

When we reached Metro's emergency room, I pulled my legs up under my white lab coat—a coat that smelled like Dad—as they slid the stretcher past me—three burly men carrying it out across the asphalt parking lot and through the ER's gleaming sliding door.

Afterward we went back to the fire station. The Oldsmobile pulled in, and Jonny and Scotty got out. Scotty came up to one of the EMTs and took the canvas navy knapsack off his back, untaping EKG electrodes from his hairy chest and arms.

"Dammit! Something's wrong with the contacts!" she

said. "We weren't getting a signal." She showed it to Dad, who fiddled with it and got it working again.

At dinnertime, we were given huge plates of spaghetti, and hot garlic bread and mountains of salad, and then chocolate cake just out of the oven. The firemen took turns cooking when things were slow, and the food was always spectacular. A few weeks earlier, my first time there, we had gone out to a street fair and gotten fantastic spareribs and collard greens and sweet potatoes, and I had seen Ray, the little black boy whom I had tutored the year before at Temple, who was there with his grandmother. All the firemen were white, and all the people at the street fair were black, but they were all friendly. It wasn't always like that, said Mr. Pollizzi, one of the firemen. On the way back to the station, he showed me bullet holes in the upstairs windows of the firehouse. Sometimes, when you were putting out a fire, he said, *they* came and shot at you.

One thing for sure, even though we didn't put in as much time as Dad thought we should, we probably knew more cardiology than any kids in America. Not only could we read EKGs in a rudimentary way, and describe the abnormalities of various heart diseases, but we knew about afterload reduction in heart failure, and the importance of anticoagulation to prevent blood clots after heart attacks. We knew our anatomy, too. We knew how in coronary artery disease the vessels supplying blood to the heart became clogged with "atheromatous plaque," and after becoming narrowed would frequently close off entirely, leading to a heart attack or death. We heard innumerable times how Dr. F. Mason Sones down at the Cleveland Clinic had accidentally stuck a catheter into a kid's coronary artery, and that his heart lit up on the radiograph machine. We also knew all about obstructions in the left main coronary artery and the left anterior descending branch, about the diffuse spread of plaque through the coronary arteries.

We were aware of the frontiers of treatment, too. By the late 1960s there were several ways to operate on the heart, to repair damaged circulation. Since 1950, Dr. Arthur Vineberg from McGill University had implanted arteries from the chest wall into the heart muscle itself. The arteries bled into the heart muscle and eventually formed "collateral" connections with other vessels, increasing the blood supply to the heart. In 1962, Dr. David Sabiston at Duke University performed a successful bypass operation— removing a piece of superficial vein from the leg and connecting one end to the aorta and the other end to the coronary artery beyond the blockage, like a plumber laying new pipes. Down at the Cleveland Clinic, Dr. René G. Favaloro was experimenting with the next step—making the bypass operation routine, and he did his first operation on November 30, 1967.

In December 1967, like every other American, we heard on the radio that Dr. Christiaan Barnard had actually transplanted a heart. He took it from a twenty-five-year-old woman who died in a car crash and gave it to Louis Washkansky, a South African man, who survived eighteen days. Like our classmates, we were astonished—but, unlike our classmates, we knew that the tissue-rejection problem was a long way from being solved.

We also knew that, miraculous as it might seem, surgery wasn't the only solution, or even the best option for patients with heart disease. One recent innovation was the coronary-care unit, or CCU, introduced in 1962 in Bethany, Kansas, by Dr. Hughes W. Day, which proliferated so rapidly that there were more than two hundred in the United States by 1967. Heart-attack patients were clustered together in CCUs, and could be monitored closely, with EKG machines running twenty-four hours a day, and given lidocaine and other anti-arrhythmic drugs to prevent ventricular fibrillation. Dad took us down to University Hospital's new CCU, where patients lay in little alcoves around a nursing station, an EKG machine connected continuously, a green trace of heartbeat flashing overhead. Buzzers sounded the moment a heart stopped beating, allowing immediate resuscitation.

And Jonny and I tagged along as Dad showed an endless stream of foreign visitors around the Work Classification Clinic. We slid across the slick marble floors, playing hide-and-seek, climbing on the bicycle ergometers, as Dad described the systematic evaluation of heart-attack survivors, the counseling about saturated fats and optimal weight and hypertension, the confidence with which you could send them back to work. Visitors kept coming, eager to set up their own Work Classification Clinics in Hamburg or Moscow or Nigeria. Dr. Susoyev from Russia, Dr. Hahter-Khan from Hyderabad, India; Dr. Sano from Japan—they came to our house for dinner of meatloaf and frozen peas, or chicken à la king, bringing as gifts carved wooden bears or papier-mâché elephants with ivory tusks, and they would make heroic efforts to continue a train of polite conversation while Danny chased Susie through the living room, or Beth smeared mashed potatoes in Kathy's hair.

At the Jewish Community Center we really saw Dad's philosophy in action. There, in an echoing basement gymnasium, Jonny and Danny and I shot baskets as middle-aged men jogged stolidly in circles around the periphery, or pedaled to nowhere on stationary bicycles, the air filled with the smell of sweat and determination. Dad would talk about his newest ideas: the use of exercise for "secondary prevention"; that is, preventing further heart attacks. And "enhancement of function"—getting the most out of damaged heart muscle. Not to mention "primary prevention"— having just about everybody in America start exercising so they wouldn't get heart disease in the first place. Jonny and

I had no doubt whatsoever that exercise was good medicine, and that it would work in preventing heart disease. No matter what, Dad would *make* it work.

And he showed us when his newest gadget arrived, an Avionics Holter monitor—a tiny EKG machine that ran continuously for up to twenty-four hours, recording onto a magnetic tape. Electrodes were attached to a patient's chest and limbs, and the Holter monitor was carried as a backpack. It could collect an enormous amount of data, which would be analyzed on a computer. With the Holter monitor, you could do what Dad had been attempting for years: determine how the heart functioned in the real world, outside the exercise laboratory. No longer did a technician have to follow along close behind. Now patients could be monitored while they exercised, after they went home, while eating, even while having sex. (And, indeed, soon enough Dad had heart-attack survivors wear the Holter monitor when they were having sex, and he wrote a famous paper proving that heart patients did not have to give up sex, after all!)

Every month or two, the extended family gathered at Nana and Papa Feil's house. The excuse was birthdays—there were always more birthdays to celebrate—but really it was just to get together. Besides fifteen or so grandchildren, there was Mom and Dad, and Mom's brothers George and Ed, and their wives Maren and Mimi, and Nana and Papa. Four doctors, a nurse, a social worker, and a medical filmmaker. Even Nana had gotten into the act as a cookbook writer, with *Gourmet Cooking for Cardiac Diets*, under the pen name Florence Field.

For once, diet was thrown to the winds. After singing "Happy Birthday" under hot floodlamps, with Uncle Ed's movie camera whirring and baby cousins crying, and Jonny blowing out somebody's candles before they could exhale, and Nana relighting candles and wiping away tears, and another "Roll 'em!" we would finally settle down to Nana's chocolate roll cake with whipped-cream filling and mocha icing, accompanied by coffee ice cream. There'd be seconds, even thirds, then candy, malted-milk balls and sweet jelly wedges and jelly beans and chocolate coins. Then the children's tables would be folded, plastic sheets removed from the carpet, and while Uncle Ed set up the movie screen Jonny and Danny would build elaborate towers almost to the ceiling with Papa's cigar boxes and Uncle Ed's old green and yellow film spools, or careen around the room on huge old metal Model T trucks that used to belong to Uncle George. Kathy, our eldest sister, and Leslie, the oldest girl cousin, both with braces and teased, ironed hair, would be giggling and whispering on the sofa, too good to play with boys.

In the dining room, over porcelain coffee cups, the air filled with smoke from Papa's cigar and Uncle George's pipe, the grownups talked medicine. Uncle George, who had a ruddy, jowly face and practiced internal medicine in Shaker Heights and was affiliated with Western Reserve Medical School, would consult with Papa or Dad on heart cases. Sometimes, if you strained to hear, there would be Mom's voice, talking about the child she'd seen who was abandoned by its mother, who had been beaten, or who had congenital heart disease, or perforated eardrums, or difficulty in breathing. Or whether to hospitalize the little boy whose mother didn't give him his erythromycin every day. But it was hard to hear her—she would be drowned out by the men.

We heard their voices rising: "Socialized medicine—it will destroy the profession!" The word: "Anti-Semites!" And: "The diet should have no more than twenty percent fats! No more!" One exciting day, we heard Dad announce that finally, *finally*, his idea of exercise as a treatment for heart disease was being given its rightful due. A multicenter study was being set up to test his hypothesis: The National Heart Disease and Exercise Project. One center would be in Cleveland, others in Alabama and Georgia and Philadelphia and Washington, D.C. Once and for all—to prove him right.

"Exercise reverses coronary artery disease!"

"Now, Herman!" we heard Papa say. "We'll see!"

And Dad: "We'll see, we'll see all right!"

Uncle Ed would call out "All ready!" and we'd turn the living-room lights off and the old black-and-white serial, one of Uncle Ed's favorites from when he was a kid, would flicker on the screen. Grownups quietly entered and sank onto the old leather chairs, and above us Buck Rogers's streamlined spaceship rose bumpily over faraway planets.

Finally, way past bedtime, the babies all sleeping, we scuffed our way down the gravel driveway and piled into the car, sticky and tired, to drive home. Dad pulled into the garage, and we all climbed out in total darkness, the whir of cicadas in the sycamores above. Frisky and Waddie would begin howling as we stood on the back porch, Dad fumbling with the keys.

If you asked then what I wanted to be when I grew up, I would say with some embarrassment, "A doctor," knowing the answer was as expected as it was inevitable. The grownups would all nod knowingly. But that was a lie—or, at best, only part of the answer. Really, I wanted two futures, to be a baseball player or a prophet. Neither, however, seemed very likely. In real baseball games I was consigned to right field, and even the laziest pop flies bounced out of my glove. As for the other possibility, I knew dozens of doctors, but I'd never been introduced to a single prophet.

If there was any philosophy of child-raising in our household—besides scientific medicine—it was that of benign neglect. We often went weeks without brushing teeth, days without baths, and once we got home from school, we were pretty much on our own. Mabel, our housekeeper, would be in the kitchen, doing laundry or starting dinner. Without television to narcotize us, we were free to get into all kinds of mischief. If we were acting up when Dad got home from the hospital, he would pull off his belt and threaten to "Patsh in tukhes until you shray 'Hurrah!' "— that is, smack our rear ends until we screamed "Enough!"—but he never did anything worse than smack the belt against the banister. For several years, we were frequent visitors to the emergency room, with gashes on our foreheads or scalps from pushing each other into radiators or window wells, with broken arms from jumping off beds. There, awaiting our casts or stitches, we regularly encountered another Western Reserve doctor, a surgeon, whose five boys seemed to require an equal number of repairs. Fortunately, despite our lack of supervision, there were no fatalities.

While I tended to read the afternoons away, Jonny specialized in torturing Kathy. As a teenager, Kathy was exquisitely aware of popular culture, and plastered the pink ballerina wallpaper in her bedroom with posters of Dino, Desi, and Billy, and Herman's Hermits, and the Dave Clark Five. Jonny tormented her for the efforts she made to keep up with her best friends, Jean and Joan Heitman, twins who lived down the street. He called her "tinsel-teeth" for her braces, and reduced her to tears by joking about the "moon rockets," the orange-juice cans which she attached to her head with bobby pins after washing her hair, and the heated iron with which she attempted to straighten her curls.

She might be a teenybopper, but she also did an elegant experiment with genetically obese brown mice, blubbery little rodents kept in the basement near the incinerator in cages with clicking treadmills, proving conclusively that if you overfed them they exercised less, and if you underfed them, they exercised more, and hence would be less likely to develop cardiac disease. From her we learned about teenage life, about crushes and moods, and the cruelty of cliques in an all-girls high school. Later on, the family spent summers at Camp Wigwam in Maine, where Mom was camp doctor, taking a month or so off from her work in Cleveland, and Kathy met Tom, a counselor and canoe instructor who had grown up in Maine, and we saw our first evidence of the transformative power of love.

Jonny was always known as the "monkey" of the family. Even as a baby, he was extraordinarily active and mechanically minded, beginning at the age of six months to climb out of his crib, as well as unscrew its wooden panels. Dad would joke that once when we went to the zoo we had mistakenly left our little brother there and come back with one of the monkeys from the monkey house. Yet Jon struggled with schoolwork, having difficulty learning to read because his mind could not clearly distinguish "was" from "saw." He got extra tutoring after school and on weekends, and Dad would stay up late at night to help him finish essays and compositions in junior high and high school. Despite these difficulties, he loved research.

Whereas I was a reluctant visitor to Dad's laboratory, Jon was in his element there, making friends with the lab technicians or getting the firefighters to demonstrate their equipment to him, or conducting a study to determine the physical fitness of high-school students.

Jonny and I were buddies, despite our opposite temperaments, and we spent many afternoons playing tennis at the Roxboro Junior High School courts, which had once hosted a Davis Cup tournament, or bicycling the twenty-mile round trip to Squire Valley View or to the polo fields. In high school, we bought a car together, a beat-up 1964 blue Buick Skylark, and on weekend nights we would go "burger-cruising" up and down Mayfield Boulevard with our friends Parker and Packer, seeking out six-packs of 3.2 beer and picking fights with "greasers," sometimes having narrow escapes, careening down dark side streets with headlights off.

As a kid, Danny, the youngest of the three boys, was a cute little curly-headed kid with a cheerful temperament. We called him "Daniel the cocker spaniel." He was always telling jokes, and Dad said he was the spitting image of Uncle Alex Zeiger, his mother's brother, except that Uncle Alex had red hair. Danny decided at an early age that he wanted to own a sports car convertible, and also that he was a Republican, neither of these being popular decisions in a family that owned rattletrap Corvairs and Rambler station wagons, and whose politics, except for Mom, were slightly to the left of the Democratic Party.

Susan was a skinny, serious, freckle-faced little girl with long, curly brown hair often braided in pigtails, and a tendency to break into goosebumps if you snuck up behind her and yelled "Boo!" Our family had a distressing habit of losing her on trips. Once in southern Ohio we accidentally forgot her at a motel; another time, when she was seven or eight years old, we left her behind at a Stuckey's Restaurant on an interstate highway somewhere in Pennsylvania. Half a mile down the highway, we realized there were only five children in the car, and Dad sent me running back along the shoulder, and he fishtailed after me, backing up the exit ramp. When we found Susie, she was nonplussed as ever.

Beth was the baby, four years younger than Susan, and even Jonny was nice to her.

Summers we went away, to Michigan or Canada or Maine. Whereas in Cleveland Mom was in the background, overshadowed by Dad and the other men, in Maine her doctoring came into its own. Dad stayed in Ohio, coming up for a week or so at the end of camp, and Mom was the camp doctor. Mom and the girls stayed in a farmhouse outside Camp Wigwam's front entrance. In a cabin down by Bear Pond, Mom treated strep throats, impetigo, influenza, sprained ankles, and she had a few cots to isolate infectious campers. Once, when the entire camp came down with severe abdominal cramps and diarrhea, Mom studied the epidemic, watching the farmboys working in the kitchen. She concluded that it came from the lukewarm water they used to clean the dishes, which did not kill bacteria from their none-too-clean hands, and indeed, after they were taught to wash with soap and water and the dishwater temperature was increased to 140 degrees, we recovered.

Then everything changed.

It hit Ohio about 1970. All at once, we were growing our hair long and wearing torn, patched jeans and tie-dyed T-shirts, listening to Jimi Hendrix and The Doors and Janis Joplin. Kids quit the swimming and basketball teams and began wandering in the woods near school, smoking pot or getting drunk on Boone's Farm Apple Wine. They began dropping out of high school, and taking hashish and uppers and downers, and getting hepatitis, and dying of overdoses—and suicide.

It was the local manifestation of the world's new madness. In 1968 alone, there was the North Vietnamese offensive, and the American counteroffensive, and then the assassination of Martin Luther King, Jr., and Robert Kennedy. French students were rioting, and Richard Nixon was elected President. In 1969 Americans walked on the moon, and Americans gathered on a Woodstock farm's endless muddy field, and there was the March on Washington, and crowds of hundreds of thousands, and millions of war protesters. Everywhere one looked, protest filled the streets. Even Dr. Benjamin Spock, Mom's former colleague from the Family Clinic, was being prosecuted for his antiwar activities! The Chicago 7 were put on trial, and the draft lottery began, the first draft since World War II.

We trembled, waiting for our numbers, making plans should we draw below 100. In 1970, my junior year of high school, four unarmed students were shot dead by the National Guard during protests at Kent State University. So what if Nixon pledged to bring home 140,000 troops? Who trusted him, who could trust any authority? Suddenly, everything was madness, every predetermined order was shaken forever.

Another nighttime scene, only a few years later, shook the predetermined order of my life. It was late evening, spring of freshman year at college, and after an evening chemistry lab at the Mallinckrodt Laboratory I started bicycling back to my dormitory in Harvard Yard. I'd been working since dinnertime, revising a program that simulated a chemical reaction, shuffling a stack of keypunched IBM cards that fed into a rumbling computer the size of a Ford Fairlane; finally I'd gotten it working.

To my surprise, I found the Yard's iron gate locked. I could see the dark outline of my dormitory, a looming mass of ivy-covered red brick, inaccessible.

I turned right, bicycling around the underpass toward the Harvard Square subway station and the Harvard Coop, since the Yard's front entrance never closed. The street was oddly deserted. There were no cars, not one pedestrian. Rounding the corner, I saw something that made no sense at all, that turned the dreamlike spring evening into a nightmare.

There, in front of the Cambridge Trust Bank and curving along Massachusetts Avenue to the Out of Town News kiosk on the traffic island where you went down into the T, stood a line of motionless helmeted figures, nightsticks held before them. You couldn't even see their faces, only the glare of red off their face masks and riot shields.

That was when I realized that dozens of students were hanging out of windows giving onto the Yard or clinging to the wrought-iron fence, silently watching. Then I saw police dogs.

I kept going, pedaling steadily the wrong way down the one-way street, the only moving object, until the dark shadow of Lamont Library appeared. On Quincy Street, just before the Freshman Union, I turned, and discovered the one gate that was open. Two City of Cambridge policemen stood guard, and after a few questions, they let me in.

My roommate—an economist's son from Washington, D.C., who never hesitated to let me know how much more sophisticated he was than I—came back very late that night, utterly exhilarated. The Harvard Center for International Affairs had been trashed. Fires had been set, records destroyed. The riot was about South Africa, he told me, and apartheid, and the CIA, and Vietnam, too. What had happened in '68 in Paris, in '69 in Cambridge and in New York and across the country, intimations of revolution, finally was coming to fruition. Right here, right now.

At 3 a.m. we were awakened by footsteps bounding up the stairs, by fists pounding on doors. My roommate jumped out of bed, and I heard loud whispering, and then he pulled on his clothes and ran out. I tried to sleep. I was not to see him again for days.

The next morning, the news was that Harvard President Derek Bok's office in Massachusetts Hall had been occupied by protesters. A cordon of police surrounded Mass Hall, and soon hundreds of protesters began to circle the Yard in the cold drizzle, chanting "Harvard out of South Africa!" and hundreds of candles flickered in the rain. My friends and I watched out the windows for hours, and then, almost reluctantly, joined them, shivering in our ponchos. A man in a trench coat stood near Massachusetts Hall, camera in hand, and every time you passed by, he snapped your picture. Rumors were that he was CIA.

Soon a general strike was called throughout the university. Students for a Democratic Society, the SDS, resurrected, called angry meetings in Sanders Theater. My roommate derided me for attending classes. How could I think of grades, of medicine and doctoring, when the corrupt old world was ending, when the new green order was beginning?

What did all this have to do with medicine? Everything! Indeed, who could study when the world was exploding in chaos? What was the point of cautious experimentation, of carefully observing symptoms and calculating medication dosages? Hadn't science itself led to so much oppression? The "science" of napalm-incinerated children and defoliated jungles, of the hydrogen bomb and the intercontinental ballistic missile and the B-1 bomber? Who cared about reducing arteriosclerotic plaque in the arteries of middle-aged businessmen, or taming the growth of cancer cells, when the world's very survival was at stake?

It was the return of a question from childhood, with a new urgency. When I was thirteen, my doubts had been assuaged by admiration for my father and his work; now they were multiplied by world events. I had changed—outwardly, I had been transformed by a summer of canoeing at North Woods Camp in Ontario, and by hundreds of miles of competitive high-school swimming; and intellectually I had left behind the complacent comfort of the Midwest for an Eastern university town.

I now returned to see my hometown for what it had become: a disaster. The city that in my grandfather's day had been the fifth largest in the country, a booming center of steel and iron and rubber production, of car and truck manufacturing, the city that had been the birthplace of some of America's greatest fortunes, Andrew Carnegie's and

John D. Rockefeller's among them, that had been called the Forest City and "the best location in the nation," now suffered from declining American industry, from unemployment and malaise, and crime and drugs. Its steel mills and machine works were idle, hulks of rusty iron and broken glass. Lake Erie was polluted, its fish dying. The city was famous now for its burning river, the Cuyahoga, which regularly ignited from industrial effluents released by factories along its banks.

My best friend from high school, who had a low draft number, spent his time smoking marijuana, sitting in a little cabin in the woods, utterly incoherent. Another friend was drinking. Two kids I'd known from high school had crashed their cars and died. Another, a talented poet, was in and out of mental hospitals, having tried to kill himself.

Now, when I came home for vacations, Dad would tell me about the National Heart Disease and Exercise Project. It was much more rigorous than Dad's earlier studies. There were five centers, including the central site at George Washington University in Washington, D.C., and four collaborating centers, including Dad's lab in Cleveland. There had been a year in which methods were standardized between sites, and equipment was calibrated, and technicians were trained, and criteria for selecting patients were set. Once the patients entered the study, they all went through six weeks of low-level exercise training, one hour three times a week. All were given the same messages about the importance of not smoking, and of changing their diets to include less salt, saturated fats, and cholesterol. Then the patients were randomly divided into two groups: half to start a rigorous exercise program carefully monitored by physicians, and the other half to be a "non-intervention" group, not encouraged to exercise.

Once I would have been excited by this study, but now the busy lives of Mom and Dad and their doctor friends became a cruel joke, a naïve palliative. Home for a visit, I found myself reverting to adolescent indolence, reading half the night and sleeping until midafternoon—or worse, returning to mute childhood, and grudgingly agreeing to join Dad for a game of chess or to meet him down at the hospital to see his latest exercise equipment, the computerized bicycle ergometer that you could program to ride up and down foothills in the Rockies, or following him on hospital rounds late at night, unshaven, a white coat pulled over my flannel shirt and patched jeans. One night at the hospital, Dad and I bumped into my old friend Jimmy Baumann, sitting in a wheelchair, gaunt and despairing. He had just returned from India, where he had contracted typhoid, and now he had hepatitis from shooting heroin. At home, under Dad's spell, I became the obedient shadow, and was nothing; when I rebelled, and rejected entirely the future mapped out for me since childhood, then I was totally at a loss.

It was not just me. Family life had suddenly become unpleasant for all of us. Jonny had grown his hair long, and became sullen and angry, staying out all night. I heard little Susie breaking into impassioned arguments with Dad, over issues I never quite understood. Dad suddenly seemed insistent, tyrannical, strident. It was even worse in my cousins' house. My cousin Mark, eldest son of Dad's younger brother, Earl (a pathologist at Harvard), had always been, like me, predestined to a life in medicine. But Mark now dropped out of school and, when last heard from, was heading west, hitchhiking to parts unknown. Rumors were that two of Mark's younger brothers had dropped out of high school.

College, medical school, residency, war. We had always expected to be doctors in a war—like Dad. What kind of war was this, though, flashing across TV screens? In dreams, my brothers and sisters and I were still in the same place. Little shadows in white coats, trotting obediently along hospital corridors, we hurried to keep up with the bigger figures before us. But now we headed toward a nightmare. The life of doctoring and research, a life not unlike Dad's and Papa's—building on the work of all the past generations of doctors—now seemed inconceivable to us all.

Nixon was bombing North Vietnam, and soon duplicitous Kissinger was going to Paris to negotiate with the North Vietnamese. In January 1973, the Paris Peace Agreement was signed, providing for withdrawal from a ruined country.

That summer, instead of returning home to work in a research lab, I lived with Lisa Perry, my girlfriend from college, and several other students in a run-down section of Cambridge. I did odd jobs, carpentry and yard work, and interviewed small-claims-court litigants for a Japanese professor. I wrote short stories and much of a novel. And I wrote a letter to the dean's office at Harvard, requesting a leave of absence, time indefinite.

In the fall, when classes started again, I drove cross-country with my oldest sister, Kathryn, who was starting graduate school in English at Stanford University, and after staying with her for a few days, I found a room in an apartment in the Castro District of San Francisco. I worked as a busboy in a downtown restaurant that doubled as a bookie joint; I did door-to-door consumer testing for Adolph's Meat Tenderizer; I rode a heavy yellow bicycle for the Speedy Messenger Service, going up and down the steep San Francisco hills, delivering packages from one business to another. I dated a Vietnamese refugee, an artist, who lived in Chinatown with her radical cousin who hated all whites and wouldn't even say hello to me. At night I hung out in North Beach with other would-be writers, drinking cheap red wine, and I found myself by third-hand invitation at parties in vast marijuana-scented Potrero Hill lofts, and walked home at 3 a.m. through the Mission District's diesel fumes. Downstairs from me lived two pleasant young women, part-time prostitutes, and when one of them delivered a baby, I visited her at the hospital, bearing flowers, and was universally mistaken for the father.

That year my father came through San Francisco several times on his way to give medical lectures. He made polite small talk with my roommates, an unmarried couple, and Rosa, a single mother with a one-year-old baby. Each time he let me know of the doctors over at University of California Medical School in San Francisco who would be glad to put me to work in their laboratories: all I had to do was ask. The forced conviviality of these visits broke down every so often into sullen silence (mine) and rejected help (his); fortunately, they would end soon enough, and he drove his rental car back to the airport on his way home to Cleveland or on to San Diego. Then I was on my own again, back to the manuscripts I hoped would make my name.

I had renounced all family expectations, and was doing exactly what I wanted to do. Naturally, I was miserable. It wasn't just the starvation wages; and it wasn't the frustrations of innumerable rejection slips, since I knew that was all necessary for me to become a writer. It was something else.

In the spring of 1975, not long after North Vietnamese tanks and troops overran Saigon, ending the war, I again wrote to the dean's office, indicating that I was interested in coming back to Cambridge to complete my senior year. That fall (still uncertain), I submitted applications to medical schools, and went around the country interviewing for positions. Despite the dubious activities of my junior year off, I was accepted by several schools. That winter, Dad had a serious emergency. While in his hospital laboratory, he suffered an acute episode of chest pain, and had the presence of mind to phone the cardiac-surgery suite to let them know that he had a patient in urgent need of a bypass procedure, and that the patient was himself. He successfully underwent an operation that restored circulation to his heart muscle. It was the middle of finals when I found out about this, hearing his woozy voice as he phoned from a hospital ward, post-operatively, to tell me that everything was all right.

He was fine by the time I graduated.

All summer, I debated whether or not to go to medical school. Finally I decided that I had no choice but to give medicine a try. The bottom line was this: I did want to be a doctor. Perhaps not the kind my family wanted me to be, not a third generation of cardiology researchers, but a doctor nevertheless.

It would be a decade or more before I knew whether I had made the right decision.

9

TRAINING YEARS: 1976–1988

IT was 1976, the Bicentennial year. Fireworks lit the sky, tricolor bunting was everywhere, and tall ships filled New York Harbor when, a college graduate, I returned to California to begin medical school. I drove cross-country through a seeming time warp: when I arrived at Stanford University Medical School, the entire town of Palo Alto, if not the state of California, seemed to belong to a new century.

In the cautious East, the theories of Dad and his fellow cardiologists about exercise and diet still met with skepticism. Since the 1964 release of the Surgeon General's report on tobacco and health, some Americans had begun to stop smoking, and a few health fanatics avoided dietary cholesterol and spent their Sunday afternoons jogging along the Charles River, or swimming laps in neighborhood pools. In California's sunny flatlands, though, the cardiologists' warnings and prescriptions had joined seamlessly with the local culture to create what could only be described as a "great awakening." The post-Vietnam era was a recovery of body, not spirit, a time of prayers to the sensual ecstasy of muscle and sweat, not for the salvation of the immortal soul.

It was the summer of the yogurt cone—a seductive metamorphosis of the bland but healthy "ice milk" with which my brothers and sisters and I had grown up. In Cambridge, we had gone to Elsie's Diner for greasy cheeseburgers and submarine sandwiches. In Palo Alto, the Good Earth Restaurant served huge salads topped with alfalfa sprouts and fresh basil and shiitake mushrooms, and morels and radicchio. Soy-soaked tofu had practically replaced red meat as a source of protein, and bread teemed with healthful bran and seeds. Californians not only embraced healthy food—their religious passion extended to exercise. Back east, exercise meant deadening hours jogging around and around the gymnasium floor, or an endless thud and whir of feet on the treadmill. Here, bicyclists on ultra-light ten-speeds whizzed along the roads, shadowed by palm trees and huge eucalyptus trees, and flew up into the foothills to commune among redwood groves. Half a mile from the medical school there was a fifty-meter outdoor swimming pool with a grassy bank along one side, where my medical classmates lay sunning after class, idly turning pages of histology or biochemistry textbooks, then popping in to swim a few dozen laps.

I found a place to live, as roommate to three biology graduate students, and I registered for medical school. Classes began. Just as California culture had changed, wholeheartedly incorporating medical advances, so, too, I soon realized, had medical school been transformed. Like Mom and Dad, I began dissecting cadavers on the first day of anatomy class; like them, I studied pathology, physiology, and bacteriology; but Stanford Medical School in 1976 could hardly have been more different than Western Reserve in the late 1930s. I knew all too well Dad's old stories about confronting his cruel medical-school professors back before World War II, his brave moments with anti-Semitic deans. Dad still relived the brutal competition of his medical-school days, where a third of the first-year class flunked out. In contrast, classes at Stanford Medical School were pass-fail. Our professors assured us that we had been so well selected at the time of admission that there was no reason for *any* of us to flunk.

I could not even take refuge in minority status. Perhaps a third of my class was Jewish, and I was much more likely to be lumped together with WASPs as a "white male," one of the privileged elite, than to be seen as a member of a discriminated-against minority. Even women could not claim that role—they constituted thirty-five percent of my class. Beleaguered ethnicity status belonged to the half-dozen black students, to the handful of Mexican-Americans, to the sole American Indian.

The defining moments of my first years of medical school were thus entirely different from what Dad and Mom led me to expect. There was physical-diagnosis class, when students were required to perform physical examinations on one another; when the women in our class protested that this violated their privacy and undermined their professionalism, the exercise was made optional. Examining one's tanned, attractive lab partner was hardly the harrowing med-school experience most of us had feared. Neither was the course on human sexuality, for which we were lectured by a professed sadist wearing a scarlet three-piece suit, and by nudists and wife swappers and sex therapists, and which culminated in a two-day marathon of pornographic movies of every kind of sexual activity known to the human animal, an exhibition intended to desensitize us to forbidden topics, but one that, at least according to my observation of eighty-five classmates, had other, unanticipated effects. One warm night freshman year, one of the deans gave our class a party at his big old mansion on the Stanford campus. Beneath eucalyptus and palm trees, we drank beer and surreptitiously smoked pot from hand-rolled joints. By midnight, half of our class was naked—shadowy white bodies playing volleyball in the pool, or lounging in the Jacuzzi, wineglasses in hand, as warm steam rose into the California night.

More important surprises came in medical-school classes. Nothing could have prepared us for the tidal wave of medical knowledge that washed over us for six to ten hours every day, for the endless hours of frantic note-taking in darkened amphitheaters. If I thought I knew about medical advances from Dad and his fellow cardiologists, biochemistry soon disabused me of that notion. Only fifteen years earlier (1962), James D. Watson, Francis H. C. Crick, and Maurice H. F. Wilkins had won the Nobel Prize for decoding the structure of DNA, the double helix of chains of "nucleotides," molecules which determine the genetic code.

Consequently, it had become possible not only to determine the exact chemical structure of proteins, their sequences of amino acids and their three-dimensional shape, but also to know the precise structure of the genes that coded for them. In 1949 Linus Pauling had decoded the structure of hemoglobin, which allowed the blood to carry oxygen. It was a "tetramer," a collection of four chains of peptide molecules connected to heme molecules, a compound whose unique structure allowed it easily to bind oxygen in the lungs and to release it throughout the body. But now biochemists could pinpoint the exact gene defects leading to hemoglobin diseases. In sickle-cell anemia, a mutation replacing a single amino acid of hemoglobin made red blood cells fragile and liable to collapse, thus leading to a host of medical complications. Specific abnormalities in protein structure and thus genes had been identified in many other hereditary diseases, from albinism to infantile diabetes to hemophilia, from porphyria to Tay-Sachs disease.

Nobel Prize–winning biochemists stood before our freshman medical-school class, outlining the complex pathway of energy through the body, teaching us intricate details of oxidation, reduction, phosphorylation, and about enzymes and coenzymes, and about the miraculous double-sided structure of cell membranes. They sketched the structure of bacterial genes, and demonstrated how bacteriophages, tiny viruses made of DNA or RNA, could be used to transplant genes from one strain of bacteria to another, and even to copy or clone human genes into bacterial cells. Soon scientists would be able to correct genetic defects.

Biochemistry was just the beginning. Advances in immunology and pathology and anatomy and physiology were equally amazing. Everywhere we looked, there was another new field to master, another telephone-book-size text to memorize, another series of complex mathematical formulas to decipher. Professors routinely began their lectures by saying, "What I am going to talk about today is the most important thing you're going to learn in medical school"—so that, before the first semester's end, we routinely broke into laughter before they finished their sentence. We laughed, but we never knew: Was the next hour of lectures indeed the most important one of our education, the one we could not afford to miss?

On entering the hospital wards in our third year, we were even more disoriented. We saw common diseases at the VA Hospital in the Palo Alto foothills and at the Santa Clara Valley Medical Center down in San Jose—diabetic ketoacidosis, gastric ulcers, malignant hypertension, head trauma, alcoholism. Even these run-of-the-mill cases could become unexpectedly complex, requiring placement of Swan Ganz catheters, and central venous lines, and calculation of the acid-base status of a patient in metabolic alkalosis complicated by respiratory acidosis, or any of a number of other complications of multisystem failure.

It was at the main Stanford Medical Center, though, that we saw the most astonishing evidences of medicine's new high technology. On my oncology sub-internship, I saw how one of our professors, Dr. Henry S. Kaplan, had virtually singlehandedly defeated Hodgkin's disease. Previously, this type of lymphoma, or tumor of the lymph glands, had nearly always been fatal. Now, by an elaborate medical and surgical workup, including dissection of many of the body's lymph nodes and removal of the spleen, as well as extensive X rays and blood tests, Dr. Kaplan had made it possible for doctors to determine the precise stage of a patient's disease, and then to target treatment to the diseased organs by highly focused "total nodal" irradiation, or by cocktails of chemotherapy—Cytoxan, Methotrexate, cis-platinum. For one patient I saw, a beautiful young woman with long red hair, advanced Hodgkin's disease was totally cured by irradiation. If her disease had struck a decade earlier, she would be dead. The day I examined her, the only signs of disease were the well-healed surgical scars on her abdomen, and her matter-of-fact discussion of the fact that she could never have children, since radiation treatments had made her sterile.

Night and day we inhabited the huge Medical Center building, and we came to know its endless hallways and windblown courtyards and vending machines and intensive-care units and operating rooms the way we were coming to know the human body. Many weekends we spent in the library, looking out at the shimmering green of wind blowing through the trees, hearing the endless twittering of unseen flocks of birds, looking up periodically from our stack of photocopied reprints as blue patches of untouchable sky turned dark with the coming of night, and many nights we were awake on the hospital corridors, seeing one shift of nurses leave and the next arrive. With the barest of skills, we grappled to understand the medical universe we would have to face for the next fifty years, and we struggled, like centuries of doctors before us, to claim a part of it for ourselves.

It was not only an education in scientific triumphs, though. There were also ample indications of crisis. We knew, for instance, that medical costs were rising dramatically by the late 1970s: from annual expenditures of $27.1 billion in 1960, spending had increased to $132.9 billion by 1975, going from 5.3 percent of the gross national product to 8.3 percent. All indications were that it would soon top ten percent. We saw the newest 1970s technology—the CT scanner, which exemplified the dilemmas of modern medicine. By use of computers, and a low-intensity X-ray beam that rotated around the body, the CT scan created three-dimensional images of the body—not only of bones and fluid-filled cavities, but of soft tissues such as muscle and fat as well. Our professors flashed up slides of indistinct images from conventional X rays, then the new CT scans, in which tumors and hemorrhages were outlined with unprecedented clarity. We watched, realizing that the CT scanner was, no doubt, only one of many astonishing machines to be introduced during our lives as doctors. The internist or surgeon could now direct treatment with remarkable specificity and precision. Yet each CT scanner cost a million dollars, and every hospital wanted one: how would it be financially possible to provide CT scanners for everyone? And yet, how could any modern hospital do without?

This dilemma was raised not only by CT scanners but by any number of new technologies and new procedures. The same debate applied to the coronary-artery bypass grafting, and to the care of terminally ill patients in intensive-care units who could be kept alive almost indefinitely even when brain-dead. Then there was the issue of transplantation. Kidneys, and livers, and hearts, and lungs, and corneas, and bone marrow, and skin—by 1976, all could be transplanted from one human being to another. What did that mean for the inevitability of death? And the cost of prolonging life? Obviously, the answers of Dad and Mom's colleagues, the World War II generation, were insufficient. In their eyes, science had always been an end in itself—the doctor's role was to produce science, to create better treatments, and society's role was to find a way to pay for them. But as our generation entered medical school and residency, it was becoming painfully obvious that scientific advances invariably created dilemmas. The benefits of any one advance were often immediately apparent, but its costs and complications might not be known for years.

The most difficult lessons often came unexpectedly and were unaccompanied by exam questions or by explanations from learned professors. One afternoon during my first year of medical school, as some friends and I were returning from the hospital cafeteria to the medical library, we heard screaming from down the hall. There was a commotion, and a Code Team—the doctors, nurses, and technicians assigned to resuscitate patients on an emergency basis—rushed past us onto one of the medical floors. They entered a patient's room and we could hear their frantic activity. We were still too ignorant to be any help, but we could not bring ourselves to leave. We watched a distraught woman, wailing in anguish, led along the hallway by a nurse, who was also in tears, leaving bloody footprints down the hall.

The next day we found out what had happened. The patient was a young woman, a twenty-five-year-old schoolteacher in the late stages of recovery from myasthenia gravis, a disorder that causes paralysis of the voluntary muscles. For several weeks she had been on a respirator. While her mother was visiting, a nurse came in to change the intubation tube in her throat. When the tube was removed, bleeding had suddenly begun—a rush of arterial blood. Perhaps the wall of an artery had been eroded by constant contact with the plastic tube, or perhaps the nurse pulled too hard and nicked the vessel wall. A Code was called; and, with the patient's terrified mother watching, surgeons arrived and tried to stop the bleeding, even cutting open the young woman's chest in a frantic effort to tie off the torn vessel. But they failed, and the young woman died, drowning in her own blood.

Not long afterward I had another eerie experience, this time astonishing rather than disconcerting. As a third-year medical student I chose an elective rotation on the cardio-vascular-surgery service run by Dr. Norman Shumway. Every morning I awoke at 4:00 a.m. and bicycled to the Medical Center, where I changed into surgical greens, ready for a day in the operating room. We did innumerable coronary-artery bypass operations, and replaced defective heart valves. We even stood by (somewhat derisively) one day as the radiologists tried a brand-new procedure, called "angioplasty," developed by Swiss doctor Andreas R. Grüntzig. In angioplasty, a guide wire is snaked from the femoral artery in the groin up into the heart. A catheter with a tiny deflated balloon at its tip is passed over the guide wire and into the heart. Then the tiny balloon is inflated, opening up the narrowed coronary artery.

One day I stood in the operating suite, tottering atop three metal stools like some character out of Dr. Seuss, watching Dr. Shumway transplant a heart. From my unsteady perch I peered down into the operative field, as Dr. Shumway clamped the aorta and the heart-lung machine took over the circulatory functions. I watched as the diseased, fatty heart was removed and dropped into a basin. Then I gazed into the patient's empty chest and was overcome with a profound, even visceral sense of shock. This empty space, this heart cavity without a heart, belonged to a human being who was still alive. Indeed, this was miraculous. At the same time, I realized, as the new heart was sewn in, with big looping stitches—not a technically difficult procedure, almost akin to repairing a sail—replacing a heart was oddly prosaic. The new heart, warming, soon began to beat, the chest was closed and the patient was wheeled out of the operating room to begin an uneventful recovery.

I was the first of our generation to begin medical school, the first of the children to confront the dilemmas and opportunities of late-twentieth-century American medicine, but each of my brothers and sisters had to confront the same legacy. We were all of us shadowed by the past, by a legacy we could sense every waking moment, but whose enormity we could not entirely comprehend. In its most tangible form, it took the shape of Dad's reputation. His cardiology colleagues or enemies would buttonhole us at medical lectures or on hospital wards and, unasked, tell us how much they admired Herman Hellerstein, and how, if you looked at any aspect of cardiology, you'd find that he wrote the first ten papers in that field. Or they'd let us know how he had enraged and humiliated them by his response to a question at a national conference, telling an audience of a thousand that theirs was the stupidest question he had ever heard, and giving five reasons why.

Each of the six of us responded differently to this legacy. My reaction took the form of a stubborn insistence that I would continue my efforts to become a writer. Thus, while my classmates at Stanford Medical School might spend evenings and weekends in biochemistry or neurophysiology laboratory, whenever I got a free moment I would bicycle over to the English Department, where, with the assistance of my sister Kathryn, I had talked my way into the fiction graduate writing program. There I met Tobias Wolff, and Allan Gurganus, and Ron Hansen, and Harriet Doerr, and Vikram Seth, and other writers. This was before any of them had written the books for which they have become well known—*This Boy's Life, Oldest Living Confederate Widow Tells All, A Stone for Ibarra, The Golden Gate,* and others. I came from dissecting cadavers, with powder from rubber gloves on my hands and the smell of formalin in my hair, and spent afternoons under the direction of Professor L'Heureux or Professor Scowcroft, dissecting short stories or the latest chapter of somebody's novel. Later, perhaps after sharing a pitcher of beer at The Oasis bar down on El Camino Real, I would hop back on my bicycle, the heavy texts in my backpack making me sway unsteadily across the road as I headed back to the med-school library for an evening of parasitology, histology, and renal physiology. I did not know then which part of medicine might be right for me, but I knew it must be a field in which the writer in me would not have to die.

Indeed, for all six of us, our family's medical heritage was like that heavy backpack full of books, making us sway as we went through life. This was true even for the two who did not become M.D.s, my older sister, Kathryn, and my brother Jonathan. They opted not to become doctors for different reasons, but they, too, were deeply marked by our family's past.

During these years of training, of uncertainty and sleepless nights, I particularly envied Kathryn. She seemed free of any obligation or desire to become a physician—she was free to follow other interests. Whether it was because she was a daughter and I was the oldest son, or whether she had just made her talents and preferences known from an early age, there was never any expectation that she would carry on the family medical tradition.

Kathryn did her share of science projects in junior high school, and she spent a college summer down at Dad's office collecting and collating his hundreds of scientific publications into several thick blue-bound volumes, but it was clear that her heart was elsewhere. After high school, Kathy spent a summer at Harvard Summer School, and then went to Wellesley, where language and poetry gave new meaning to what had often seemed mere moodiness. Encouraged by her professors, she began writing poetry, and studying literature, and submitting poems for publication, and even though she was miserable enough at Wellesley that she transferred to Brandeis after two years, she had gained something in Waltham, Massachusetts—a sense of her talents as a writer. After college, she was admitted to the Stanford University graduate program in creative writing, in the poetry program. I followed her out to California twice, once when I was taking a year off from college, and again after being admitted to medical school.

After she finished her Masters in Fine Arts in poetry, she transferred into the English Department's Ph.D. program. Rather than choosing to write her dissertation on T. S. Eliot or Faulkner or Joyce, or delving into then-becoming-fashionable semiotics or deconstruction, she became passionate about Yiddish literature, particularly about the poetry written in Yiddish by immigrants to America in the early twentieth century. A Yiddish poet named Malkah Heifetz Tussman who lived in Berkeley, a woman in her seventies who had been part of the Yiddish renaissance half a century before, began to teach Kathryn the language and to help her translate poems from Yiddish to English. On visits home to Cleveland, Kathy would collect Yiddish books from the houses and apartments of elderly immigrants, often Dad's patients, cartons of dusty, irreplaceable treasures. She wrote her Ph.D. dissertation on Moshe-Leyb Halpern, one of the leading immigrant Yiddish poets in New York, and in 1982 she published a book of translations of his poems, called *In New York*. As she became active in writing papers, poems, and translations and critical essays, she was led also to observant Judaism.

Similarly, Jonny decided not to get an M.D. In college at

Macalester, in Minnesota, Jonny developed an interest in environmental sciences. During summers, he worked at the Case Western Reserve University Dental School, assisting in research projects, and Dad tried to convince him to become a dentist. But Jon had decided on environmental sciences, and began graduate school at the University of Minnesota. After earning his degree, he married Peggy Atwood, a nurse-practitioner who had grown up in Mankato, Minnesota, and they moved back to Cleveland. After Papa moved into a nursing home, Jon and Peggy bought Nana and Papa's house on Ardleigh Drive. Jon went to work replacing rotten timbers and cracked stucco in the Tudor façade, and replastering the textured ceilings of the living room and dining room. In the kitchen, he sanded cabinets and molding down to bare wood, and stripped layers of paint off brass fittings. Upstairs, in one of the maid's rooms, he installed pipes and put in a laundry. Finally, the house looked new—no doubt, better even than when Nana and Papa finished building it in 1924.

At his job, Jon began to work to set standards for levels of toxins in synthetic compounds, such as sealants and roofing materials, and to evaluate workers' exposure to such compounds during manufacturing and construction processes. I always saw his work as being rather distant from medicine, but when I began writing this book, and questioned Dad about his studies of firefighters and factory workers, the connection became clear to me: in a way, Jonny became a healer of the environment, working to decrease health risks in the work world.

Four of us were to become doctors. My other brother, Daniel, and the two youngest girls, Susan and Elizabeth, all chose medicine, and each was to map out a different territory to call his or her own.

Danny, the youngest boy, always had a keen sense of

market forces. He chose to go to college at Vassar shortly after it became coeducational, when the female-to-male ratio was more than ten to one. He majored in economics, and after graduating in 1979, he was tempted to go to Wall Street to earn his fortune, but he could not turn his back on medicine. He became the fifth generation of the family to enter medical school at Case Western Reserve University. When it came time to choose a specialty, his decision was hardly a surprise. On our marathon drives from Cleveland to Canada and back, our family always passed through Niagara Falls, New York. As we walked across the puddled concrete of the promenade, and approached the misty edge of the Falls, and looked down into the surging chasm, Danny, age four or five, always had one response: to clutch his knees together and insist that Dad take him to the bathroom immediately. To this day Daniel insists that his acute experience of the "oculo-urologic" response led him to urology, a field of medicine that no one in the family had ever considered, and one, incidentally, in which buying a red sports car convertible is well within one's financial means.

Much younger than Kathy and Jon and I, Susie was still a little kid when I left home. Immersed in my own concerns in Boston and Palo Alto, I knew only the outlines of her life, her fights with Dad over issues of which I was unaware. In college at Brown University, Susan majored in literature and society, and took pre-medical courses. She was torn between becoming a doctor and getting a Ph.D. in comparative literature, and in the third year of college, 1979–80, she went to France and studied at the Sorbonne and at L'Institute des Etudes Politiques. I visited her in Paris that year, my senior year of medical school, and found a self-possessed, beautiful young woman with long, curly brown hair and Katharine Hepburn features who had innumerable friends and who seemed to be comfortable just about anywhere on the face of the earth. She had an enormous collection of Parisian posters stripped off the side of kiosks, and thought nothing of hopping over the turnstile for a free ride on the Metro. She was taking courses in history, and in the exotic field of semiotics, struggling to decipher her professors' enigmatic pronouncements. The further her studies went, though, the more absurd and disconnected from reality they seemed. Kathryn was trying to finish her Ph.D. at that time, in the sixth or seventh year of what seemed like an endless effort, and the opportunities afterward seemed limited, to say the least.

The following summer Susan went to Poland and worked in a hospital in the city of Cracow, in the south of the country, not far from the border of Czechoslovakia. It was the summer of the Olympics, and the Solidarity movement was actively organizing strikes and demonstrations. She worked in a hospital, doing the tasks of a first-year Polish medical student—assisting nurses, taking blood pressures, bringing medications. She lived in a steel-mill town ten minutes by bus from Cracow. It was an exhilarating, frightening time. After stifling decades of Communism, the air was filled with talk about change. Every accepted value was being challenged, and books critical of the Polish system were being furtively circulated. News was hard to come by—there were no foreign newspapers, and her only sources of reliable information were telephone calls to Paris or the United States. By midsummer, a crisis loomed. There were reports of Soviet troops massing on the Polish border, preparing for invasion, and soon the foreigners began to leave.

Susan's year abroad had made the decision easy: after returning home and finishing college, she began medical school at University of California at San Francisco. The summer after her first year, she decided to go to Mexico. In France she had become friends with a group of Chilean exiles and had begun to learn Spanish, and she had taken

Spanish classes in college, so she found little difficulty in working at a cardiology institute in Mexico City. In her view, this was just a first step. The next was China. She began to prepare a grant application to study obstetrical care in the People's Republic.

During her third year of medical school, Susan took an intensive course at Berkeley in Mandarin, studying the language eight hours a day for two months, learning a thousand characters, and the basics of grammar. She took another semester of Mandarin in Chinatown that fall, and in the winter she went to China.

She began in Shijiazhung, an industrial city of about one million in northern China, about two hours by train southwest of Beijing. She was to spend three months working in the Hebei Provincial Hospital. In the entire city, there was only one other foreigner, a man teaching English at the local university. She worked with an elderly woman obstetrician-gynecologist, seeing outpatients, doing basic examinations, learning how to do abortions, and administering a questionnaire she had developed, which asked about women's attitudes toward China's one-child policy. Later, she began to work in the operating rooms, where regulations required that a certain percentage of operations be done under acupuncture. Conditions were primitive, and while Chinese doctors had sedative medications, and ether, and could do spinal blocks, they could not afford to use the inhaled anesthetics standardly used in the United States. Furthermore, acupuncture might be effective for local surgery, but did not work well for major abdominal operations.

She then spent three weeks with traditional Chinese doctors, who taught her traditional theories of medicine, and acupuncture, and techniques such as massage and moxibustion (the application of suction cups filled with steam and herbs), and began to learn to make diagnoses by feeling the pulse and looking at the patient's tongue. Next she went to the countryside, a provincial area outside Shijiazhung. The people there had never seen foreigners, and every morning, when she walked to work, hundreds would line the streets to watch her. There Susan worked with indigenous doctors, people with only about a year of medical training.

After that, she spent three months in cosmopolitan Shanghai, on China's coast south of Beijing, at the Second Medical College of Shanghai. She lived in a dormitory with other foreign medical students. There were many Africans there, students from Zaire and the Ivory Coast, and Arabs from Cyprus, Syria, Iraq. Susan had the strange experience of trying to get to know the Arabs through their only common language—Chinese. She worked on an obstetrical ward, and an endocrinology ward, and went on tours of many hospitals that referred patients to the Second Medical College hospital. Again she was struck by the dramatic differences in technology. While there were some incubators at the hospital, the doctors did not know how to use them. There was one fetal heart monitor, but it, too, was rarely used. The only treatments available for premature babies were oxygen, intravenous fluids, and a few antibiotics. The most commonly used antibiotic, gentamicin, was a highly toxic one that American doctors only used in resistant infections.

Then Susan's boyfriend, John Triedman, also a medical student, met her in Shanghai, and they set out to travel. They went to southwest China, to Kunming, Szechuan province, near the border of Burma and Laos, the Chinese part of the Golden Triangle, seeing the various tribal cultures living near the Mekong River, and then headed toward Tibet. She and John were planning to go overland to Katmandu, Nepal, but she began to have high fevers, which came in regular cycles. Most likely it was malaria. She treated herself with chloroquine and fansidar, antimalarial drugs, but had to return to the United States early.

The greatest shock in China was not the state of medicine, which was roughly comparable to American medicine in the 1920s or 1930s, but the different way in which the Chinese culture viewed the individual, as only existing in relation to the group. Her entire time in China, Susan could hardly be alone for five minutes. Privacy was unheard of, and her hosts were insulted if she expressed a desire for time by herself. Even more striking was the enormous impact of dense population, the vastness of a country in which every possible inch of land, every natural resource, was being used to support its enormous population. In such a world, China's much-criticized one-child policy seemed essential, even inevitable. While Susan had come to China expecting to witness late-term abortions and to hear about such drastic measures as infanticide (especially of baby girls), she found that IUD use was the norm, and that the vast preponderance of abortions were done early in pregnancy. If there was any common approximation of infanticide, it fell more under the category of neglect: parents would be slower to bring a sick baby girl to treatment than a sick baby boy.

After her return to San Francisco, Susan had six months of medical school to complete. She took courses on international health issues. And she began a project to study Norplant, a form of long-acting contraceptive, containing the hormone progesterone, that is implanted under a woman's skin. A logical, effective form of contraception, Norplant had been largely abandoned by drug companies, which feared being sued in the wake of multimillion-dollar lawsuits over complications of IUD use; thus, the study had to be funded by the Population Council. Susan interviewed black and Latino and white patients, to determine whether this form of contraception was acceptable to different groups of women, and found that there was a high level of satisfaction, regardless of the woman's background.

As Susan completed medical school, it seemed to me that the biggest problem she faced was whether any field of medicine could be broad enough to engage her interests.

Elizabeth, the baby of the family, was only eight years old when I left home for college; and on my visits home, I would see the little blond girl regularly transformed by time-lapse photography. When the time approached for her to decide on a career, she, like me, was uncertain whether to become a doctor. As a little girl, she followed Dad to the hospital a few times, but when she went into the coronary-care unit she tended to feel faint and need to sit down. Dad didn't take Beth or the other girls to the hospital in the middle of the night, as he had done with the boys, but Beth often would eat a second dinner with Dad when he came home from the hospital at 8 or 9 p.m. and hear about the lives he had saved that day.

Like the rest of us, Beth heard students and patients telephoning Dad and Mom at all hours of the day and night, the crises and solutions of a doctor's life. As the youngest child, she was at home during various family health crises—our grandmother's illness and death in 1979, Papa's gradual decline in health in the 1980s, and Mom and Dad's medical problems as they entered their sixties. Beth began college at Smith, our grandmother and mother's alma mater, but after two years decided she could not bear being at an all-women's college and transferred to Brown, where Susan was in school. Beth majored in geology and spent summers out west. One summer she went to Princeton's Yellowstone Big Horn Research Association in Montana to map geologic formations. She took classes, learning about synclines and anticlines, the folds of rock that had risen to form the vast Rockies, and she wandered over southwest Montana, and into the northeast entrance of Yellowstone, going down into the wildflower meadows of Wyoming. The next summer she worked for the U.S. Forest Service in Oregon, in an experimental forest. Her group went to Mt. St. Helens. They mapped flora and fauna that had begun coming back to the scorched landscape in the five years since the massive eruption, and they wandered through old growth stands at Mt. Rainier. She did not relish spending her life as a geologist, though, and the next year, after graduating from college, she tried medicine, as seen through the research lab.

She began to work in the laboratory of Dr. Joseph Ilan, a molecular biologist who was doing research on recombinant DNA. Using plasmids, they embarked on a laborious process of constructing a gene, which coded for a hormone called somatomedin C, or "insulin-like growth factor 1." The goal was to make genes that could turn on and off cell growth, and then to transplant them into living organisms. However exciting this was theoretically, much of the work itself was extremely tedious: adding one amino acid, washing the solution, adding another, washing, then another. Afterward, there was a purifying process, using electrophoresis on agar gels— that is, putting the solution on a gelatinous surface across which a weak electrical current runs, which causes molecules with different electrical charges to move different distances along the gel. The experimenter sees different bands on the gel, corresponding to different-sized fragments of molecules that have been synthesized, and can select the desired one.

Beth liked research, and she appreciated the significance of the possible applications of their work—for diabetes, or for cancer. Dr. Ilan spoke of how in a type of children's brain tumors, glioblastoma, a "reverse" growth factor could potentially be inserted to stop the tumor from growing. But, like Mom forty years earlier, Beth could not imagine a career focused solely on research. Before the end of her year of molecular biology, she applied to medical school. She was admitted to several—Case Western Reserve, Ohio State, Boston University, Tufts—but chose to go to Case

Western Reserve because of its nontraditional educational philosophy, and because it admitted many older students, who had done other things with their lives besides take pre-medical courses.

As the four of us began to make decisions about our medical careers, Dad and Mom would hear our stories, and advise us, and tell about their own doctoring lives. Dad and I continued to meet during his cross-country trips—when he had given a lecture at a San Francisco hospital, or on his way to or from the Far East. We would have lunch in Berkeley, or dinner at the San Francisco airport during a few hours' layover, and we would talk.

In retrospect I realize that it was a difficult time for him, because his major project, the five-center National Heart Disease and Exercise Project, which had begun in 1974, was being threatened, and then torn apart. It was an enormously ambitious study, organized to prove definitively whether exercise could be used as a treatment for heart patients.

Over coffee, as jets taxied across the runway outside the airport restaurant, Dad would hear about my medical-school adventures, and he would tell me the latest about Heart Disease and Exercise. It had turned out, he would tell me excitedly, that mortality from all causes was thirty-six percent lower in the exercising group of heart patients. They had fewer heart attacks than the control group. Among those who did have heart attacks, the exercise-group patients more often survived, presumably because exercise had created better collateral circulation in their hearts.

One trip brought discouraging news: as a result of President Nixon's cuts in medical research, the Office of Management and Budget was ending the study early. Rather than continuing for ten or twelve years and enrolling several thousand patients, the study was going to be stopped after only three years and 650 patients. The irony was this: just at the moment when American society seemed to have begun to take the cardiologists' message seriously, just when important data were emerging, their work was being sharply curtailed. Dad would be fighting back: although most other centers were being closed, he was determined to keep his center open, even if it meant finding other ways for financing it, including donations from "GPs," e.g. grateful patients, who regularly gave tens of thousands of dollars to his research projects.

I would hear Dad's recital of the latest details on this study with mixed feelings: not only interest and pride, but also a certain degree of guilt and regret, because as I continued through medical school it was becoming clearer that my own path in medicine would take a different direction. Through four years of medical school, I was having the unparalleled luxury of sampling different fields, of developing momentary passions and interests—oncology, cardiac surgery, radiology, neurology—while knowing that I was always free to move on to something else. On cardiology rotation, although I had surprised my professor the first week by diagnosing a "multifocal atrial pacemaker" (an abnormal, fluctuating source of the heartbeat within the atria) on a patient's EKG, I felt no special sense of excitement during rounds on the coronary-care unit, no thrill of anticipation while listening to a patient's heart murmur. Perhaps what I was seeing was too familiar, or perhaps I was dissuaded by the high-technology side of cardiology, by its increasing reliance on numbers and radiographic images, and its increasing distance from the patient. Perhaps there was a remnant of the anti-Establishment feelings from my college days, too.

Or perhaps I felt the battle was won. Even though Dad's study was ending prematurely, every day in California brought proof that his theories had been accepted—by the nation's joggers and swimmers and bicyclists and restaurateurs, by our generation. The rate of smoking was dropping (from fifty percent of men in 1965 to forty percent in 1978), and deaths from heart disease were falling as well (from 286 per 100,000 per year in 1960 to 202 per 100,000 per year in 1980). Cardiology had become a big business, with hundreds of millions of dollars in research moneys, and thousands of doctors eager to practice and do research—it hardly needed one more pair of hands. Whatever the reason, though, cardiology bored me. And other fields did not.

This was a surprise to me, and to my family, and when it came time for me to decide on the direction of my career, my choice was not a popular one. Turning my back on internal medicine, and on cardiology, I chose to apply for residency training in psychiatry, a field that to many doctors hardly seemed to be a part of medicine. I sent for catalogues for programs across America, and in the fall of my fourth year of medical school, I began to interview for a position, traveling to Boston and New York and Philadelphia. My grandfather, Harold Feil, who had just closed his medical practice at the age of eighty-six, did not understand at all—not that he said as much, but I could tell by his silence, his brusqueness, when I came home for a visit that winter, a year after my grandmother's death. My father, too, responded unenthusiastically, although he did point out that his studies had always included the psychological aspects of heart disease, and that he had often collaborated with psychiatrists and psychologists.

Psychiatry was a visceral, instinctive choice, and in a way it surprised me as much as anyone in my family. I had worked on the country's best heart-surgery service, and one of the top cancer services, yet I was entering a specialty that had low prestige, that paid poorly—at least compared to cardiac surgery—and that was torn by disagreement and infighting. It took me several years even to begin to understand why.

My exposure to psychiatry in medical school was limited: I spent a summer working in a sleep laboratory at the Palo Alto VA Hospital, on a project that was attempting to find distinctive brain-wave patterns in the EEGs (electroencephalograms) of sleeping schizophrenic patients, high-frequency spikes that were thought to indicate abnormal electrical discharges from the limbic system, one of the primitive centers of the brain that regulates consciousness. For weeks, I flipped through thousands of pages of multi-channel sleep-EEG recordings, searching among the various levels of sleep: the "hypnagogic" moments before the brain goes into Stage I sleep; the restless moments of dreaming REM sleep, when the eyes move following dream images but the body's muscles are actually paralyzed; and the deeper, slow-wave periods of Stage III and Stage IV, the soothing times of night. Unable to distinguish with certainty between sharp spikes from deep brain centers and the brief muscle movements of a restless sleeper, I found little of value.

My first hospital rotation in the third year of medical school was on a locked inpatient unit of the county medical center down in San Jose. Schizophrenic and manic and depressed and drug-abusing patients were admitted there for a week or two of medication treatment. Compared to the sleek, gleaming cardiac surgical suite, or the rows of tiny incubators of premature babies in the pediatric ICU, the psychiatric ward was chaotic, smoke-filled, noisy; science was hardly noticeable. Instinctively, though, I knew I was encountering only the unfriendly frontier of an endlessly fascinating field, one with unparalleled promise.

As the oldest son, I was accustomed to having first choice, and the four of us entering medicine began to joke about how we had divided up the human body in choosing our specialties. Choosing first, I picked the head—not just the brain, but the mind as well.

Yet I had chosen a field in chaos, a deeply divided field. In the late 1970s, psychiatry seemed to be at a low point. Psychoanalysis, which had swept through American culture after World War II, was being challenged by the new biological psychiatry. On the basis of the work of Sigmund Freud, psychoanalysts had become proponents for intensive psychotherapy, often four or five times a week, and their various theories—Kleinian, Kohutian, Sullivanian, and others—had come to permeate American culture, affecting literature, movies, child-rearing, the expression of sexuality, and popular ideas about human motivations and beliefs. Medicine had gone through a brief period of infatuation with psychoanalysis, too, with the popularization of "psychosomatic" theories of diseases from asthma to ulcers to heart disease, theories which held that unconscious conflict was the cause of physical illnesses and that the best treatment was not medical but psychological.

By the 1970s, psychoanalysts were under attack from multiple fronts. Behavioral psychologists derided their broad, sweeping claims for the efficacy of their treatment in the absence of any convincing research. In the medical community, the failure of psychoanalysis to cure psychosomatic illnesses had alienated many internists and surgeons. Within the field of psychiatry, the most telling attacks came from biological psychiatrists. Biological psychiatry had its own checkered history, with enthusiastic use of dubious treatment, including lobotomy and insulin shock, which injured many patients. But beginning in the 1950s and 1960s, the history of biological psychiatry could be seen as one triumph after another. The antipsychotic medication Thorazine (chlorpromazine) had been introduced in the early 1950s—the first specific treatment for the symptoms of schizophrenia, the delusions and hallucinations and disordered thinking that do not respond to mere sedation. It worked by blocking the action of dopamine, a "neurotransmitter" chemical, in centers of the brain which regulate the perception of reality. Thorazine freed millions of psychiatric patients from state hospitals, where the average length of hospitalization had been twenty-five years, and allowed them to be returned to the community after hospitalizations of a few months or less (whether they received enough social supports in the community to make their lives tolerable was another issue). In the 1960s, antidepressant medications including amitriptyline (Elavil) and imipramine (Tofranil) were introduced. These were equally revolutionary in that they specifically treated the symptoms of "major depression," a disorder that, untreated, often led to prolonged suffering and, in as many as fifteen percent of cases, to suicide. Then came lithium carbonate, which was proven to treat the mood swings of manic-depressive illness, both the giddy, grandiose highs in which a patient can think himself capable of billion-dollar business deals, and spend all his savings in a day, and the black, despairing lows in which suicide is common. Lithium was able successfully to treat over two-thirds of manic-depressives. This, as any student in Psychiatry 202 could see, was merely the beginning.

Now the biological psychiatrists were on the warpath, complaining that psychoanalysts were frauds, that psychotherapy was useless, that the only treatment of any value for psychiatric disorders was medication. In their eyes, psychotherapy was a useless, expensive placebo in which suffering remained untreated for years, even decades. The analysts did their best to fight back, claiming that drugs were useful only to mask symptoms, and that premature relief from psychic pain could rob patients of the motivation to work in psychotherapy for a "cure" to their problems—but it was obviously a rout.

In my last year of medical school, something occurred which mirrored the experience of four years earlier, when I was a senior at college. Then Dad had his emergency bypass after diagnosing an impending heart attack; now Dad diagnosed another illness. Having noticed a continual blurring in the left upper corner of his vision, Dad spoke to an ophthalmologist and said he needed an examination immediately. "I have a pituitary tumor," he said, explaining that his visual disturbance resulted from the growing tumor's pressure on the optic chiasm, the spot behind the eyes where fibers of the optic nerve cross just below the lower brain.

The ophthalmologist laughed, saying that such a diagnosis was extremely unlikely, but the findings on the eye examination were indeed consistent with such a possibility, and later the CT scans and X rays revealed that a benign mass was growing in the area of Dad's pituitary gland, at the base of his brain, and was pressing on the optic chiasm.

In testimony to medical progress, Dad underwent a second revolutionary, life-saving surgical procedure. In previous years, operating on the pituitary gland required entering the brain from above, and dissecting through many layers of brain tissue before reaching the tiny sella turcica at the base of the skull, the bony cave that houses the pituitary. Bleeding and brain damage were common complications, and many patients suffered significant paralysis or memory loss. A new procedure, though, the trans-sphenoidal hypophysectomy, developed only a few years earlier by Dr. Ole Pearson and Dr. Gerald Brodkey of University Hospital of Cleveland, made that approach unnecessary. In this procedure, an incision was made through the lining of the nose, and the pituitary gland was approached from below, through the sinuses, using a tiny instrument which could scrape out the tumor.

Dad had this operation, and by the time I graduated from

medical school, he was well enough to travel to California, where he stood unsteadily by my side as Mom took photographs, the medical diploma held between us as though it would erase all our differences. Over dinner at a vegetarian restaurant, Mom and Dad and my girlfriend Lisa (who had moved to California after graduating from Harvard) and I, and my sister Kathryn, discussed the miracle of his recovery, the fact that the only complication of the procedure was that he would have to take thyroid medication for the rest of his life. We discussed Kathy's Yiddish translations, and the dusty boxes of books she had received from one of Dad's patients, and the consulting Dad was doing for NASA, in which astronauts were going to be trained on bicycle ergometers in outer space so that they would maintain cardiovascular fitness in the low-gravity environment of space capsules. And I tried to explain my plans for the future.

That June I shipped all my possessions back to my parents' house in Cleveland—except for a carload of clothes and books, enough to get me started in New York City. On July 1, the beginning of the medical new year, the date when medical students become interns, interns become residents, residents become Fellows, and Fellows become unemployed, my psychiatry residency training at New York Hospital began. It was to be the longest four years of my life, the most excruciating and, in many ways, the most exciting.

To non-doctors, residency training—that period of three or four or five years after medical school—appears to be only a time of extra learning, of specialization, after the major education received in medical school. Nothing could be further from the truth. Residency training is a total assault on the young doctor's self, an entire remaking of personality, of patterns of thinking and responding, of belief systems. It is as intense as the brainwashing my elementary-school principal Mrs. Adams warned us might come any day at the hands of North Koreans, and perhaps more unrelenting.

The reality is that, as demanding as it might be, medical school is merely a preamble, a period of extended play and make-believe. I spent a month pretending to be a cardiac surgeon, a month pretending to know how to treat Hodgkin's disease. In residency training, though, you become irrevocably what you have only been playing at. A neurologist, a pediatrician, a thoracic surgeon, an ophthalmologist. Those specialties have nothing in common, other than the M.D. after the physicians' illegible signatures. They think entirely differently, they have willfully unlearned the common language they memorized when they were innocent medical students. In fact, their paths barely cross in the hospital, and when they are forced to communicate, in the patient's chart or in a hospital corridor, they resort to a sort of medical Pidgin English.

My four years' becoming a psychiatrist differed little from Dan's six years' becoming a urologist, or Susan's four years becoming an obstetrician, or Beth's three years becoming a pediatrician. Only the content of our learning differed. I spent half a year on medical and neurological floors, then moved to inpatient psychiatric units for the next year and a half. I worked with geriatric patients on a research unit, and with patients with "borderline personality disorder" (patients with unstable personalities, who often make impulsive suicide attempts) on a long-term inpatient unit, and on alcohol- and drug-abuse rehabilitation units, and for about a year with a general inpatient psychiatric population. Then I moved to the outpatient clinic. I learned psychopharmacology, and techniques of crisis intervention, I learned something about group therapy and behavior therapy, and I trained in intensive psychoanalytic psychotherapy, in which patients were seen two or more times a week for several years. I spent six months on consultation-liaison psychiatry, treating the psychiatric aspects of medical illnesses, including severe burns. Over four years, I gradually realized that the war between biological psychiatrists and psychoanalysts was symbolic of a greater battle between mind and brain, an increasingly dubious conflict—and that the real challenge for psychiatry was to learn how best to combine an understanding of both to illuminate the human psyche, and to best treat mental illnesses.

You could say that Daniel went the opposite direction in medicine from me. Our medical-school educations were similar; but our choices for residency training could hardly have been more different. I chose the most low-technology specialty of medicine, Dan one of the most high-technology specialties. I moved up the human body from the heart; he moved downward.

He graduated from Case Western Reserve University Medical School in June 1983, and then began a six-year residency in urology. His first two years were general surgery, beginning on the "Red Service" at University Hospital, the busiest surgery service in Cleveland, with a huge caseload of trauma and emergency surgery. The first year Dan mostly worked as an assistant in the operating room, but by the second year he was able to take out appendixes or gallbladders himself. General surgery was grueling and highly competitive, based on a "pyramid system" in which residents competed with each other for a dwindling number of positions in each advanced year, and Dan hated it. On his last night of call in general surgery, Dan had to cover three different services. Two patients were dying, one in the surgical ICU, the other in the medical ICU, despite a "full-court press" of medications to increase blood pressure and despite being placed in Trendelenberg position, with feet elevated and head low, to increase blood flow to the brain.

Dan swore he would not let them die on his shift (in part because he would have to dictate summaries of their enormously complicated treatments). When dawn came, both patients were still alive—and Dan had made it to urology.

The four years of urology training came as a relief, with much less pressure, much more teamwork and camaraderie. First year, as a junior resident, Dan did rotations at the VA Hospital, at University Hospital, and at Metro, the city hospital. It was like starting from scratch—learning basics about fluid and electrolyte balance, learning to look into the bladder using a cystoscope, helping senior surgeons take out cancerous prostates, and managing severe urological diseases, including patients with massive kidney stones, and patients who had developed sepsis, or infection of the blood, as a result of untreated bladder infections. He also worked on a spinal-cord unit, which was filled with young men, former soldiers, paralyzed as a result of gunshot wounds or motor vehicle accidents; only one patient, a former Green Beret on secret assignment in Guatemala, had been injured in combat. The second year Dan spent four months at each of three Cleveland hospitals. He worked at the Cleveland Clinic, a "tertiary care hospital" where patients came from all over the world; at Mt. Sinai Hospital, on a "community" service; and at St. Luke's Hospital, where he helped implant "penile prostheses," or mechanical devices in the penis that help impotent men get erections. He learned to do "percutaneous stone manipulations," or remove stones in the urinary tract without invasive surgery. His third year, a "multidisciplinary year," Dan spent time outside urology, working in kidney-transplant surgery for two months, then in pathology, then in radiology, then in nephrology (kidney diseases). He spent a few months doing research in an infertility laboratory. His final year, his "chief year," Dan worked as a chief resident on a pediatrics unit, then at a private hospital, then at Metro Hospital. As the end of residency training approached, the question was: What should he do next? Should he do specialty training, or should he look for a job as a general urologist?

After her return from China in the fall of 1985, Susan faced a different dilemma. In her last year of medical school, she debated whether to apply for training in obstetrics or in internal medicine. Which was the better way of pursuing her goal of working on international women's health-care issues? She finally decided on obstetrics, feeling that that specialty would give her unquestioned access and legitimacy to work on the issues which interested her. She interviewed at obstetrics residency programs around the country.

Then came what medical students know as the Match. In the Match, all American medical students and residency training programs rank each other by preference, and a computer program sorts out which doctor should go where in the country. It is a logical, efficient system, but it generates much anxiety, since the final decision of where a young doctor will spend the next three to seven years of his life, and perhaps the rest of his career, is being decided by electronic circuitry, and there is virtually no room for second thoughts.

Susan's decision was complicated by the fact that she and John Triedman, who were both graduating in 1986, had decided to apply together for residency training, to do a "couple's match," so that they would be able to live in the same city. Their first choice was Seattle, which offered excellent programs both in obstetrics and in John's special interest, pediatric cardiology. However, the computer in its infinite wisdom decided that Boston, their third choice, was a better match. And thus, in the spring of 1986, the year that Dad retired, Susan and John got ready to send all their possessions cross-country, and to spend the next several years of their life at Harvard.

They found an apartment in Jamaica Plain, not far from the medical school, and began their residencies on June 15, 1986. Susan's obstetrics residency at Massachusetts General Hospital and the Brigham and Women's Hospital stood in dramatic contrast to Marcus Rosenwasser's studies over a century before. While Marcus had a few months' training in obstetrics clinic during medical school, and perhaps two dozen evenings on "watch" at the hospital, delivering babies, Susan's four-year residency (following medical school) was a highly structured educational experience, exposing her to every standard aspect of both obstetrics and gynecology, inpatient and outpatient, medical and surgical. Of the eight residents in her year, six were women, a proportion fairly typical in today's obstetrics programs, whereas only one of her junior professors was a woman, and none of the senior professors.

Internship was six months of general surgery, followed by three months of obstetrics and three months of internal medicine. Then came three years of residency. There were three months per year at Mass General, and nine months at Brigham and Women's. Each year was divided into half obstetrics and half gynecology. Susan worked on inpatient units, in clinics, with "benign gynecology," and in the oncology or cancer ward, and with normal obstetrical cases and high-risk obstetrics. She learned how to do cesarean sections, and amniocentesis, and even (since Brigham and Women's Hospital has preserved some of the obstetrical craftsmanship of an earlier era) how to do complex forceps deliveries. She learned prenatal monitoring, and the optimal management of labor, and the management of complications of delivery. Since Brigham and Women's Hospital performs over 12,000 deliveries annually, Susan delivered hundreds of babies each year—until she could practically deliver babies in her sleep.

While obstetrics is not seen by other doctors as a field of

great innovation, the changes since the era of Marcus Rosenwasser (and since the time Mom was in residency training) are notable. By 1991, infant mortality dropped to 8.9 deaths in the first year of life per thousand babies born, fewer than half of what it was in 1960, and perhaps one-thirtieth of what it was in 1880. Hospital maternity stays, eight days in Mom's residency years, have decreased to three, even two days. Premature babies that weigh as little as 500 grams, or about one pound, are routinely delivered, kept in incubators, their skin hardly able to retain fluids, their eyelids fused shut—and they often survive. Prenatal testing makes it easy to identify when the fetus is in "distress"—though not necessarily easier to decide when it is best to intervene with surgery. And at some hospitals, notably University of California at San Francisco, doctors are actually beginning to operate on the fetus in the uterus, to correct congenital defects.

Gynecology has made even more enormous and dramatic advances, particularly in infertility techniques. During her residency training, Susan had some exposure to "in vitro" fertilization, in which the sperm fertilizes the ovum in a petri dish, and the tiny organism is then implanted in the uterus. She had more exposure to a procedure called "gamete intra-fallopian tube transfer," or, as its acronym is known, GIFT. In GIFT, a woman who has difficulty conceiving is medicated with Pergonal, a combination of two hormones (follicle-stimulating hormone and leuteinizing hormone), which causes production of a large number of "follicles" or egg sacs in the ovaries. Using a laparoscope, an instrument which allows them to see inside the abdominal cavity, doctors suction eggs, or "oocytes," out of the follicles while the woman is under anesthesia, and combine the oocyte with sperm in a thin cannula or tube; this tiny gamete, the beginning of a human being, is then put back into the fallopian tube, the tube leading to the uterus. Doctors believe that the fallopian tube may contain local factors—chemicals or hormones—that may improve the rate of fertilization.

Another great advance in gynecology is "operative laparoscopy," which residents commonly call "video-game surgery." In these procedures, doctors operate through multiple small puncture sites in the woman's abdomen, and can avoid making large incisions. Susan learned to do laparoscopic surgery on ovarian cysts, on adhesions, or scar tissue, and on ectopic pregnancies, a dangerous condition in which a fetus escapes from the uterus and begins to grow in the woman's abdominal cavity.

Like Susan, Beth had to make a choice among all the different fields of medicine. Before deciding, she took an extra year in medical school to study pathology. She spent six months doing autopsies at University Hospital, and then three months doing surgical pathology, going into the operating room during surgery on breast or colon or prostate cancer, and making "frozen sections" of tumor tissue and lymph nodes, to help surgeons determine the stage of the cancer's spread, and thus the degree of surgery necessary. That winter, 1988–89, she spent time at the Cuyahoga County Coroner's Office, doing autopsies on murder victims, suicides, unexplained deaths. She saw car-accident victims, and children who had drowned after falling through ice, and in one unusual case, she even went to the scene of a crime to investigate the death of a well-dressed twenty-five-year-old man who had been found in the backseat of a rented car that was pulled inside a stranger's garage, a bullet wound to the back of his head. A drug rub-out, they finally concluded.

During her year off, Beth realized again how much she missed contact with patients. Life in the pathology lab, like that in the research laboratory, kept her too far from what interested her in medicine. And, like Mom, Beth chose to enter pediatrics. She began her residency training at Case Western Reserve's Rainbow Babies and Childrens Hospital in July of 1991. There were twenty-one interns in her class, five men and sixteen women.

Internship year was a series of rotations in which she learned to treat all ages of children, from newborns to infants to teenagers. She began in the neonatal intensive-care unit, or the NICU, where she worked with premature babies. She would be called to the delivery room to examine newborn babies where there might be a problem, such as "deceleration of heart rate" or "stained fluid"—slowing of the infant's heart, or amniotic fluid that was discolored with meconium (the fetus's stool) or blood, any of these things being possible indications of threats to the fetus's life. After the baby was born, she would resuscitate it, and check its heart rate, its breathing, and the color of its skin; if necessary, she might have to intubate the baby, to place a tube into its throat to allow it to breathe. Then she would escort it to the NICU.

Her next rotation was on 7 West, the "NICU Stepdown Unit," a ward accommodating babies that had successfully been treated on the NICU—so-called gainers and growers. Babies were discharged from the NICU when they reached the weight of a thousand grams, or about two pounds; before they could be sent home from 7 West, they had to grow to 1,800 grams.

Then she moved on to 5 West, a floor for toddlers and babies, where she saw patients with asthma, meningitis, cellulitis, and other infections, as well as children with the types of cancer common early in life—acute lymphocytic leukemia, neuroblastoma, Wilms' tumor (a type of kidney tumor seen in young children that commonly spreads to the lungs), and tumors of the posterior fossa of the brain. These children would be admitted for treatment with various combinations of anti-cancer drugs.

Next she moved on to 4 West, where she worked with grade-school and teenage children, including patients with cystic fibrosis, who would come into the hospital for a "clean-out" of their lungs with antibiotics, and aerosol treatments to their lungs. Finally, she moved to the outpatient clinic, and spent a month treating colds, wheezing, earaches, and rashes.

The highlight of the year came in January, when she rotated back to the NICU and was assigned to treat newborn twenty-three-week-old twins—among the smallest ever treated at Rainbow. There was a 500-gram boy, and a 460-gram girl—each weighing about a pound. Despite intensive treatment, the baby girl died, but the boy survived. Although he had some bleeding in his brain (which is common in premature babies), he had no obvious damage, and by the end of her rotation, he was gaining weight. Eventually he was transferred to a rehabilitation facility, to receive intensive physical therapy.

Second year consisted of work in the pediatric intensive-care unit (PICU), where she treated older children, particularly patients who had undergone repair of congenital heart defects, such as the tetralogy of Fallot, or ventricular septal defects, and as well she treated children in "septic shock," requiring intubation, placement of central lines, and various types of antibiotic treatment. Much of the time was spent in the emergency room, seeing everything from colds and rashes to car accidents and sudden-infant-death-syndrome babies.

In contrast to Mom's experience forty-some years earlier, the pediatrics Beth learned was a highly interventionistic, highly technical specialty of medicine. She learned to intubate babies, to place "umbilical lines" into the umbilical vein of newborns, to put in chest tubes and arterial lines, and to do spinal taps and take urine samples by "suprapubic taps," to search out the source of infection in desperately ill babies. The 500-gram preemies brought home to her another aspect of pediatrics—the way technology had outstripped ethics. Many of her fellow pediatricians, while capable of saving tinier and tinier babies, harbored intense doubts as to the purpose of their hard work, not only because many of the babies would have substantial defects should they survive, but because many of the smaller babies were the children of drug-addict parents, and their very prematurity was a result of social chaos and ignorance and untreated drug abuse.

Thus, over the course of a decade, one or more of us was immersed night and day in a new medical world, learning to make decisions within the discipline of our choice so that merely being awake for thirty-six hours, merely being exhausted, would not warp our judgment or thinking. As such, we were each remade. We would appear at weekend family get-togethers, pale and drowsy or excited and enthusiastic, and we would seemingly return to our childhood roles—youngest child, middle daughter, youngest or oldest son. Our new selves, our special learning, remained largely hidden. It was almost as though time had not passed. When the weekend ended, we returned to our different worlds—to the psychiatric clinic, the delivery room, the urology operating room, the neonatal ICU. There our new self reemerged.

For the four of us, it was indeed a new, infant self. In a sense, we were at the same point where Marcus Rosenwasser was when he returned to Ohio from his medical grand tour in 1868, where our grandfather Harold Feil was in 1920 on his return from working with Thomas Lewis in England, where Dad was in 1947, when he finished cardiology training in Chicago with Louis N. Katz, where Mom was in 1952 when she finished pediatrics residency.

That is, emerging from medical training—having received state-of-the-art late-twentieth-century medical education—we faced the daunting task of deciding how to apply it, of deciding where to go. We might be living in utterly different medical worlds, but all of us—Dan and Susan and Beth and I—faced identical questions. Mom and Dad were at the stage of concluding their careers, of summing up the results of half a century of doctoring. Our lives as doctors were just beginning.

What problems were worthy of our energies? What disease demanded to be cured?

10

SETTING OUT:
1989–1992

MY career began to take direction during fellowship year in 1984, when I encountered a group of difficult, baffling patients—patients with schizophrenia who also abused cocaine and alcohol. By any standard, they were sick. They suffered from a disease that remains poorly understood even in this age of PET scans and brain metabolic studies. They heard voices, they acted bizarrely in response to delusional ideas, and they experienced the world through a frightening prism of distorted perceptions that nobody else shared. At the same time, these patients had become addicted to drugs—occasionally to heroin, but more often to cocaine, alcohol, Valium, marijuana. They were a lost tribe—outcasts both from the psychiatric world and from the world of addicts. Psychiatric professionals (and other patients) ostracized them as "drug addicts"; addiction-treatment professionals (and addicts) rejected them as "crazies."

Finally—after years of halfhearted interest in what were supposed to be exciting medical problems—I had found a clinical challenge worthy of the effort. I would never have predicted that schizophrenic substance abusers would have attracted my intense interest. Nevertheless, they were what brought me into the world of medical research.

After completing psychiatric residency training in 1984, I took a year of fellowship at New York State Psychiatric Institute, located at Columbia Presbyterian Medical Center, in the field of public psychiatry. It was not exactly what my family had envisioned as an ideal career, but it was the right choice for me. Dad's advice, as usual, had been clear: he suggested that I do advanced training in PET scanning, a new technology which could show in a rainbow of colors the metabolism of various parts of the brain during thought processes. Alternatively, he thought I might do well to learn some basic neurophysiology.

Instead, I had realized that I leaned toward what essayist and doctor Lewis Thomas has called medicine's "non-technologies"—toward curing by words, by persuasion and interpretation, and by the organization of services, rather than the "high technologies" of scalpel, catheter, and radioopaque dyes. So I spent fellowship year learning family therapy, group therapy, medical and social history, public policy, even reading business-school management texts. There were eight Fellows. Each of us spent three days a week at Columbia and two days at a clinic, hospital, or community mental-health center. My clinical placement was unusual, given that the fellowship was in public psychiatry: I worked at Beth Israel Medical Center, a private hospital on the Lower East Side of Manhattan, in a clinic treating primarily Medicare and Medicaid patients—that is, a private hospital that served the public.

As far as I could tell, that clinic treated one of the most fascinating and diverse populations one could imagine. There was every diagnosis—chronic and acute schizophrenia, major depression, atypical depression, manic-depressive disorder, substance abuse, borderline personality disorder, multiple personality, and paranoia. There were panickers and obsessive compulsives, and the psychiatric complications of cancer and AIDS and diabetes, and the consequences of a thousand kinds of trauma. The clinic had every imaginable ethnic group and social class as well. There were Chinese and Vietnamese and Cambodian refugees, and Hasidim from Crown Heights and Russian immigrants from Brighton Beach, and Poles and Ukrainians from the East Village, and painters and dancers and conceptual artists from SoHo and Avenue B, and Dominicans and Puerto Ricans and Peruvians and Mexicans from "Loesida," as Latinos call the Lower East Side, and retired garment workers and socialist organizers and schoolteachers from Stuyvesant Town and Peter Cooper Village, and chronic mental patients living in single-room-occupancy hotels off lower Madison Avenue, and the homeless who congregate around Houston Street and the Bowery, who came seeking hospitalization when the weather turned cold, and a sprinkling of advertising and publishing executives who worked around Union Square and Park Avenue South.

The Beth Israel clinic treated all these patients, and, as far as I could tell, did a pretty good job, especially in view of its limited resources. But one group of patients was sent away virtually untreated—those with "co-morbid," or concurrent, schizophrenia and drug abuse. These patients would go in and out of the hospital every few weeks or months, and they constantly visited the emergency room, in one crisis after another. Sometimes they were admitted to the psychiatric unit, sometimes to the drug detox unit; equally often, they ended up in jail. In the old days, when mental patients were sent to state hospitals for decades at a time, when the average length of hospitalization for schizophrenia was twenty-five years, such patients did not exist: most schizophrenics did not have access to illicit drugs. Since the 1960s, and the introduction of antipsychotic medications, a process of deinstitutionalization has occurred, and the mental-hospital population has dwindled rapidly. Nationally, it decreased from 600,000 to 100,000 between the 1950s and the 1980s. In New York State, state hospital census dropped from 93,000 in 1953 to 64,000 in 1970, and 23,000 in 1985. Since the 1970s, the number of mentally ill drug-abusing patients had increased rapidly nation-wide. Clearly, I could see, here was a large and growing problem, and one that almost no one in psychiatry had yet addressed.

With the supervision of Dr. Christian Beels, my professor at the New York State Psychiatric Institute, I began work-ing with a number of such patients at Beth Israel. My inter-est came partly from a stubborn, and perhaps naïve, refusal to believe any patients were untreatable, and partly from curiosity. Why would some schizophrenic patients use illicit drugs? Did drugs dull symptoms of psychosis, somehow help them to escape the world, or did they merely provide entertainment or pleasure? Some illicit drugs, such as co-caine, make psychotic symptoms worse—why would even a "crazy" person want such a thing? Just as interesting, there was the treatment question: How could such patients be engaged in outpatient treatment? After all, our clinic was right across the street from a large city park in which one could purchase just about any known drug. Why come to a clinic at all?

Every Thursday, Dr. Beels and I met in the cafeteria of the Psychiatric Institute overlooking the Hudson River and Riverside Drive; through the smeared window glass we watched traffic moving across the George Washington Bridge, and the roar of the West Side Highway down below nearly drowned out all conversation. Over tuna-salad sand-wiches and Cokes we plotted how to seduce such patients into treatment, and how to keep them in treatment once they began.

It was best, we decided, not to insist on total abstinence from drugs, at least at the beginning: if such patients were capable of abstinence, they would probably not be so sick to begin with. Given the chaotic nature of their lives, it was unrealistic to assume they could attend all group meetings—even coming to half of scheduled sessions might be a sign of progress. On the other hand, it seemed obvious that such patients were suffering—their frequent hospital admissions and ER visits spoke of more than the need to get a roof over their heads. Was there a way to get them to share their experiences, to break their isolation, to give them a sense of community, of belonging? After all, has not all successful medical treatment begun by giving a name to suffering?

At Beth Israel, I began working with Elizabeth Meehan, a social worker who had several years of experience working with drug abusers. Every week we went up to the inpatient dual-diagnosis unit, a special unit treating only patients with both psychiatric and drug-abuse disorders, and after talking with the staff, we would meet with any patient who seemed a likely candidate for our group. Whenever possible, we had patients come down to visit the group for a session or more before they left the hospital. Soon enough, we had several such patients meeting for about an hour on a once-a-week basis.

There was Ricardo, a barrel-chested former carpenter who had lived in the Bowery for twenty years, steadily drinking himself into oblivion, periodically getting himself admitted to Bellevue; there was Darryl, who looked like Ratzo Rizzo from *Midnight Cowboy*, and who had ruined a promising career as a Long Island Railroad conductor when he became a heroin addict and crazy as well; there was Edmund, a thirty-five-year-old from a small town upstate, who had become psychotic in his senior year of college, and despite numerous halfway houses and rehabilitation programs had also ended up in the Bowery. There was Daphne, an articulate twenty-year-old college student who supported herself as a prostitute between hospitalizations, keeping her spirits up with IV cocaine and heroin; there was Annette, a gaunt black woman; and Arnell, a tough-talking homeless man; and Clive, a friendly plump black man from South Carolina who in his better moments found his way to Georgia to pick peaches a few months a year; and Ivan, a Ukrainian who lived with his elderly parents and abused barbiturates and had delusions about the police.

First they talked—week after week—about all the ways they had tried to kill themselves. They spoke about what their voices said to them. They talked about getting high. Of all the things in their suffering lives, drugs had a magical ability to bring momentary pleasure, brief respite from the torture of psychotic illness. We taught them about the symptoms of schizophrenia, and the biological effects of illicit and psychotropic drugs. We learned from them, too— that we needed to "set limits," to insist that they couldn't come to the group intoxicated, and couldn't use drugs in the clinic's bathroom or stairwells. That they could only talk one at a time, and that they needed to listen to each other, to learn when to be silent. When indicated, I medicated them, writing prescriptions or giving shots of antipsychotic medications. Beth Meehan did outreach, helped them find a place to sleep, and talked with their methadone counselors, and the aunts and brothers who had given up on them. We were hopelessly naïve.

At the end of a year, we were astonished to realize that the majority of the group members were still in treatment. If a patient came to *any* group meetings after leaving the hospital, he was likely to still be in treatment six months or a year later. Of the first ten patients, seven were in treatment at six months. At one year, five were still in treatment, and if Ivan—who never missed a meeting—had not followed his retired parents in their move to Florida, the count would have been six. Given the disorganized and chaotic nature of their lives, it was remarkable that any of them were still in treatment.

Further, although our treatment program was extremely modest, many of the patients seemed to be doing pretty well. Not that their schizophrenia was cured—there is at present no cure for schizophrenia. But they had been stabilized. They took antipsychotic medications fairly regularly, and they did not "decompensate" (become severely psychotic) very often, at least to the point of requiring hospitalization. Moreover, though they had not all entirely stopped abusing drugs, many had cut back significantly. Their lives had been given some order for the first time in years. For such sick people, to become "chronic patients" was a sign of major progress. The question, though, was whether there was any quantitative way to demonstrate their improvement.

Beth Meehan and I sat down in front of the clinic's registration computer, and began the laborious task of compiling hospitalization data for the ten patients. We counted all hospital days in the three years prior to the creation of the group, and in the first year of treatment. When we added up the figures, we realized that the first ten patients had averaged 15.5, 20.0, and 38.2 days in-hospital three, two, and one years before the group began, and only 7.8 days in the year after our group began. This included the patients who dropped out as well as those who stayed in treatment. While this was not the world's most rigorous study (after all, it was "naturalistic," was not randomized or double-blind, and had no comparison group), I knew from the psychiatric literature that nothing comparable had been reported on such patients. Beth raised the issue that we were writing about only ten patients—what kind of research was that?

"We have to start somewhere," I told her, recalling my

grandfather's small study on EKG changes in angina pectoris, and my father's early reports from the Jewish Community Center study, describing only eighteen patients. "A case series *is* a reasonable beginning. You have to know whether it's worth spending a million dollars to do a more scientific study. Think of this as pilot data."

Over the next several months, Beth and I struggled to write up our results. More difficult than tracking down the patients' hospitalization histories was the task of getting a secretary to type our drafts, since the clinic staff did not view research as a priority. I ended up typing the paper, entering text into my IBM PC at home with its two 5¼″ disk drives, having to load in the Wordstar word-processing program each time I turned the computer on, and then printing out on my daisywheel printer, which made a heavy "ka-thunk!" when it reached the end of a line. The department's chief psychologist advised me on which statistical tests to use, and I calculated chi-squares and Wilcoxon sign tests by hand on my solar-powered Radio Shack calculator.

When the paper was done, we were daring enough to submit it to the *American Journal of Psychiatry*, one of the top psychiatric journals. The paper was soon returned, with the recommendation that we shorten it to a 1,200-word "brief report." I pared it down to the bare essentials, and a month later it was accepted for publication. It was printed in October 1987, and I felt that I had done my duty to Darryl and Ricardo and Daphne and the others.

After all, I saw myself as mostly a writer. During the last year of medical school and throughout residency, I had started publishing essays and articles and stories in literary and popular magazines. I won a few awards, got an agent, and started collecting essays for a book. I also began a novel. During fellowship year, I finished my first two books, and wrote a dozen or more magazine articles. I met editors for drinks after work to discuss article ideas. I was particularly interested in the misuse of medical technology, in ethical dilemmas raised by modern medicine, and in iatrogenic disease—disease caused by treatment. After my fellowship year, I was hired as a full-time staff psychiatrist at Beth Israel, working in the outpatient clinic. I saw clinic patients, continuing the dual-diagnosis group and starting work with other patients, including those with panic disorder and mood disorders. I taught and supervised residents, and I started private practice. Things seemed settled for me: I would do clinical work as a psychiatrist, and have time to work on my books and articles.

By the late 1980s, my brothers and sisters, too, were beginning to establish themselves. Almost every year, one of us got married. Jon had been first, marrying Peggy Atwood, a pediatric nurse-practitioner, in the spring of 1983; I was next, marrying Lisa, after a nine-year courtship, in the fall of the same year. After receiving a graduate degree from the Kennedy School at Harvard, Lisa had gone to work at the New York City Health and Hospitals Corporation, which manages New York's public hospitals. After two years, she took a job at Bellevue, in the field of hospital reimbursement, and then moved to New York University Medical Center, Bellevue's sister hospital. Then Kathy married David Stern, a University of Pennsylvania professor in Jewish Studies, and she began to practice orthodox Judaism. Then Danny married Karen Berman, an architect. Next, Susan married John Triedman, who had become a Fellow in pediatric cardiology at Children's Hospital in Boston. And Beth married Dan Jaffe, a newly graduated lawyer.

Grandchildren began arriving. First Jon and Peggy had a little girl, then Lisa and I had a daughter, then Kathy and David. Then Peggy got pregnant again, and then

Lisa, and then Kathy. Then Susan, then Karen. Every year it seemed there were one or two more babies. When our daughter Sarah was born in February 1987, we converted my study into a baby's room, and the apartment soon filled with stuffed animals and walkers and baby swings, and colorful hard plastic toys that we would be certain to step on in the middle of the night. Lisa took three or four months off from work, and then returned on a four-day-a-week schedule.

No longer were our family reunions just the familiar meetings of Mom and Dad and six offspring. Now they were complex logistical operations with half a dozen spouses, and armsful of babies and diaper bags and stuffed animals, and pots boiling on the stove, and tape players blaring Sharon, Lois and Bram, or Raffi, and Lego blocks everywhere, and video cameras running. Now when the family got together we had to commandeer Jon's house and Dan and Karen's extra bedroom, and rent rooms at the Alcazar Hotel down Cedar Hill. In smaller groups we met in Philadelphia, New York, Boston, and one winter on Florida's Gulf Coast. Periodically, we would all get together in Cleveland. All eighteen, twenty, twenty-two of us.

Even though Dad had officially retired in 1986, he seemed busier than ever. He had to pack up his exercise laboratory at Western Reserve to move to smaller quarters, and every year he fought off the inevitable time when he would have to close down entirely. He began a project with an obstetrics professor who was studying exercise training in pregnant women. He became interested in cardiac diseases in menopausal women, beginning to discover, like his colleagues, how years of research had neglected half the human race. He consulted for the World Health Organization. He and a coauthor prepared a new edition of their classic book on rehabilitation of the cardiac patient. And now that all the kids were out of the house, Mom was free to work the way she always wanted to: and despite the fact that she was sixty-eight years old, she began working full-time—as a pediatrician at the Metzenbaum Center with foster children, and visiting newborn babies at boarder homes.

Everything began to change for me when, one day at work, I received a pamphlet from the National Institute of Mental Health, describing a new initiative for research into treatment of patients with both psychiatric and substance-abuse disorders. It was what is called an RFP, or "request for proposals." Clearly, somebody in Washington had realized the significance of the growing population of such patients, and the pressing need for devising effective treatments. Suddenly the idea of "co-morbidity"—that many patients had two or more serious illnesses—was hot. So was addiction psychiatry, especially considering the huge increase in drug abuse that began with the early 1980s introduction of crack cocaine, a smokable, quick, cheap high. As many as forty to sixty percent of chronic mental patients abused drugs. They were now known as "MICAs"—mentally ill chemical abusers—and the newspapers were filled with accounts in which desperate or psychotic MICAs had committed crimes or bizarre acts. The spread of AIDS, which had been discovered only half a dozen years before, was particularly rapid among drug users, and the Reagan Administration was belatedly starting to allocate more money for drug-abuse treatment.

By this time Beth Meehan had left the staff of the clinic, so I sent a copy of the RFP to one of my colleagues, Dr. Richard N. Rosenthal, chief psychiatrist of the inpatient dual-diagnosis unit. He called me back immediately.

"Let's go for it," Rick said. "What should we study?"

"Well," I said, "we only have data on ten patients, but

that's ten more patients than anyone else in the country!"

On weekends, Rick and I began working on a grant proposal. I would walk from my apartment to his high-rise apartment in the East Eighties off Third Avenue, and he would warm up his Macintosh computer, which occupied the only corner of his living room not filled with crates of vintage wine. Mid-afternoon, when our energies flagged, we would remove a bottle from a crate and open it, swirling French burgundy around our glasses as we stared at the flickering screen. Besides my pilot data from the group of ten schizophrenic substance abusers, I had also collected information for a Grand Rounds presentation on all 1,792 patients admitted to the psychiatric hospital over a one-year period, including 602 schizophrenics, of whom a quarter (146) were also severe substance abusers. And there was Rick's collection of index cards, on which he had noted in tiny handwriting the pertinent demographic and clinical data on every patient admitted to his inpatient unit since he had arrived in 1984, over 450 patients, of whom 292 were schizophrenic substance abusers.

It was not much to go on, but if you put it all together, it demonstrated that we had a large population of such patients, that we could manage them as inpatients, and that we had devised a promising preliminary outpatient program which at least kept many of them in treatment and out of the hospital. As we began writing sections of the grant on Rick's Apple, our more important work began— that of dreaming out the details of something that did not yet exist. Where should we set up this program? In the clinic or in a separate space? How should we staff the program? What kind of budget should it have? More important, what was our hypothesis? What was the best research design?

I had never imagined myself doing research; in fact, in

my battles with Dad, I had always defined my interests as anything *but* research. Yet, as Rick and I worked, the project began taking on a life of its own. What was important, I knew from Dad's talks about the early days of the Work Classification Clinic, was not fancy statistics or a complex research design but rather the ability to see a problem anew, to sense the fault lines in the scientific literature. It was alchemy, transmuting the burdensome problems of everyday hospital work—"difficult" patients—into the gold of important research questions. It required an ability to see what is *not* explained by the available literature, to understand which conditions receive short shrift, which disorders or diseases are on the outside, neglected, which afflicted patients suffer needlessly. Next it required the ability to tell a convincing story, to convince anonymous reviewers of the significance of your work, to induce them to give money to your project rather than to someone else who had worked equally hard at his (in that regard, it didn't seem altogether different from writing a good book).

Our final hypothesis was so simple as to be almost elementary. What Beth Meehan and I had done was an integrated treatment approach in which substance-abuse treatment (after all, she had been trained as an alcoholism counselor) had been combined with psychiatric treatment in one setting and with one philosophical framework. In our new project (we called it COPAD, combined psychiatric and addictive disorders treatment), Rick and I would compare this integrated treatment approach with standard community treatment, where dual-diagnosis patients received psychiatric treatment in one location and substance-abuse treatment in another. We believed that this sort of splitting of treatment led often to dropout and rehospitalization.

Our new integrated treatment would be twice a week rather than once, and would be run by a psychiatrist, a social worker, and an addiction counselor. In the non-integrated treatment, our clinic's doctor would provide psychiatric medication, and the patient would attend substance-abuse groups at other drug-treatment programs, which dealt primarily with non-schizophrenic addicts.

Research assistants would meet with the patients every few months, and would assess them. How many remained in treatment in each group? How severe were their psychiatric symptoms? How much drug use was there? (Urine samples would be tested periodically.) They would give batteries of psychiatric tests. And they would collect data from New York City hospitals about rehospitalization.

In May of 1989, we completed our grant application. Rick did the bulk of preparation, running around the hospital to get signatures of hospital vice presidents, and to secure budget approval (the cost of our proposed three-year study totaled nearly a million dollars). Finally, we sent the package down to Washington. Rick's official title on the grant was principal investigator, and I was co-principal investigator. It was like being emperor and prime minister of a mythical country.

We waited. Our friends who were more experienced in the grant-writing business advised us to be prepared for rejection—after all, the chance of a new study getting funded was about one out of seven—and predicted, even assuming the best, that we would have to refine and resubmit our application at least two or three more times before it was approved.

We were therefore amazed when, in October of that year, our grant was approved and funded in full. Rick and I then began a frenzied process of getting office space (the parlor floor of a brownstone next to the hospital, which had to be gutted and rebuilt), interviewing and hiring a project coordinator, and then finding research assistants, who needed to be trained. By spring we were ready to recruit patients.

In retrospect, I suppose, the parallels to Dad's and Papa's work seem obvious. The choice of an ignored, undertreated group of very sick patients, the effort to define disease amid a welter of symptoms, and to fashion an effective treatment approach—in many ways, this is what Dad was doing in 1950 with heart-attack survivors, and what Papa did in the 1920s with arrhythmia and angina patients. In a way I can even see connections with Marcus Rosenwasser's work after the Civil War with obstetric patients, who suffered and died from a hundred undiagnosable maladies. What was strange, though, was the reversal between Dad and myself: he, who had been talking of nothing but research as long as I could remember, was now working with a co-author on a popular book, called *Healing Your Heart*, about reversing heart disease through a strenuous program of diet and exercise. And with another co-author (commissioned by a wealthy businessman patient), he began writing his autobiography. I, who had a passion for writing, was suddenly boring my wife and friends and in-laws with stories about research.

I was not the only one in the family to undergo such a transformation. Similarly, my brother Dan the urologist and my sisters Susan the obstetrician and Beth the pediatrician, as they finished residency training, were to begin to encounter groups of patients who called forth from them a need to cure. Perhaps it is a process of imprinting like that observed by Konrad Lorenz in the new-hatched duckling who affixes the label "mother" to anything that moves into its line of sight during a certain, brief, vulnerable stage— and for the rest of its life follows that object with unmatched reverence. So, too, a young doctor, after a dozen or more years of education, rises into the world at a certain time, primed to grasp a disease to cure. In this process, conscious choice plays a minor role. Certainly, I never would have imagined becoming passionately interested in drug-abusing schizophrenics.

At first I only hypothesized about my brother's and sisters' transformations, since at our family meetings we rarely talk about anything remotely related to work. We might ask, "So, where are you working now?" Or: "What are you going to do next year?" Or: "So, are you on call tonight?" When you saw a pale, washed-out sibling leaning against the door frame in the pantry at Mom and Dad's house, answering a page from the hospital, that was about as detailed as conversations got. I would start to scrawl notes as three-year-olds ran around the dining-room table, but after a few minutes invariably I gave up. Instead, we were more often talking about the babies, or houses bought and sold, or what Dad and Mom were up to. But I could sense in Dan's and Susan's and Beth's lives echoes of the same process I was experiencing. Traces of their new passions were reflected in their latest change of address, or in the title of a conference presentation.

When I got a new computer at the clinic with a modem, I could connect with the hospital's medical library and do database searches. Just by typing the name Hellerstein, I could find out what my family was up to, things that a weekend home did not reveal.

My computerized search of the Index Medicus revealed that Dad had finally published his articles about exercise in pregnancy, "Maternal left ventricular performance during bicycle exercise," in the *American Journal of Cardiology*, as well as "Umbilical artery wave-form during bicycle exercise in normal pregnancy" in the journal *Obstetrics and Gynecology*, and that Dan was writing about "Trans-rectal ultrasound and partial ejaculatory duct obstruction in male infertility" and about "Sonographic measurements of transition zone of prostate in men with and without benign prostatic hyperplasia," both in *Urology*, that Susie had completed her study on "Acceptance and perceptions of Norplant among users in San Francisco, USA," in *Studies in Family Planning*, and even that my cousin Mark (who had returned long ago from his cross-country odyssey to earn an M.D. and a Ph.D. in nutrition from Yale, and now works at University of California at San Francisco and Berkeley) had published fourteen articles on liver physiology and metabolism in the past four years.

So I pressed on, beginning a round of late-night telephone calls, after the kids were asleep. Dan and I could never seem to find a good time to talk, so he made a cassette tape describing a typical day's activities, and sent it to me.

After finishing his residency in urology, Dan took a fellowship in Houston, Texas, in male infertility. Texas, of course, is now one of the international meccas for medical training, like Germany in 1870, London in 1920, or Chicago in 1947. Dan's mentor was Dr. Larry I. Lipshultz, professor of urology at Baylor College of Medicine. Dan was one of two full-time Fellows, in addition to several other doctors who rotated through the service for a few months at a time, learning microsurgical techniques which could scarcely have been imagined fifty years ago. Dr. Lipshultz has a super-subspecialty practice, seeing men with a variety of disorders leading to infertility. Each week Dr. Lipshultz performed about a dozen "varicocele ligations"—twenty- to thirty-minute operations in which dilated veins in the scrotum were tied off, and about four reversals of vasectomies, microsurgery procedures which took two to three hours each. There would be several operating rooms active at once, and after Fellows began the procedures, Dr. Lipshultz would come in and perform the operation. During that year Dan also treated patients with benign prostatic hypertrophy, or swelling of the prostate, which surrounds the urethra, the tube through which urine passes, resulting in difficulty in emptying the bladder. He treated patients with impotence, and with prostate cancer, and even assisted in sex-change operations, in which patients' genitalia were transformed from male to female.

In his tape, he described a typical day of work:

I got to the hospital at 7:30 a.m., for a sex reassignment surgery case—it was a man on estrogen hormones, who had been cross-dressing for four years, wanting to become a woman ... A guy in his 30's, he's married and lives in Oklahoma, in the oil and gas business. We did surgery which inverts the penis, making the glans of the penis into the new cervix. The skin is pushed up in a space created between the rectum and the prostate. It is done by careful dissection. He'd already had an orchiectomy before. She had already had an orchiectomy before, so that part of the procedure wasn't necessary this time. Sometimes you have to do it concurrently. All in all, it was relatively bloodless. A neo-urethral meatus is made where the scrotum was, and the scrotum was reshaped after some excision to the labia majora. The labia minora really doesn't exist in a concrete fashion. The corpora cavernosa are partially amputated and then sewn with the distal tips toward each other to create a new clitoris. A butchery surgery when you see it done, but the end result if you see it a few months later is actually quite remarkable. We had one "trans" in the office who from the neck to the mid-thigh looks for all intents and purposes like a woman, without any suggestion of male history.

Later that day, I went over to work with Dr. Lipshultz. We had three electro-ejaculations. These are conducted for men who are anejaculatory on the basis of either psy-

chological illness (often patients who may have had primary impotence in the past), or for spinal cord patients, paras and quads, and on occasion a diabetic or so. The primary diagnosis for the fifty or sixty I've done in the last six months has been paraplegia or quadriplegia. However we have had three patients in the past three months who've been psychogenic anejaculatory patients. This one guy is from Seattle. He's married and had primary impotence and anejaculation. Through sexual therapy he was able to cure his impotence. However, he remained anejaculate. The couple has tried self-insemination but this has failed. We've done about five, six electroejaculations. The device itself is about one and one-quarter inch in diameter, with three linear electrodes running the length of it. It's made of plastic and the electrodes are metal. It's placed inside the rectal vault under anesthesia and a low voltage charge is given to stimulate the nerves around the prostate and seminal vesicles and also the ejaculatory duct. He's always had a poor result in terms of sperm count and motility, but there still may be some hope.

Dan went on to describe two other electroejaculation cases, both paraplegics. Listening to Dan's voice on the tape, I was struck by the incredible power of education—six or seven years specializing in urology, and he was doing procedures none of the other doctors in our family had ever imagined, much less done.

Dan's voice continued:

In the afternoon, Dr. Lipshultz has a clinic where we see patients who come from far and wide—internationally if not intergalactically—to be seen for infertility problems. He's got the busiest infertility practice for men in the entire world. Every day we see the textbook cases come to life. We see people in follow-up and people who come for consultation for vasectomy reversal—microsurgery is usually part of the process. And people who are in for general urological problems, including people requesting a vasectomy. There are some purists who won't do vasectomy or reversal because of religious reasons, but Lipshultz doesn't have that problem, he does what the patient wants.

A lot of these guys are dragged into this office by their wives and don't really care about having another kid. They go through the reversal procedure for the wife, because their kids (from their first marriage) are already fifteen or twenty years old. The typical patient is in his forties, remarried, and has good means, and the wife is generally a lot younger. The neat thing about this fellowship is that I get exposed to all aspects of infertility.

During the week the nurses do most of the inseminations, and on weekends the fellows and nurses split the work. Four to eight are done on weekends—for extra money for the fellow and the technician. Patients' ovulation is monitored by the nurse. When a day is chosen, a donor is selected and semen is provided, usually fresh, though sometimes frozen. The patient undergoes a standard gynecological exam, and through use of a syringe the semen is placed into the area around the cervix, and a cap is placed on it to hold it in place. The patient sits there for about fifteen minutes. Sometimes semen is placed directly into the uterus through the cervical os . . . One or two of them have gotten pregnant—that's good to hear.

After his fellowship, Dan interviewed for jobs across the country, back at Western Reserve, in Texas, in New York, and at the Mayo Clinic. He decided to accept a position at the Jacksonville, Florida, branch of the Mayo Clinic, beginning October 1990. First, he went to Rochester, Minnesota, for about two months to be "Mayonnaised," or introduced to the Mayo Clinic's unique ways of performing medical and surgical procedures (including putting the left surgical glove on first, instead of the customary right, a tradition begun because one of the Mayo brothers was left-handed!). Then he and his wife Karen moved to Jacksonville.

At Mayo, Jacksonville, Dan began a practice of general urology, with about ten to fifteen percent in his specialty of infertility. He continues to use the electroejaculation procedure he learned during his fellowship year. He was appointed a senior associate consultant at the Mayo Clinic, Jacksonville, and assistant professor of urology, Mayo Medical School.

He, too—after years of telling Dad that he couldn't care less about it—has begun to develop an interest in research. He is interested in finding better treatments for benign prostatic hypertrophy (BPH), or enlargement of the prostate gland, which causes obstruction of the flow of urine. Treatment of BPH is one of the frontiers of urology. Over 500,000 prostatectomies (removal of the prostate gland) are performed annually in the United States. Surgery requires two to four days in the hospital, and carries risks, including reactions to general anesthesia, and post-operative complications such as impotence.

Consequently, urologists are competing to develop better, non-surgical treatments of BPH. One medication, Proscar (finasteride), shrinks prostate tissue; another, called Hytrin (terazosin), traditionally used to treat high blood pressure, has been found to "relax" the prostate and increase urine flow. Both drugs have side effects, and patients must often take them for a lifetime. Thus the appeal of high-technology non-surgical procedures. There are two such approaches at present, both experimental—one uses a laser beam, another uses microwaves.

Dan has been researching the microwave technique. He uses an experimental instrument made by a French company, Technomed International, which has not yet been submitted for approval by the Food and Drug Administration. A customized catheter or tube containing a microwave antenna, it is placed in the part of the urethra that passes through the prostate gland. Fluid circulates within the catheter, keeping the urethra cool, so the patient does not feel pain. The microwaves radiate out, heating the prostate and altering its tissue in a way that causes it to shrink, relieving obstruction. Afterward, urine flows more rapidly, improving symptoms such as straining, dribbling, intermittent flow, incomplete emptying, and frequent daytime and nighttime urination.

Dan has participated in two microwave studies, one Phase I study in which five urology programs were assessing whether the procedure was safe, and a Phase II study in which he is one of two investigators attempting to determine whether the procedure is effective, each comparing forty patients who receive microwave treatment with twenty who receive "sham" treatment, or insertion of the catheter without a microwave treatment.

Susan finished her four years of residency training at Brigham and Women's Hospital in 1990. Though she learned high-technology procedures, Susan's heart remained with her early interest, international women's health issues. That fall, she began a master's program at the Harvard School of Public Health, specializing in "maternal and child health." While getting her MPH, she took a job at Beth Israel Hospital, one of Harvard's teaching hospitals, as director of the outpatient obstetrical and gynecology teaching clinic. She supervises OB-GYN residents and nurse practitioners, and has begun to reorganize the clinic and improve its teaching program. She also began a private practice, as part of the hospital's faculty practice plan, doing general obstetrics and gynecology, and taking call once a week for twenty-four hours at a time.

The lock-step years of residency training did not allow much time for pursuing special interests. Neither did her new schedule, since she had gotten pregnant in her last year of training. Her first baby, Nellie, named for our grandmother, was born in April 1991. But somehow Susan found the time to begin working on a project on home uterine monitoring. A new instrument for monitoring the fetus had received limited approval by the Food and Drug Administration, and Susan and her colleagues, including Dr. Benjamin Sachs, the chairman of obstetrics at Beth Israel, wanted to determine whether it was a useful technology, a worthwhile way to spend resources, before it was wholeheartedly embraced by practitioners, patients, and insurance companies. My computer literature search (but not our conversations!) revealed that a paper based on this study ("Home Monitoring of Uterine Activity, Does It Prevent Prematurity?") was published in the *New England Journal of Medicine* soon after Nellie's birth. The fetal monitoring instrument, which "detects and records uterine contractions," is attached to the mother's abdomen twice a day for one to two hours, between weeks 24 and 36 of pregnancy; a recording can be transmitted by telephone to a central station. Susan and her co-authors wrote:

In our opinion, even though the approval of this device by the FDA was limited, the door has been opened to the widespread marketing of this system for the prevention of premature births. We do not believe that the efficacy of the Genesis system for this purpose has been proved, and we see disturbing implications for the practice of obstetrics if this form of technology is introduced.

Susan jokes that her marriage to John Triedman is proof that she had a happy childhood—not only did she marry another doctor, as Mom did, but one who is both a pediatrician (like Mom) *and* a cardiologist (like Dad). And, in the extended family, John is the only one of our generation who is continuing the heart physiology research that meant so much to Dad and Papa. John does research on the reflex control of the cardiovascular system, especially how breathing affects heart function, working primarily with Dr. J. Phillip Saul. (While Dad is an enthusiastic booster of John's work, more than occasionally he will point out that he or another researcher made the identical observation forty years ago!) John's recent work focuses on how the heart rate, on a moment-by-moment basis, controls blood pressure. In one experiment, by putting patients' legs in a special "negative-pressure" chamber, and using a bank of three computers, John was able dramatically to demonstrate the relationship between breathing and heart rate. In another group of patients, in which the heart's "autonomic" nervous system had been blocked by various drugs, thus making the heart rate completely constant, he discovered that "central venous" blood pressure (pressure in the large veins near the heart) began to fluctuate greatly. Like the work of Carl J. Wiggers and his students over fifty years ago, John's work in basic physiology has little direct application but may turn out to be important in unanticipated ways.

In his work with patients, John sees children with various kinds of heart disease, many with congenital disease. He is working with "interventional catherizations," doing what are called "radiofrequency ablation of arrhythmias." Like angioplasty in the 1970s, which offered a non-surgical way to treat coronary-artery disease, radiofrequency ablation offers a non-surgical treatment of arrhythmias. It was pioneered by Dr. Warren M. Jackman of the University of Oklahoma Health Sciences Center in Oklahoma City, first using electrical direct current, which caused complications, including perforation of the heart muscle, and more recently (and more successfully), using radio waves. It is an intricate procedure, requiring five to seven hours in the catheterization laboratory, and the co-operation of an anesthesiologist, several doctors, a nurse, and a number of technicians. First, doctors identify the exact location in the heart where abnormal heartbeats are generated. Then they slide a catheter through blood vessels into the heart. Once they have reached the exact location, they deliver "radiofrequency energy," which coagulates the diseased part of the heart muscle. Often (particularly in children with congenital arrhythmias), the disorder is permanently cured.

Like the rest of us, John is working with new groups of patients, who present complications and disorders never seen before. For John, the most dramatic cases are adults who had successful surgery during childhood for congenital heart diseases. In the past, such patients never survived to adulthood. Today, twenty years after surgery, they have complex arrhythmias and need to be managed with complex regimens of medications; cardiologists are just beginning to determine how best to treat them.

In 1989, after having our second child, a son, Benjamin, Lisa and I sold our co-op apartment and moved to suburbia, becoming house owners and commuters. I was promoted to director of my clinic, running an operation of over 30,000 visits per year, with eighty staff members, serving over 4,000 patients—like being mayor of a small town. In spare moments I kept working on my family history. I carried diskettes back and forth between my computer at work and the one at home. I stuck drafts of chapters (printed out single-spaced to minimize weight) in my appointment book, to peruse during less-than-scintillating conferences, or during rides on the Metro-North commuter train. When several chapters had accumulated, I emptied the contents of a hospital Attending Staff Manual, a blue plastic three-ring binder, and put the manuscript in there—thus ensuring that no one would read my book if I happened to leave it lying around the clinic.

The project Rick and I began also continued, and by the summer of 1992 we had enrolled about fifty patients, and had begun writing papers, using the huge mass of data that had accumulated—with special urgency once our three-year grant entered its last year and the necessity of applying for more funding became clear. Our findings supported the generalization that it costs a million dollars to prove what good pilot data tell you for essentially nothing. Patients generally stay in integrated treatment but drop out of non-integrated treatment. Patients who started treatment (that is, attended as few as two group sessions after leaving the hospital) had dramatically fewer days in-hospital than those who never started treatment— four or five days over four months, versus twenty-two days for dropouts. Symptoms and drug abuse also improved for patients staying in treatment. We were also able to identify the patients most at risk of dropping out—those with high levels of both "positive symptoms" such as delusions *and* "negative symptoms" such as social withdrawal, and lack of energy. Fortunately, our laborious hand calculations are a thing of the past, now that the computer age has democratized statistics. With a two- or three-thousand-dollar computer and a standard, incredibly powerful statistics program, one can store and manipulate hundreds of thousands of bits of information. With the click of a mouse, we were able to do

MANOVAS, ANOVAS, Fourier transformations, scatter diagrams, to rotate graphs in three dimensions, and make beautiful multicolor slides to present our results.

My newfound interest in research has spread. With other doctors at the hospital, residents and staff psychiatrists, I have begun a series of studies of "dysthymia," or chronic low-grade depression—a condition traditionally believed to be psychological in origin, and treated with psychotherapy, but which more recently has been thought to be often biological in origin, and which seems to respond to medication. Like the COPAD study, we started small. Using free medication samples cadged off the drug-company reps who always hang around the hospital, we treated a series of thirty-eight dysthymic patients. About two-thirds responded to medication. We presented that pilot data at a national conference, wrote it up for publication, and used it as the basis to apply for money from a drug company to do a more rigorous double-blind, placebo-controlled study with Prozac (fluoxetine), a new drug that specifically affects the brain chemical serotonin. Again, over sixty percent of patients on medication got better. In contrast, fewer than twenty percent of patients treated with placebo improved—a dramatic difference. When that study was finished, we did a follow-up study, looking at the patients from both studies to see whether their medication response at two months was maintained nearly a year later. (It was.) Next came an offer from another drug company to participate in a large, fifteen-center study of a different antidepressant in dysthymia, which we have just begun.

Each of us, as doctors, has begun making a mark in the world. The conditions which my siblings and I are addressing reflect aspects of the state of medicine at the end of the twentieth century. My work with crack-abusing schizophrenics reflects the effects of deinstitutionalization and social decay, and my work on dysthymia reflects the growing use of new classes of effective antidepressant drugs—as well as a surprising, well-documented worldwide increase in the prevalence of clinical depression, manic-depressive illness, and suicide, over the past seventy-five years. Danny's work with male infertility reflects Americans' unwillingness to live with the givens of biology, as well as the sophistication of science in undoing the effects of chronic diseases. His work with microwaves in BPH reflects another sort of medical advance: whereas in the early 1900s doctors were limited to the body's surface, by the middle of the century they were routinely able to do major surgery, even inside the heart and brain. By the 1980s and 1990s, doctors are able to do the equivalent of major surgery without large incisions—either operating through narrow scopes or catheters, or targeting various kinds of rays or waves to diseased tissue. If the Technomed microwave device is safe and effective, it may replace the transurethral prostatectomy, which itself replaced the open prostatectomy, a massive surgical procedure. And radiofrequency ablation of arrhythmias, as it is further refined, may make long-term medication treatment unnecessary for many patients.

Susan's work on the overuse of diagnostic tests in pregnancy addresses our society's tendency to place undue faith in the newest technology—rightfully, doctors must make sure it is used effectively.

And then there is Beth, who has not yet finished her training. I called her one Sunday night during a snowstorm in New York; it was raining in Cleveland, and we talked for an hour about the changes in pediatrics, and about what she was seeing in the emergency room, in the middle of the second year of residency.

She was working twelve hours on, twelve hours off,

seeing everything from colds and rashes to sudden-infant-death-syndrome babies, and serious car accidents. It was exhausting, and fascinating. Next she would be assigned to a "transport" rotation, picking up sick kids at community hospitals and doctors' offices, to bring them to Rainbow Babies and Childrens Hospital, children in need of a level-three nursery, or heart patients requiring surgery. Then came a community hospital rotation, followed by electives.

She talked about how pediatrics is in the throes of organizing into specialties, as internal medicine did fifty years ago; and how increasingly there is pressure to do three more years of fellowship training after the three years of residency. About half her classmates planned to specialize, the other half to remain generalists, working in the community.

"Which way will you go?" I asked.

"I'm not sure," she said. So many things interested her. Maybe a fellowship in adolescent medicine, or behavioral pediatrics. Maybe something having to do with prevention. Over and over again, her work in the pediatrics emergency room and intensive-care unit impressed on her that the advances of medical technology desperately cry out for advances in ethical thinking—and even more for advances in prevention. Many of the children she was working so hard to treat were sick as a result of behavior—prematurity because of a mother who abused drugs or did not get prenatal care; brain damage from preventable accidents; asthma worsened by the parents' cigarette smoking. Infant mortality among blacks was twice as high as among whites—largely because there were so many more black low-birth-weight babies. This in turn was the result of poor prenatal care, poor nutrition, poverty, drugs. Accident prevention, health education, immunization, lead intoxication, the relation between smoking and asthma. There were so many areas it was hard to know where to start.

"And my work in molecular biology and pathology—maybe I'll get back to that somehow in pediatrics . . ."

We said good night, and I hung up. Afterward, as I helped Lisa get the kids ready for bed, I found myself wondering how it would all come together for Beth. At University Hospitals, Dad is always being stopped in the hallway by pediatrics professors who tell him how wonderful a clinician Beth is, how warm with children and their parents, how good a teacher with medical students. Perhaps she will be primarily a clinician, and a teacher. On the other hand, there are her interests in molecular biology, and in pathology. Is there some way in which she will use her skills from the laboratory to investigate disease or to treat patients? Will she go back to the lab as well?

Clearly, Beth's story remains to be told. In her life as a doctor, she has just reached the beginning.

EPILOGUE

IN the summer of 1992, all six of us returned home to Ohio. The stated reason was Dad's ultimatum: we each had to claim our belongings, because finally it was time to clean house. In forty years, Mom had never done that, and now he was delegating the responsibility to us. The real reason, though, was Dad's illness, and his desire to bring order and closure. In 1990, he had been diagnosed as having prostate cancer, and had an operation to remove the tumor. For nearly two years, he had been fine. Twice before, medical advances had prevented certain death—with his heart, his pituitary. Was there a third reprieve as well?

Recently, his lab tests had become abnormal. In particular, his PSA, or prostate specific antigen level, a marker for tumor cells, was rising. Hormone therapy had been instituted, which had worked for a while, but now the numbers were rising again. We kids began to brace for news, for late-night phone calls, our experience as doctors making us deeply aware of the causes and consequences of disease, but providing no emotional respite.

A week here, a weekend there, we began to fly back home. It was an unsettling time, a time of many changes. Beth and her husband had just bought a house, and Mom's brother George was in the hospital, and Jon had accepted a new job in Toledo, putting Nana and Papa's house on the market. Each of us kids came back to Ohio, and we went through our rooms, filling plastic garbage bags and large file boxes, sorting through remnants of our childhoods. I came in August. I did more interviewing, finally progressing through the nineteen-forties, -fifties, -sixties, -seventies, and -eighties, arriving near the present, where history turns into journalism, and memory becomes observation. And I did my share of housecleaning.

In my attic room, I discovered a time capsule of virtually every possession I had ever had, every piece of clothing, practically every classroom assignment. There was a small metal box filled with an eight-year-old's treasures: strips of birchbark, a little Indian in a canoe, a penknife, a compass, a ribbon from Space Camp, smooth white and black rocks, cuff links, a Cub Scout patch. There was my hundred-page report on New York State in fifth grade for Mrs. Crowell: "It is impossible to describe more than a small amount about New York, only an outline of the past, some of the present, but nothing of the future—I will leave that to future students of Roxboro, or to those lucky enough to attend exhibits at the World's Fair, at which that subject will be addressed . . ." There was my seventh-grade science project: "Effects of Reversing Day and Night on the Circadian Rhythms of White Mice." And there was the letter I had written to Dad before taking a year off from college in 1974: "to relieve you of the obligation of being caretaker to my dreams."

Kathryn, Susan, and Dan had all been there the week before, doing their best to straighten up "the mess." They had filled innumerable garbage cans, and dozens of boxes filled with books and clothes were stacked on the upstairs landing and even in Dad's library.

There was another problem: the bedrooms, study, and basement were filled with boxes and file cabinets of data from a hundred studies (among them the Heart Disease and Exercise Study), with fliers and newspaper clippings and anti-smoking posters, and thousands of patients' charts. Finally, at the age of seventy-six, six years after retiring, Dad was giving up his laboratory—and while deciding what to throw out, what to give to the medical society, he had brought everything home.

One evening Jonny came over to help me look for old baseball cards. Mom hovered around us as if we might accidentally discard priceless heirlooms.

"Keep that! Don't throw that out!" she kept repeating.

"It's junk! It's garbage!" we responded.

We stayed up till 1:30 in the morning, looking through drawers and cupboards, filling garbage bags, but all we found were a dozen Batman cards, a few Beatles cards, even some Laugh-In cards. Finally we discovered two cards from the 1960 World Series—in which the Pittsburgh Pirates defeated the New York Yankees 4 to 3, despite Mantle, Maris, and Berra.

Over the weekend, I packed half a dozen boxes with books, notebooks, "treasures," and various memorabilia. I picked out a few lamps, an oak desk chair I had refinished years ago, a small desk that my son might want. I went through the back closet, sorting through box after box of college books and medical-school texts and notebooks. I piled everything up, ready to take with me what I wanted from home. I found myself promising to drive my mini-van back from New York at Thanksgiving to pick it all up.

On Labor Day, the entire family met for a week-long vacation in Maine. We rented three houses on a lake in the White Mountains. Everyone was there—Mom and Dad and all six of us kids, and all the spouses, and eight grandchildren. We alternated having dinner at the different houses, the Tennis House one night, the Porch House another, the

Lake House the third, cooking up huge batches of spaghetti or baked chicken or vegetarian chili. Dad was revising his autobiography, which was almost completed—only the last chapter still to write. He spent much time sitting in a green metal chair between the tennis court and a baseball field, editing the manuscript, and watching us play with the kids.

"You know I'm not feeling as well as I wish I was," he said. "I would like to participate more."

"We know," we said.

Watching the kids playing, we returned to our eternal subject: medicine. It was amazing how medicine had changed since Dad started practicing during the war, even more amazing how many changes there had been since the time of Marcus Rosenwasser. The flood of new diagnostic techniques, of new ways to investigate disease, of new treatments, was mind-boggling. In the old days, new technologies came in one or two at a time—the X ray, the EKG. Today there were hundreds at once. "In vitro" fertilization; surgery on fetuses; brain-cell implants for Parkinson's disease; implantable defibrillators, which could automatically deliver a jolt of current the moment a patient's heart began to go into ventricular tachycardia or fibrillation; the Human Genome Project, beginning to map all human genes! Not to mention computers: in the old days, they would measure one heartbeat at a time; now John Triedman was collecting a hundred megabytes of data for one experiment! It was endless. In the dozen years since I had graduated from medical school, two or three new generations of medication had been introduced. In my field, psychiatry, rigorous new research has shown the effectiveness of psychotherapy for some conditions, of medications for others, the benefits of new classes of medication for old diseases, and the value of new uses for old medications. Urology, obstetrics-gynecology, pediatrics, cardiology—

each was rushing headlong into new frontiers of diagnosis and treatment.

I knew the statistics. Life expectancy has increased in the United States and is now 72.0 years for men, 78.9 years for women. Infant morality has continued to drop, and most infectious diseases as well. Polio went from 33,300 cases in 1950 to none in 1990. Typhoid and diphtheria have also almost disappeared. Heart disease has continued to decline: after its big increase from 7.9 percent of deaths in 1900, it peaked at 28.9 percent in 1960, then fell to 24.1 percent by 1987. Since cigarette smoking has decreased (so that only 25.5 percent of Americans over age eighteen smoked by 1990, compared to 42 percent in 1965), no doubt, down the line, lung cancer deaths will start to drop as well.

And yet, as of the summer of 1992, medicine was in worse trouble than ever. Its difficulties seemed to multiply with each new advance. Since Dad retired in 1986, medical spending had gone from about ten percent of the GNP to more than fourteen percent—$808 billion for 1992!—and was projected to rise to nearly twenty percent of the GNP, or $1.7 trillion, by the year 2000. At least a quarter of the money goes for administrative costs—for the endless stacks of insurance forms, for the review of claims, for appeals of denials of payment, for the millions of clerks and claims adjustors and reimbursement officers and lawyers (lawyers are not too popular in our family, and Beth's husband, the only attorney in the family, has taken more than a fair share of ribbing). With the current recession, the number of uninsured Americans keeps rising: from 31.5 million in 1990, to 37 million in 1992—11.7 percent of whites, 20.2 percent of blacks, 26.5 percent of Hispanics. Even worse, worldwide, there are incalculable numbers of deaths from preventable diseases, millions of children dying from schistosomiasis because of the lack of simple concrete-block toilets at the edge of fields, tens of millions dying from malnutrition—and millions more destined to die from AIDS.

We sat on the lawn, throwing tennis balls and Frisbees to the kids. We got up to separate them when they started fighting. We discussed ideas, dilemmas, conundrums. Not that we had any terrific solutions—we're just doctors, not politicians. We joked with Dad—how easy his generation had it. All *they* had to do was be brilliant clinician-scientists. Now we have to be administrators, businessmen, computer specialists, ethicists, politicians, grant managers, and experts in hospital reimbursement. In our spare time we get to practice medicine and, if we're lucky, do science.

Besides, new diseases seemed to keep arising, like something mythological, two hydras to replace each head cut off. AIDS is spreading rapidly in the United States: between 1986 and 1990, in four short years, cases increased from 40,000 to 165,000, and deaths rose from 23,000 to 105,000. According to the Centers for Disease Control predictions, as many as 215,000 more Americans will die of AIDS by the end of 1993. Old diseases are returning, among them hepatitis, measles, malaria, multiple-drug-resistant tuberculosis. We remarked on other old disorders returning as well, with the end of the Cold War, old ethnic and religious hatreds in Russia and Eastern Europe, not so different from what Marcus Rosenwasser saw in Bohemia in 1866, and Papa saw in 1920, and Dad saw in 1944.

We watched the kids playing on the lawn before us: Sarah and Ben and Jessica and Julie, and Leah and Nellie and Rebecca and Jonah. If some of them became doctors, a sixth generation, who could imagine what kinds of medical problems they would face? How would they deal with the diseases of the mid-twenty-first century?

We played tennis, we went canoeing, we worked on handwritten manuscripts or on notebook computers after the kids fell asleep. We talked about our plans: Danny's work with microwaves to shrink prostate tissue; the new grant proposal Rick Rosenthal and I were working on, for $2.7 million; Susan's plans for an international health expedition to Armenia to address women's medical care. At night, hearing the splash of waves, and baby Nellie—who had an ear infection—tossing, and the cry of loons, we slept restlessly.

One afternoon we took a trip to Camp Wigwam, the boys' camp we attended for several years, where Mom had been camp doctor.

As we walked through the pine woods, past cabins and tennis courts and the amphitheater, and along the banks of Bear Pond, Dad walked slowly, conserving his energy.

"Damn it!" he muttered.

"I hope you don't think I'm lazy," he said.

We had straightforward discussions—about the huge number of pills he takes every day, about the daily radiation therapy he was receiving for six to eight weeks, about chemotherapy. On his leg and abdomen we could see indelible markings used to guide the beam of the collider. We talked about "the plan"—to try testosterone-blocking drugs, then an experimental drug from England.

On the last day, we all met at the Porch House for a conversation with Mom and Dad. No spouses or kids, just the eight of us. It was around the issue of dividing things up, continuing to clear house. Sorting through the past, and coming away with that which is worth keeping. Which, I guess, is what I had been doing for the past six years, reading medical history books and letters and journals and scientific articles, and interviewing everyone endlessly.

Through the trees, you could see the gleam of water, and the hazy green summit of Mt. Washington.

"After I'm gone," Dad said, "I don't want your mother to have to face a mess. I want things to be in order."

"I'm scared," said Mom.

Mom and Dad held hands, both in tears, all eight of us in tears, and we sat there making a list of what goes to whom, how to "decompress" things. We knew it was symbolic, we did not really care much about Nana's cookbook collection, or the Whistler engravings, or the eighteenth-century English desk, or our great-great-great-grandmother Colman's first edition of the *Leatherstocking Tales*, or the ugly Dresden vase that somebody brought over from Germany in 1840.

We made plans to meet again at Thanksgiving: all eight of us and the spouses and kids. The whole family. Rather: all the families. Then we packed our cars, strapped our kids in their car seats, and got ready to drive back to what were now our homes, in different cities scattered across America. Tomorrow we were due back at our hospitals. Our patients were waiting for us.

BIBLIOGRAPHY

I

The following books were useful in giving a background of nineteenth-century medicine and its social context in Cleveland:

Medicine in Cleveland and Cuyahoga County, 1810–1976, ed. by Kent L. Brown. Cleveland: Academy of Medicine, 1977.

Inside Looking Out: The Cleveland Jewish Orphan Asylum, 1868–1924, by Gary E. Polster. Kent, Ohio: Kent State University Press, 1990.

The Birth of Modern Cleveland, 1865–1930, ed. by Thomas F. Campbell and Edward M. Miggins. Cleveland: Western Reserve Historical Society, 1988.

History of the Jews of Cleveland, by Lloyd Gartner. Cleveland: Western Reserve Historical Society and the Jewish Theological Seminary of America, 1978.

The Lives of University Hospitals of Cleveland, by Mark Gottlieb. Cleveland: Wilson Street Press, 1991.

A Place to Heal: The History of the National Jewish Center for Immunology and Respiratory Medicine, by Mary Ann Fitzharris. Denver: National Jewish Center, 1989.

Other books which gave a perspective on the changes in medicine and medical education include:

Medical Education in the United States and Canada: A Report to the Carnegie Foundation for the Advancement of Teaching, by Abraham Flexner. Boston: Carnegie Foundation for the Advancement of Teaching, 1910.

The Principles and Practice of Medicine, first ed. by William Osler. New York: D. Appleton and Company, 1892.

The Principles and Practice of Medicine, seventh ed., by William Osler. New York: D. Appleton and Co., 1910.

Learning to Heal: The Development of American Medical Education, by Kenneth M. Ludmerer. New York: Basic Books, 1985.

American Doctors and German Universities, by Thomas N. Bonner. Lincoln: U. of Nebraska Press, 1963.

The Structure of American Medical Practice, 1875–1941, by George Rosen, ed. by Charles E. Rosenberg. Philadelphia: U. of Pennsylvania Press, 1983.

The Social Transformation of American Medicine, by Paul Starr. New York: Basic Books, 1984.

Several books were helpful in describing obstetrics and gynecology in the late nineteenth and early twentieth centuries, giving a context for the obstetrical log and medical papers of Dr. Marcus Rosenwasser, and forming a basis for comparison with present-day techniques:

Lying In: A History of Childbirth in America, by Richard W. Wertz and Dorothy C. Wertz. New York: Free Press, 1977.

Obstetrics and Gynecology in America: A History, by Harold Speert. Chicago: American College of Obstetricians and Gynecologists, 1980.

Operative Gynecology, by Richard F. Mattingly, John D. Thompson. Philadelphia: Lippincott, 1985.

The history of cardiology in the early twentieth century has been described in a number of personal reminiscences, as well as in scholarly works, including:

My Life and Medicine, by Paul Dudley White, with assistance of Margaret Parton. Boston: Gambit Inc., 1971.

Reminiscences and Adventures in Circulation Research, by Carl J. Wiggers. New York: Grune and Stratton, 1958.

The History of Coronary Heart Disease, ed. by J. O. Leibowitz. Berkeley: U. of California Press, 1970.

"The Emergence of Modern Cardiology," ed. by W. F. Bynum, C. Lawrence, V. Nutton. *Medical History*, Suppl. No. 5. London: Wellcome Institute for the History of Medicine, 1985.

"The angina pectoris controversy during the 1920s," by Reidar K. Lie. *Acta Physiologica Scandinavica*, Suppl. 599, 1991, pp. 135–47.

Dr. Harold Feil's medical papers, and those of his colleagues and contemporaries, provided a sense of the frontiers of cardiovascular research.

In addition, a number of obscure and/or unpublished works were essential to my reconstruction of turn-of-the-century medical life, in addition to the diary and obstetrical log of Dr. Marcus Rosenwasser. These include:

Pes Anserinus. The Cleveland College of Physicians and Surgeons, 1909. My grandfather Harold Feil's medical-school yearbook.

Old Nic in Nicotine: Tobacco Lure and Cure, by Nathan Rosewater. Cleveland, 1925.

The Life and Times of Edward Rosewater, by Victor Rosewater, 1945. Unpublished biography of Edward Rosewater, by his son Victor.

Also, I used letters from Dr. Thomas Lewis to Dr. Feil, as well as letters between Harold and Nellie Feil, and their correspondence with various relatives, including a series of letters from London addressed to Mrs. Nathan Rosewater, Hotel Statler, Cleveland. My grandmother Nellie Feil's genealogical notebook, sketching the history of her family back to the eighteenth century, was an important discovery for me, as was the Rosenwasser family tree, compiled by Sidney C. Singer, 1942, a mimeographed family tree and history of the Rosenwasser/Rosewater/Kohn families. In addition, my parents' attic contained boxes of records of Dr. Feil's patients (including the original EKG of Mr. Edward J. Moore's anginal attack, mounted on a card), and clippings, detailing activities of family members, from newspapers, including the *Cleveland News*, *Cleveland Plain Dealer*, and *The Omaha Bee*, from the 1870s to the present.

II

Developments in medicine since World War II have not yet been adequately captured in any sort of comprehensive historical review. The written sources for this section of the book have been primarily technical reports and the personal accounts of individual investigators. There have been a few more scholarly accounts, including two by my father. Particularly useful were:

"The Impact of Chance: Three Examples: Bioelectricity and electrophysiology of the heart," by H. K. Hellerstein. *Cardiology: The Evolution of the Science and the Art*, ed. by Richard J. Bing. Switzerland: Harwood Academic Publishers, 1992.

"Electrocardiography," by Louis N. Katz and H. K. Hellerstein. *Circulation of the Blood: Men and Ideas*, ed. by Alfred P. Fishman and Dickinson W. Richards. Bethesda: American Physiological Society, 1982. (Original by Oxford University Press, New York, 1964.)

"Reminiscences of Cardiac Resuscitation," by Claude S. Beck. *Review of Surgery*, 1970, pp. 77–86.

"History of Coronary Care Units," by Hughes W. Day. *American Journal of Cardiology*, vol. 30, 1972, pp. 405–7.

Original accounts of the first successful case of defibrillation are included in:

"Ventricular Fibrillation of Long Duration Abolished by Electric Shock," by Claude S. Beck, William H. Pritchard, Harold S. Feil. *Journal of the American Medical Association*, Dec. 1947, pp. 985–6.

"Sudden death during surgical operations, with report of efforts to revive . the heart," by Harold Feil and Herman K. Hellerstein. *Ohio State Medical Journal*, Feb. 1950, pp. 125–26.

In contrast to the lack of comprehensive histories of recent developments in cardiology, there are two excellent histories of pediatrics in America, from colonial times to the mid-to-late twentieth century:

History of American Pediatrics, by Thomas E. Cone, Jr. Boston: Little, Brown and Co., 1979.

History of the Care and Feeding of the Premature Infant, by Thomas E. Cone, Jr. Boston: Little, Brown and Co., 1985.

A particularly useful account of military events was included in:

The Lucky Seventh. Dallas: 7th Armored Division Association, Taylor Publishing Co., 1982. A history of the 7th Armored Division.

A useful summary of the role of women in medicine in Cleveland was published by Linda Lehmann Goldstein, in the Case Western Reserve University Medical Alumni Bulletin.

III

The tremendous medical progress in the last two decades has not yet begun to be assessed in any meaningful way. The vast expansion of new medical technologies and treatments, the growth of the medical-industrial complex, and their impact on the lives of physicians and patients, are at this point almost impossible adequately to characterize. In this section, interviews of family members provided most of the information, along with medical articles in selected areas.

My father's work on rehabilitation of cardiac patients has been described in publications of the National Exercise and Heart Disease Project in the 1980s, and also in:

Healing Your Heart, by Herman K. Hellerstein and Paul Perry. New York: Simon and Schuster, 1990.

Rehabilitation of the Coronary Patient, third ed., ed. by Nanette Kass

Wenger and Herman K. Hellerstein. New York: Churchill Livingstone, 1992.

My father's autobiography, *The Heart of the Matter* (Caldwell, Idaho: Griffith Publishers, 1993), written in conjunction with Adam Snyder, has provided additional background, both personal and professional.

Accounts of the medical work of myself, my siblings, and other relatives over the last decade draw on a number of recent publications in medical journals.

ACKNOWLEDGMENTS

Over the course of half a dozen years, my parents, Herman K. Hellerstein, M.D., and Mary Feil Hellerstein, M.D., have made themselves available for innumerable conversations, interviews, and discussions that have provided the background for this book. Time after time, they have dug through the seemingly endless archive in their attic, and emerged with previously unsuspected documents, clippings, and old letters. Their patient assistance has made this book infinitely richer. Arthur Wang, my editor at Hill and Wang, has provided tireless encouragement through the long gestation of this project, and his sense of form and language have allowed me to find order and narrative in a deluge of personalities, history, and scientific information.

Other data about my family have come from a variety of organizations, which have been generous in opening their archives to me. For the earlier generations, Genevieve Miller from the Allen Memorial Library in Cleveland, and its Dittrick Medical History Museum, provided medical papers from Marcus Rosenwasser's and Harold Feil's generations. The Case Western Reserve University Archives supplied information about nineteenth-century Cleveland medical schools. The Western Reserve Historical Society provided access to contemporary accounts from newspapers such as *The*

Jewish Independent, The Jewish Review and Observer, The Jewish Orphan Asylum Magazine, and others, and their Rosenwasser collection contained invaluable documents such as Marcus Rosenwasser's medical-school diary. Dr. Stanley Marguiles generously sent me Rosenwasser's obstetrical log. The Rocky Mountain Jewish Historical Society, at the University of Denver, provided information about Dr. Gustave Feil. I obtained other important material and background from historian Judah Rubenstein, my uncles Edward and Dr. George Feil, and distant cousins Dorothy Belding, Kay Bang Donovan, and Betty Mintz. Gail Stuehr, of the Case Western Reserve University Public Affairs Department, generously provided a number of photographs of family members.

For more recent generations, materials were gathered in a series of interviews. Besides my parents, my siblings (Kathryn, Jonathan, Daniel, Susan, and Elizabeth) and my brother-in-law John Triedman have tolerated endless questions, often late at night, on weekends, or during family reunions, and have unselfishly allowed me access to their recollections and private thoughts.

Robley Wilson, editor of *The North American Review*, has been generous in allowing me to publish essays about my family over more than a decade; several of these were explorations and prototypes for chapters in this book. The MacDowell Colony granted me intervals of peace and solitude in 1986 and 1988 essential to the early development of this book. More recently, such intervals of reflection have been provided twice a day by the Metro-North Commuter Railroad.

Finally, and especially, I would like to thank my wife, Lisa Perry Hellerstein. She has shown more than a reasonable degree of patience and good humor in accommodating to my trips, absences, late-night telephone marathons, piles of documents throughout the house, and my general air of preoccupation. This has allowed me to stay on track despite the innumerable distractions of a doctor's life. Her love, support, and encouragement have been invaluable, too, in giving me perspective on what has at times seemed to be a daunting legacy.